ENVIRONMENTAL VALUATION
New Perspectives

Environmental Valuation
New Perspectives

Edited by

K.G. Willis

Environmental Appraisal Research Group
Department of Town and Country Planning
University of Newcastle upon Tyne
Newcastle upon Tyne
UK

J.T. Corkindale

Environmental Protection Economics Division
Department of the Environment
London
UK

CAB INTERNATIONAL

CAB INTERNATIONAL
Wallingford
Oxon OX10 8DE
UK

Tel: +44 (0)1491 832111
Telex: 847964 (COMAGG G)
E-mail: cabi@cabi.org
Fax: +44 (0)1491 833508

A catalogue entry for this book is available from the British Library.

ISBN 0 85198 966 7

Typeset by Solidus (Bristol) Limited
Printed and bound in the UK by Biddles Ltd, Guildford

Contents

Contributors

Professor W.L. Adamowicz: *Department of Rural Economy, Faculty of Agriculture and Forestry, University of Alberta, Edmonton, Alberta, Canada T6G 2HI.*

J.T. Corkindale: *Economic Advisor, Environmental Protection Division, Department of the Environment, Romney House, 43 Marsham Street, London SW1P 3PY, UK.*

G.D. Garrod: *Environmental Appraisal Research Group, Department of Town and Country Planning, University of Newcastle upon Tyne, Newcastle upon Tyne, NE1 7RU, UK.*

N. Glass: *Chief Economist, Department of the Environment, Romney House, 43 Marsham Street, London SW1P 3PY, UK.*

Professor W.M. Hanemann: *Department of Agricultural and Resource Economics, University of California at Berkeley, 207 Giannini Hall, Berkeley, California 94720, USA.*

Dr N. Hanley: *Environmental Economics Research Group, Department of Economics, University of Stirling, Stirling FK9 4LA, UK.*

Sir Martin Holdgate: *Formerly Director General, IUCN, The World Conservation Union, Rue Mauverney 28, CH-1196 Gland, Switzerland;* now *President, The Zoological Society of London, Regent's Park, London N1W 4RY.*

A. Holland: *Department of Philosophy, University of Lancaster, Lancaster LA1 4YW, UK.*

Dr C.W. Hope: *The Judge Institute of Management Studies, University of Cambridge, Mill Lane, Cambridge CB2 1RX, UK.*

Professor M.W. Jones-Lee: *Department of Economics, University of Newcastle upon Tyne, Newcastle upon Tyne NE1 7RU, UK.*

R. Laslett: *Managing Consultant, London Economics Ltd, 91 New Cavendish Street, London W1M 7FS, UK.*

Professor G. Loomes: *Centre for Experimental Economics, Department of Economics, University of York, York YO1 5DD, UK.*

Professor D.M. Newbery: *Department of Applied Economics, University of Cambridge, Sidgwick Avenue, Cambridge CB3 9DE, UK.*

Professor C. Perrings: *Department of Environmental Economics and Management, Institute of Biology, University of York, York YO5 1DD, UK.*

Dr C. Price: *School of Agricultural and Forest Sciences, University College of North Wales, Bangor, Gwynedd LL57 2UW, UK.*

Professor K.G. Willis: *Environmental Appraisal Research Group, Department of Town and Country Planning, University of Newcastle upon Tyne, Newcastle upon Tyne NE1 7RU, UK.*

Preface

Public and private sector projects and policies are increasingly appraised in terms of their environmental costs and benefits. In 1991 in the UK the Department of the Environment published *Policy Appraisal and the Environment* which provided a guide for government departments on how environmental impacts could be taken into account, how non-priced environmental effects could be valued in monetary terms, and how these values could be incorporated into the development and appraisal of policy. This book essentially follows on from that path-breaking document in carrying the debate a further stage forward.

Since the publication of *Policy Appraisal and the Environment*, various government departments have used and applied its methodology in a number of studies. By 1994 the Department of the Environment considered it an appropriate time to take stock of this accumulated knowledge and experience, and published *Environmental Appraisal in Government Departments* to share the lessons learnt from these empirical studies evaluating and appraising the formulation of environmental policy and decisions. The Department of the Environment also considered it pertinent to explore the comprehensiveness of environmental values and cost–benefit analysis, and the context in which environmental values were formulated. This was all the more imperative in the light of the academic controversy surrounding the valuation of the environmental damages resulting from the *Exxon Valdez* disaster in Alaska, and the subsequent National Oceanic and Atmospheric Administration Report in the USA on how environmental valuation of damages to environmental resources, particularly that element known as passive or non-use values, should be assessed. In this debate on environmental valuation, disciplines other than

economics – such as psychology and sociology – were also seen to have
something to contribute to the enumeration and assessment of environmental values. The need to engage in dialogue with experts in
academic disciplines other than economics, to learn about their perspectives on environmental values, and hopefully produce a synthesis
and consensus on values, to replace the mutual antithesis between
disciplines, prompted the Department of the Environment to sponsor
the second of two conferences on environmental valuation. This second
conference was held at St Aidan's College, Durham on 24–25 March
1994, and discussed the social context and future directions for environmental valuation and appraisal. (The first conference had been held
two years earlier at the University of Newcastle upon Tyne.) The
Durham Conference was held in recognition of the fact that in
environmental valuation, as in other environmental fields, it is desirable and sensible that a multi-disciplinary approach be adopted. This
is the first approach in the UK to this end, and initiates a dialogue
between economists and others.

The editors, who were also the conference organizers, are grateful
to the Department of the Environment for sponsoring the conference,
and to Norman Glass, Chief Economist at the Department of the
Environment, and Philip Lowe, Duke of Northumberland Professor of
Rural Economy at the University of Newcastle, for jointly chairing it.
Norman Glass and Philip Lowe have provided enormous encourage-
ment to the effort to explore a multidisciplinary approach investigating the formulation of environmental values.

As conference organizers we were pleased both with the participation in and the outcome of the meeting. Indeed, demand to attend the
conference was so overwhelming that some wishing to participate
were unable to do so because of limited capacity at that time at St
Aidan's College. We hope this publication of these proceedings in some
measure compensates for their disappointment. The 76 who did
participate heard papers that provided an insight into some new
perspectives on environmental valuation, by a variety of researchers
from a wide range of institutions.

Participants also came from a wide range of public and private
agencies and academic establishments, and represented a diverse range
of disciplines: philosophy, sociology, geography, statistics, as well as
economics. Discussion of each paper revealed a greater consensus of
views between economists and other disciplines than the organizers
had expected a priori. The main message of the conference was that
economists, and the critics of the assumptions in economic theories and
methods, can have a meaningful dialogue, thereby mutually improving their respective analytical methods, assumptions, and the practical
application of their techniques in policy analysis. However, much

remains to be accomplished in developing a consensus between economists and others in agreeing a common approach to environmental appraisal and valuation.

Ken Willis
John Corkindale

Acknowledgement

The chapter by Michael Jones-Lee and Graham Loomes was originally published as a paper in the *Journal of Transport Economics and Policy* 28, January, 1994. The paper is reproduced by kind permission of the *Journal of Transport Economics and Policy.*

1

Introduction[1]

John Corkindale

Department of the Environment

The Environment White Paper, 'This Common Inheritance', (Cm. 1200), published in September 1990, announced that the Government had carried out a review of the way in which the costs and benefits of environmental issues are assessed within Government.

> The review has looked at a range of analysis which is available on environmental costs and benefits, recognising the need for an integrated approach which takes account of all the consequences of a measure for the environment, favourable and unfavourable. It has concluded that there is scope for a more systematic approach within Government to the appraisal of the environmental costs and benefits before decisions are taken. The Government has therefore set work in hand to produce guidelines for policy appraisal where there are significant implications for the environment. These will be published in due course. The aim is to provide general guidance to departments, not to set out a rigid set of procedures to be followed in all cases.

The guide-lines referred to were published by the Department of the Environment the following year under the title *Policy Appraisal and the Environment* (Department of the Environment, 1991). More recently the Department has also published *Environmental Appraisal in Government Departments* (Department of the Environment, 1994) which provides information about how the guidance set out in *Policy Appraisal and the Environment* is being applied in research and analysis.

---

[1] Any views expressed in this chapter are those of the author, and should not necessarily be interpreted as being held by the Department of the Environment.

1

An important aspect of *Policy Appraisal and the Environment* – and one which has given rise to a good deal of controversy – is its espousal of the monetary valuation of environmental impacts. Appendix C of the guide in particular is devoted to describing the available techniques for monetary valuation and how they might be applied. The case for environmental valuation is easily stated: if environmental costs and benefits deriving from the introduction of new policies and projects are to be weighed in the balance with other costs and benefits deriving from the same policies and projects, there is a need for a common measuring rod and it usually happens that the most convenient one is money.

This argument and the assumptions behind it have not gone unchallenged either by economists or by people from other academic disciplines notably ecology, geography, law, philosophy, psychology, sociology, and statistics. At the same time, even those economists who are fully persuaded by the argument are coming to recognize that the application of the principles of welfare economics in the environmental field could benefit from interdisciplinary dialogue. (The dependence of economists on others to provide physical data has always been recognized.)

This tension between economists and others has already manifested itself in various ways. Perhaps best known are the deliberations of the expert panel set up by the US National Oceanic and Atmospheric Administration in the wake of the *Exxon Valdez* disaster (Arrow *et al.*, 1993). In the UK the debate has been somewhat more muted but evidence for it exists in the decision by the Economic and Social Research Council in 1992 to fund a series of seminars on environmental valuation under the chairmanship of Philip Lowe, Duke of Northumberland Professor of Rural Economy at the University of Newcastle upon Tyne.

Against this background, the Department of the Environment decided to sponsor a conference on the theme 'Environmental Valuation in Context' held at St Aidan's College, Durham in March 1994. The decision to ask Philip Lowe and Norman Glass, Chief Economist at the Department of the Environment, to act as joint chairmen was deliberate; it was hoped that most if not all parties to the debate about environmental valuation would regard at least one of them as sympathetic to their views.

The conference itself was divided into seven sessions. For each session there was a main paper and a second opinion. In virtually all sessions the second opinion proved to be every bit as substantive as the main paper and this is reflected in the equality of treatment afforded to the authors of the chapters of this book.

The first session consisted of an assessment by Robert Laslett of

London Economics of the theoretical underpinnings of cost–benefit analysis, and its strengths in appraising projects with environmental attributes with case examples. The second opinion was provided by Alan Holland, of the University of Lancaster, who reviewed the neoclassical underpinnings of cost–benefit analysis, the limitations of utilitarian assumptions, and future directions for the philosophical development of environmental valuation methodology. This was followed by Nick Hanley's paper which explored the problems of integrating environmental values into cost–benefit analysis.

The differing approaches of economists and ecologists were compared and contrasted in the third session. The two speakers, Martin Holdgate, Director of the World Conservation Union and Charles Perrings of the Department of Environmental Economics and Management at the University of York, indicated substantial areas of agreement despite their very different backgrounds.

Session 4, the last of the first day, was a discussion by Vic Adamowicz of the University of Alberta and Colin Price of the University College of North Wales of the pros and cons of alternative valuation methods. The former speaker in particular presented a detailed analysis of the valuation method known as stated preference, drawing attention to the advantages the technique has over other questionnaire based approaches.

In the first session on the second day, Michael Hanemann from the University of California, Berkeley provided a fascinating insight into experience in the United States with contingent valuation, including the controversy surrounding the *Exxon Valdez* case and the subsequent report by the National Oceanic and Atmospheric Administration. The implications of the NOAA report for contingent valuation work in Britain are discussed by Ken Willis in Chapter 8 of this volume.

Critical responses to Professor Hanemann's paper were provided by Chris Hope of the University of Cambridge (presented in Chapter 11) and by Barry Hedges of Social and Community Planning Research. From rather different viewpoints, both speakers focused attention on the psychological influences on people's perceptions and decisions affecting their ability to formulate rational judgements on environmental values.

Session 6 was devoted to a discussion of the transferability of environmental cost and benefit estimates. Ken Willis and Guy Garrod of the University of Newcastle upon Tyne addressed an issue of major concern to government departments in the appraisal of environmental impacts; namely the extent to which it is legitimate to apply values estimated for one particular policy or project to others. A detailed examination of this question in relation to the valuation of life and safety in transport appraisal is provided in the paper by Michael Jones-

Lee and Graham Loomes in Chapter 13.

The final session was devoted to a consideration of the factors governing the establishment of priorities for environmental valuation research. The papers by David Newbery, Director of the Department of Applied Economics in the University of Cambridge, and by Norman Glass and John Corkindale of the Department of the Environment, in Chapters 14 and 15 respectively, capture the main points.

It seems clear that the need for good research on environmental valuation will continue to be with us for a long time to come. As the UK Sustainable Development Strategy (Cm. 2426), published in January 1994, puts it:

> (The market) cannot give proper weight to environmental considerations unless the costs of environmental damage or the benefits of environmental improvements are built into the prices charged for goods and services.

Although internalizing environmental externalities is only one aspect of the need for research on environmental values, the framework of welfare economics, particularly as applied in cost–benefit analysis, evidently has an important role to play. Like any model it is inevitably a simplication of the real world. The advantage of simplication is that it makes it possible to bring rational analysis to bear. The drawback is that simplication may involve some questionable assumptions. It is incumbent on practitioners not to lose sight of these problems and to address them wherever possible. If this conference and the papers in this volume have provided some stimulus to such critical scrutiny they will have served their purpose.

References

Arrow, K., Solow, R., Portney, P., Leamer, E., Radner, R. and Schuman, H. (1993) Report of the NOAA Panel on Contingent Valuation. *Federal Register* 58(10), 4601–4614.

Department of the Environment (1991) *Policy Appraisal and the Environment.* HMSO, London.

Department of the Environment (1994) *Environmental Appraisal in Government Departments.* HMSO, London.

HM Government (1990) *This Common Inheritance: Britain's Environmental Strategy*, Cm. 1200. HMSO, London.

HM Government (1994) *Sustainable Development: The UK Strategy*, Cm. 2426. HMSO, London.

2

The Assumptions of Cost–Benefit Analysis[1]

Robert Laslett

London Economics Ltd

Introduction

The main reason for talking about the 'assumptions' of cost–benefit analysis (CBA) is that CBA is a subject that causes difficulty in discussions between economists and non-economists, and not just in the context of the environment. What one group finds obvious, the other may find obscure and vice versa. This is because the assumptions of economics itself are deeply embedded in CBA, and are not widely shared outside the profession. It is these assumptions that are examined in this chapter.

CBA attributes a social value to everything affected by a project. Some things are negatively affected (costs) and some are positively affected (benefits). CBA adds up the costs, and the benefits. It takes the resulting estimate of the costs away from the benefits. It gives a social decision rule: economics says a project whose benefits exceed its costs is worth considering, while one whose benefits are less than its costs is not.

There are at least four sticking points in this formula:

1. How, exactly, does CBA attribute social values?
2. What do we mean by everything that is affected?
3. Can you add up and take costs away from benefits and believe in the resulting figure?
4. Should society do something just because economics says so?

[1] I am indebted to Alberto Pototschnig and Michael Webb for comments on the draft. Mistakes, and the views expressed, remain my own.

These questions are addressed in reverse order. The last of them is perhaps the easiest to deal with, especially in the environmental context.

Societies tend to do rather few things that economists say they should, even in areas where it is acknowledged that economics is quite important. There are a few cases where economic principles have guided policy, such as progress since 1945 towards global free trade in manufactures under the General Agreement on Tariffs and Trade (GATT). But, for counter examples, think of the way agriculture is heavily protected. Or the ways in which the tax system departs from what would be economically desirable, for instance taxing saving as well as consumption.

Economics is only one of a set of forces bearing on any social decision. But it does have a claim to attention, namely that it gives a judicious balancing of the gains to unnamed people (e.g. those who would work in industries that would grow under free trade) against the losses to vocal known people (e.g. French farmers), who claim they would lose. It thus claims to give results that better reflect the welfare of society as a whole than do purely consultative processes, where the most vocal tend to dominate the outcome.

We will see in reviewing the other difficulties with CBA how far this claim on behalf of economics is really justified. At the end we will return, as good economists should, to the question of alternatives to CBA.

Before going on, it is worth noting that many exercises involving the assessment of costs and benefits using economics are not full social CBA. Such studies, which might be termed impact assessments, are the subject of a good deal of consultancy work. Most business clients are interested only in financial costs and benefits. And while public bodies often look at some non-financial costs and benefits, they do not always try to assess all of them. The Department of Trade and Industry's Compliance Cost Assessments for evaluating policy proposals for instance are concerned mainly with first round effects such as the cost of filling in forms. The results of such analyses are interesting, but they do not reflect the full range of sophistication of CBA as an approach to policy and project analysis.

It is also worth noting that economists have spent some time analysing the difficulties of social decision rules, and appreciate the difficulties involved in setting rules that are appropriate to all situations. While rules such as majority voting respect many of the basic values one would want to see embodied in social decisions, there can be configurations of preferences that make them intolerable. For instance, if I have 'meddlesome' preferences and care more about what you do than you do yourself, almost all decision rules based on consultation and preferences break down. Such preferences may be relevant to environmental issues, for example in the tension between local and expert views about the relative priorities of conservation and development in a given region. CBA is no exception to these difficulties, and so it does not work equally well in all contexts.

Netting off Costs and Benefits

One of the key points about CBA is that it takes a balance: it weighs information about costs and benefits and decides on the basis of net benefits. This is inevitable in any sort of policy or project analysis, however quantitative or qualitative it may be. There are always losses and gains and there has to be some way of weighing them up and deciding what to do. Otherwise, societies would be paralysed and unable to act at all on contentious policy questions. This sort of paralysis can be just as great a risk to the environment as over activity. For example, logging in the old-growth forests of the Pacific Northwest goes on partly because logging-town special interests make it impossible to reach what might be a socially optimal decision to stop it.

CBA recognizes the need to look at both sides, and sets a so-called compensation test:

> if benefits exceed costs then, in principle at least, the gainers could compensate the losers and there would still be something left over for everyone.

In practice, compensation has generally only been paid for the most direct kinds of environmental loss, such as when land is acquired for transport schemes. Law courts are extending the reach of the demand for compensation, especially in the USA. And they are reaching for an economic basis for such compensation, as with the use of survey results to help assess the damage inflicted on the environment by the *Exxon Valdez* disaster.[2]

There are several problems with the compensation test. The first is that compensation might radically change the distribution of income. Let us think about global warming: if CBA suggested that it was not worth investing in widespread carbon abatement measures, there would nevertheless be a case for compensating the poor people in developing countries who would have gained much of the benefit of abatement, at the expense of much richer people in developed countries who would otherwise have faced much of the cost of taking

---

[2] These surveys tried to elicit willingness to pay through contingent valuation techniques, in which respondents are asked how much they would pay to protect the environment, or how much they would need to be paid to compensate them for damage to it.

abatement measures. But if such compensation were paid, it would result in a huge redistribution of income, and would produce large changes in world energy demand and prices. It might be that, if the CBA were repeated after these changes, it would show that abatement was worthwhile. If such a reversal were to occur, it would undermine the usefulness of CBA for assisting social decisions.

The second problem is that the results may not accord with our conceptions of social justice. A policy change might take income away from the poorest;[3] this is, for instance, a problem in raising fuel prices to efficient levels in countries of the former USSR and elsewhere: the poor find fuel impossible to afford. It is also one possible interpretation of why it is difficult to agree on measures to control global warming: developing countries would be further impoverished if they had to compensate developed countries for the abatement costs they would face.

A third issue is that not all losses can be compensated, even in principle, perhaps because they are irreversible. An obvious example is the loss of human life. Societies are unwilling to sanction such a loss as the price of a broader social gain, especially if the identity of the likely victims is known in advance. They sometimes do, for example when the National Health Service decides to withhold treatment from smokers, but normally the losses that it is permissible to inflict have to be constrained by a system of laws. We may want to constrain them in other ways as well. For instance, the UK may want to protect Sites of Special Scientific Interest, or National Parks, through rules that would prevent their destruction in the name of broader policy gains. This is a theme we will return to in the discussion of values below.

So compensation issues can cause difficulties, especially for large-scale projects which produce large effects, and for irreversible effects. This is not a problem with CBA in principle: rather it is an aspect where the theory of CBA is perhaps in advance of alternative techniques, and of many of its critics, in identifying and recognizing the problems of analysing the pros and cons of projects or policies. But it does suggest a daunting set of practical difficulties in carrying out adequate CBAs in practice.

What Do We Mean by Everything That Is Affected?

CBA requires that all the effects of a project need to be taken into account and brought into the same framework. This framework is one that compares the world after the project takes place with the world as

---

[3] This would violate the Rawlian concept of maximum justice (Rawls, 1971).

it would have looked without it; the so called counterfactual world. Often the counterfactual is no more than a continuation of the previous state of affairs, but sometimes it involves considering what the next-best alternative investment or policy might be. For example, in performing its CBA on the National Forest project, London Economics had to consider the likely level of housing and industrial development in the area in the absence of new tree planting (London Economics, 1993).

There are various distinctions to be made between categories of effects:

1. large effects focused on small groups, and small but widespread effects;
2. effects on quantities or prices;
3. effects on marketed and non-marketed commodities;
4. direct and indirect effects;
5. current and future effects; and
6. certain effects and risks.

The only effects that CBA deliberately leaves out are those on people who are not members of the society for which the decision is being taken. For a UK project, the relevant society usually consists of UK residents. But, as the implications of our EU membership become clearer, it becomes more difficult to portray costs to other EU residents as matters of no concern for UK policy. Many environmental issues require a focus on global benefits and costs, and on effects on future generations. And it is an open question whether it is reasonable to include the effects on non-humans (or at least our evaluation of the effects on them) into policy and project analysis.

This attempt to be inclusive results both in some strengths, and in the acknowledgement of some weaknesses. One of CBA's strengths is that it takes into account not only large effects on small groups (for instance the effect of a new bypass on villages in its immediate proximity) but small effects on large groups (for instance the effect on city centre residents and motorists using the road). Techniques that do not do this fall prey to special interest lobbying much more easily than CBA, which really does try to keep society as a whole as its focus. But there is plenty of room for debate about the way in which the two types of effect should be weighed up.

Because of its rooting in economics, CBA is also quite good at bringing quantity and price effects into the same framework. Various techniques exist to bring effects on non-marketed things, such as landscape and air quality, into line with those on marketed commodities. These techniques are the focus of a number of other chapters in this volume. For the present purpose it is worth noting that economics is not very good at recognizing value in contexts where there is no market price. Generally, non-economists have been at the forefront of establishing the value of non-marketed goods, and mainstream economics has only come to a belated recognition of their importance.

What about the weaknesses? Direct effects are those within the market under consideration: in assessing the effects of the Montreal chlorofluorocarbon (CFC) protocols, for example, the direct effects would be those on the makers and users of CFCs, and those who suffer from the pollution they cause. The indirect effects would be on other markets – those for alternative refrigerants for example. It is only feasible to look at the direct, and the most obvious indirect effects in CBA, and this reveals one of its limitations. It is not very good with very large projects or changes in policy, because they have very widespread indirect ramifications. The limits on CFCs will probably affect the prices of many other materials and final products, and wages, investment and economic growth could all be affected. The indirect effects may dwarf the direct ones. So one would be very wary of a CBA of the CFC issue which only looked at the direct effects.

The relationship between current and future effects is one of the most difficult areas for CBA, and will be discussed further below. It is related to the question of what society CBA is deciding for; can we take the welfare of future people any less seriously than that of those alive today?

Some of the effects of a project are more or less bound to happen – such as a rise in electricity prices if the nuclear levy goes up. Others are much less so – such as the change in the risk of a nuclear accident as a result of taking additional safety measures. CBAs typically try to include any effects on risk by using the expected value of the risk, that is by weighting welfare under each outcome by the chance of its occurrence. This assumes that society does not mind about risk, except for the costs of the alternative outcomes, and the costs of risk bearing are not typically included in CBA.[4] But it is people, not society, who bear most risks. The personal costs of risk-bearing – in this case the agony of lying awake at night worrying about a nuclear accident – can be high, and they clearly have an effect on welfare. There is a case for thinking they should be included in social decision rules.

Revealing the weaknesses in the CBA approach is not the same as discrediting the approach. Rather it reveals the sorts of situation to which it can readily be applied, and those where the complexities are likely to get out of hand.

---

[4] There is no reason in principle why CBAs should not include the cost of risk-bearing, particularly if the risk in question is priced in insurance or other markets.

How Does CBA Attribute Social Values?

This is the most fundamental question of all. The answer, as one might expect from economists, is that it does so according to the market. And this can often end the debate and rule out the use of CBA in a particular context. Non-economists are likely to contend that social values, especially in emotive contexts like the environment, are the stuff of moral statements and political principles, not markets. They may even contend that economists, like cynics, understand the price of everything and the value of nothing.

Economists' descriptions of the market to which they are referring invite another set of doubts, this time about their realism. This is because the market behind CBA's attribution of social values is not just any market, but the theoretically ideal market of abstract analysis; where, among other things:

1. there are so many small sellers and buyers that no one individually can affect the price;
2. everyone is perfectly informed;
3. there is a mechanism to make sure no one trades at a different price from anyone else.

How can this peculiar theoretical construct be a useful way of understanding what happens in real markets, in predicting when they will go wrong and in suggesting what can be done about it?

The economist's fundamental criterion of value is: what are people willing to pay for something? What are they prepared to give up to acquire or defend it? It is because of this focus on payment that markets – which do otherwise seem rather irrelevant to social values – are useful.

The economist's old, familiar demand curve for a product, is in one light a way of summarizing society's willingness to pay.[5] On the leftmost edge of Fig. 2.1 lies the individual who is willing to pay most – the millionaire dying after being assaulted and prepared to part with everything to get medical attention. On the rightmost edge are those who really don't care at all.

Looked at in this way, as an ordered summary of people's willingness to pay, the demand curve for a product is of obvious importance in measuring social benefits. In fact, the area under it (leftward of a given quantity) is the economic benefit of that product. And, more realistically, the change in the area between one quantity of

---

[5] This is in principle a Hicks-compensation demand curve, which keeps welfare constant as prices and quantities change, but in practice the more easily measured Marshallian demand curve which keeps income constant will do as an approximation. Even so, measuring the shape of the demand curve can be a serious practical obstacle (Pearce, 1983).

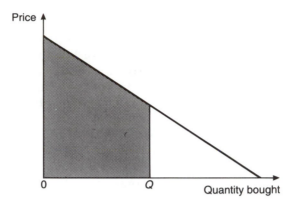

Fig. 2.1. Demand curve.

a product and another is the benefit of having more of it. The aim of survey techniques that assess willingness to pay in non-market situations is to approximate the demand curve that would have existed, had there been a market.

So much for benefits, what about costs? Well, a supply curve is the same sort of ordered summary. On the left of Fig. 2.2 are the cheapest sources of supply, on the right the most expensive. Coffee plantations for instance differ in their fertility and ease of access. Those which are fertile and nearby will tend to produce beans cheaply; they are on the left. Old, small and remote ones will be costlier and will be on the right. The area under the curve is the aggregate costs of production of a given quantity. And the area between two quantities is the cost of having more.

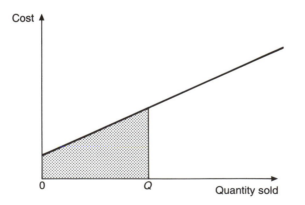

Fig. 2.2. Supply curve.

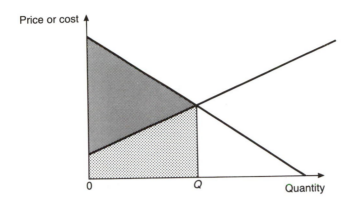

Fig. 2.3. Market equilibrium.

The quantity which economics says that society wants to reach is the one where net social benefit, measured by the heavily-shaded area in Fig. 2.3, is greatest. And this is where the supply and demand curves intersect. Further to the left, an increased quantity would mean more net benefits and vice versa. So the market, whose role is to find a price that equates supply and demand, has got us to a quantity where everyone's demands are met, just up to the point where it is worthwhile doing so.

Thus the market price summarizes an enormous amount of information. It provides, in a single figure, a measure of social value that takes account of the strengths of everyone's preferences and the costs of production facing all suppliers, and delivers maximum net social welfare.

But just what hidden assumptions have been made in getting to this point? They concern at least four things; preferences, the distribution of income, conditions in the supplying industry, and externalities.

Preferences

Market prices reflect the preferences of the current moment, based on the information, income, fashions and prejudices of the moment. Cost–benefit calculations tend to assume that such preferences will remain constant enough over a long period of time to be a parameter of the analysis. But preferences do change over time, and over long periods of time they can change out of all recognition. This can be very important for the environment.

Think for instance about the way in which the design and use of zoos has changed over the centuries. In the 19th century, they were largely concerned with the display of animals, whose welfare was not an objective in itself. It was even common for visitors to poke them with walking sticks and otherwise discomfort them, as a means of entertainment. Now we judge zoos much more by the extent to which they enable the animals in captivity to enjoy the privacy, interest and – to the extent possible – freedom they would have in the wild. This transformation of values can be attributed to many things. Increasing income and leisure, the increasing separation of city dwellers from the life of the farm, and increasing information about the natural environment of animals are all probably at work.

Changes in preferences can occur much more rapidly than this. An example is the radical change in the prices of paintings over quite short periods following an artist's death; for instance the paintings of Van Gogh. Part of the explanation is the scarcity value with which paintings by dead artists are endowed. As aspects of the environment acquire scarcity value, society's preference for them may increase out of all recognition.

A final question is the relative strength of the preferences of the gainers and the losers from a project. As we have seen, it is generally a strength of CBA that it tries to incorporate the diffuse as well as the specific effects of a project. But it is not always desirable to inflict large costs on small groups to the slight benefit of the rest of us. CBA would probably show net benefits from projects that further destroy the peace of English villages for the sake of rapid motoring. This is an area where we can be grateful that CBA is placed in the context of a political system that listens to loud small groups.

Distribution of income

Why is income distribution important in CBA's attribution of values? Let us start with our example of the man dying after being assaulted. Why is he at the left hand side of the demand curve? Because he is desperate? Well, he is, but it's not just that. It is also because he is a millionaire. If he had been a refugee, he would perhaps have been unable to pay much at all, and he would have been way over to the right. Maybe so far to the right that he was beyond the market's recommended quantity. So the market would have left him to die. Which would be inconsistent with the fundamental moral judgment which drives normal social values. We are taught to approve of the Samaritan who helps the victim, not the Levite and the Pharisee who pass him by.

More generally, by saying that the market value gives the social value, one accepts the pattern of willingness to pay given by today's distribution of income. This may be fine, or it may not. There are often substantial disagreements over the distribution of income, and if you think the current distribution is wrong, you can consistently question every CBA based on market prices. Where the distribution of income is widely acknowledged to be wrong, as in the imbalance between rich and poor countries, markets may provide very poor guidance as to whether the right amount of goods are being produced, consumed or traded.

Supply conditions

Another issue for valuation is the competitive conditions under which the market is supplied. We assumed that producers simply take the market price as given. This seemed reasonable, for coffee producers are small and none of them can affect the market price very much. This situation is stable, as the unsuccessful attempts by coffee producing countries to cartelize the industry have demonstrated.

But what if we leave our after dinner coffee and turn our attention to the video that is playing on the TV. Hollywood produces films which are cheap, in the relation to the number of viewers they attract, and they enjoy economies of scale. European film makers sometimes cannot compete. Hollywood could easily satisfy the entire European film market. Over the last 10 years, in fact, it has come close to doing so. And as it gets bigger and more successful, its competitive advantage grows.

In the end, Hollywood's film makers might get together and say, 'Hey, we're selling all the pictures in this market, why not make more profit out of it?' And they could – a single seller can make more profit from a market by restricting supply and pushing up prices. And the price where profits are greatest may be far from the point where social net benefits are greatest. So in monopoly or cartelized industries, one may not be able to trust the market to guide suppliers to do the right thing for society. Rather the suppliers are pushing the market.

Many supplier-dominated markets are in important areas for the environment. Think of the market for electric power in this country. National Power and PowerGen between them control over half the capacity in the system, and the regulator OFFER is always on its guard against their influencing the market, for instance in the recent decision to force them to divest capacity and set a limit on prices.

Externalities

The final issue to mention here is that of externalities. An externality is when someone lights up a cigarette at the next table just as I am starting my soup, and my enjoyment of my meal goes down. In the end, I go to restaurants less often because they are likely to be smoky. My welfare is reduced, my health is threatened, and I eat out less frequently than I would like.

Markets often don't solve the externality problem very well: a few restaurants may voluntarily create no-smoking areas or have no-smoking policies. But the business of smokers is too important for most of them to give it up, and the more non-smokers stay at home, the greater the market power of the smokers.

Markets are bent out of shape (distorted, in economists' parlance) by externalities like these, and it takes a non-market intervention to bend them back. Perhaps local authority would have to set rules on providing no-smoking zones to get me out to eat as often as I would like.

And externalities may be very widespread. Think of the environmental externalities resulting from the production of goods and services that go directly or indirectly into meeting our daily requirements: electricity generation produces CO_2 and SO_2 pollution as well as power; vehicles produce NO_x, lead, and noise as well as transportation services; agriculture produces fertilizer and pesticide runoffs as well as food.

Having acknowledged that externalities are widespread, we have admitted that many market prices really do not provide an adequate structure of social values on which to hang our cost–benefit analysis.

CBA does have an answer to this, in the form of 'shadow prices', the prices that would have existed, had there been ideal markets without distortions.

There is a literature (e.g. Scott *et al.*, 1976) on how to do such CBAs in developing countries, where distortions are widespread and severe because markets are not working properly. This literature runs into difficulties because of the enormous complexity of constructing the necessary shadow prices, the inevitable limitations on the data available, and the fact that allowing economists to say what shadow prices are puts them in the position of deciding what social values should be.

Theoretically, the appropriate shadow prices could be determined as those that solve the problem: maximize social welfare, given society's resources. But this is what central planning tried to do, and it failed. It failed for many reasons, but a chief one was the impossibility of collecting enough information on preferences and production costs. A central planner (or CBA expert) could never have all the information needed to say what a single market price would really be in the absence of a distortion. And if distortions are serious and widespread, he would have to calculate all shadow prices for all markets, a doubly impossible task. The great beauty of relying on market prices – which as we saw was that they encapsulate a great deal of information about production costs and people's preferences – is lost in this approach.

For this reason the sort of CBA that tried to put a shadow price on every individual product affected by a project never really took hold. In practical project appraisal in developing countries, it came to be accepted that shadow prices could only really be applied in two contexts: the price of labour and the rate of discount.

The price of labour is of concern because of the very high level of unemployment in many developing countries, and the fact that different wages are paid for the same kind of labour in different markets, suggesting that supply and demand in the labour market are out of balance. This we can pass over fairly quickly in the case of the UK. For better or worse, even with millions collecting unemployment benefit, it is generally assumed that actual wages do clear the labour market. But it is worth remembering that economists count labour used as a cost, not a benefit, to society. It is possible to argue with this view, as Robert Lane (1991) does in *The Market Experience*. His evidence suggests that work is not a disutility but a major source of lifetime satisfaction, while money income contributes relatively little to a sense of well-being.

The second area where shadow pricing is common is the rate of discount, which affects the price of everything in the CBA today, relative to future periods. It tries to encapsulate society's attitude to the value of things in the future, relative to today. The discount rate is, if you like, the shadow price of capital.

In developing countries, capital markets are often rudimentary and interest rates do not provide a reliable indicator of the social tradeoff between today and tomorrow. But why in Britain, with its highly developed capital and futures markets, do we need to set a shadow price for capital?

The reason is that there are several possible views of the social price of capital. One is the marginal product of capital, or the rate of return one would get by investing funds in the best available project. Another is the social rate of time preference, or the rate you would have to pay to compensate people for postponing consumption.

The social rate of time preference may be lower than the marginal cost of capital, which is raised by company taxation, or because society as a whole can afford to take risks no individual or company can.

The discount rate has been the subject of enormous controversy. Using any rate greater than zero in a CBA implies that society regards a benefit to tomorrow's citizen as less important than an equivalent benefit to today's. This is all right, say, for valuing a pint of beer. Tomorrow's citizen will probably be richer than today's and will be able to pay a bit more for that last pint.

But what if we are talking about landscape, or some other diminishing resource? Is it legitimate to suppose that Britain's future citizens will have a richer landscape than today's? Many feel that, under these circumstances, the use of a discount rate may lead CBA to recommend seriously incorrect social decisions. Others argue that lowering the discount rate will lead CBA to sanction so many environmental projects as worthwhile that it becomes useless for making social decisions about them.

But the rules of CBA do not compel us to use a single price to represent the tradeoff between future and present value. As Markandya and Pearce (1991) show, it may make sense to assume that the prices of certain goods will rise in relative terms in the future. In our example, the social value of a particular unspoilt piece of landscape will quite probably rise in relation to that of a pint of beer as people get richer and as more unspoilt landscape is lost. This was in fact a technique that London Economics used in its analysis of the costs and benefits of the National Forest landscape improvement project in the Midlands.[6]

To sum up, for environmental projects at least, there is a wide range of serious market distortions to consider even in the UK. This means that environmental CBA in the UK has to operate in the same sort of world as the one surrounding non-environmental projects in developing countries. Thus shadow prices will probably have to be widely used. And this is difficult territory for CBA.

Conclusion

The note I would like to end on is that CBA does what any serious tool for analysing policies or projects has to do:

1. it evaluates their pros and cons in a consistent framework;
2. it recognizes its own limitations, for instance the fact that it works better for small changes than for large ones;
3. it recognizes the need for a consistent view of what the world would have looked like without the project;
4. it looks forward and explores gains and losses through time;
5. it brings in as much information as possible on preferences and costs.

There are of course in practice severe limits to the ability of CBAs to meet the criteria that are set for them. At worst, CBA can be a 'black box' technique where economists blind the public with complex assumptions and calculations, without adequate safeguards and cross checking. And, to return to the opening list of sticking points,

---

[6] It is in fact the assumptions involved in deriving a monetary equivalent to welfare in each period, rather than the exchange rate between money in the two periods, that is often at issue.

economists who do this reduce the impact of economics and of CBA in particular on practical decision making.

An instance of this occurred at the World Bank in the 1970s. The focus of the institution was on maintaining a high level of lending, while demonstrating a convincing net social benefit using CBA was a necessary condition for projects to pass the Board. Not surprisingly, this did not ensure that the Bank's projects were good – in fact they got worse. What had happened was that the Bank's economists became expert at producing certain results from the CBA process. The result was to devalue CBA in the Bank. In the 1990s, CBA is still required for most World Bank projects, but it is less of a focus of attention and analysis as a result of this episode.

This to me is a pity, because I believe CBA is a framework to critique and refine, not to discard. And it was unnecessary – a more flexible approach to targets combined with more real respect for the technique succeeded in companies like Exxon that relied heavily on project analysis but were willing to let their investment decline. What is most necessary now is wide professional discussion of the tricky issues such as valuation, the beginnings of which can be found in some of the other chapters in this volume.

I would also contend that economists need to further develop the system of peer review for CBAs. In the UK, the role in the process of an expert and sceptical funding agency like the Treasury is very valuable for keeping consultants and staff of the Government Economic Service alike on the straight and narrow. But the Treasury has its own public finance objectives that are not necessarily at one with social welfare on every issue. I have no doubt that as economists we could ourselves do more to ensure professional discipline and integrity in carrying out these important pieces of analysis.

Finally, I would like to return to the question of the alternatives to CBA. Economics is a discipline that encourages us to think in terms of costs and benefits in relation to a defined alternative. It is not realistic to compare CBA with an idealized decision rule that would satisfy all interest groups. So what alternative decision rule might society realistically use? The problems of a *laissez-faire* model in which business makes all the decisions are clear from the discussion of market failure. While paternalism does hold some appeal for environmental protection – much of the bird life of England owes its preservation to aristocratic estates – few people would want a system where decisions are made centrally on the basis of the values of an elite. And I would contend that techniques such as environmental impact assessment are too narrowly focused to substitute for CBA.

The real alternatives are to be found in the structures which provide the context for CBA to work in, namely the legal and political systems. I am sure I am not alone in being far more comfortable with using CBA to assess projects and policies in the UK's context of deeply embedded respect for law, for personal rights and for minority constituencies, than I would be in some other parts of the world where conditions are very different.

References

Lane, R.E. (1991) *The Market Experience.* Cambridge University Press, Cambridge.

London Economics (1993) *National Forest Cost Benefit Analysis.* Final Report. London Economics, London.

Markandya, A. and Pearce, D. (1991) Development, environment and the social rate of discount. *World Bank Observer,* July 1991, pp. 137–152.

Pearce, D. (1983) *Cost–Benefit Analysis,* 2nd edn. Macmillan, London.

Rawls, J. (1971) *A Theory of Justice.* Harvard University Press, Cambridge, Massachusetts.

Scott, M.P.G., McArthur, J.D. and Newbery, D.M.G. (1976) *Project Appraisal in Practice: The Little–Mirlees Method Applied to Kenya.* Heinemann, London.

3

The Assumptions of Cost–Benefit Analysis: A Philosopher's View[1]

Alan Holland

University of Lancaster

Introduction

This chapter focuses on some of the framework assumptions that are implicit in cost–benefit analysis as it is currently practised and applied in environmental contexts, involving: (i) its concept of the environment, (ii) its picture of human nature and (iii) its role in the social and political process. Central to its application in valuing the environment is the 'itemizing' of environmental goods; central to its picture of human nature is the 'homogeneity' of preferences; central to its role in the political process is the 'privatizing' of judgement. Each of these aspects is discussed and assessed in terms of whether each frustrates rather than promotes the objectives that many practitioners of environmental economics hope to achieve. Some steps which might help to remedy the situation are suggested.

Queer Questions

Some things in our lives matter to us more than others; some things are particularly precious and have a particular significance. For a long-standing member of the Church of England, for example, it may matter very much whether women are to be made eligible to be ordained as priests. For a person with a longstanding love of the countryside, it may

[1] Both the conception and the development of the themes of this chapter owe a great deal to the discussions of the Environmental Economics Research group at Lancaster University, held under the auspices of the Philosophy Department and the Centre for the Study of Environmental Change. I am most grateful to the members of this group for their support.

matter very much whether a new road is to be built through a tract of ancient forest.

In the environmental case, the practice has grown up of approaching such questions by pretending that the situation is akin to that of a market, where the continued existence of a forest is regarded as a good which we must purchase. This, of course, is the procedure which economists know as contingent valuation (CV). According to CV, how much a forest matters to us is established by asking how much we would be prepared to pay to secure the continuance of this good. An example of the procedure can be found in a recent paper discussing the viewing value of elephants. An average 'willingness to pay' (WTP) of $89 was elicited from those asked how much they would pay to help ensure that the population of African elephants was maintained at current levels (Gardner Brown, 1993, 152–154).[2]

It is worth asking how a similar approach would work for the religious issue or, say, for an issue such as hanging. Economists might consider these issues as raising questions about 'existence value', and 'irreversible loss' by which they mean the value that we attach to the fact that something exists, irrespective of any actual or potential use we may make of it. The equivalent questions might be: 'how much would you pay to secure the ordination of women priests/have the Church of England maintain its all-male priesthood?' or 'how much would you pay to see hanging retained/abolished?'. Looked at dispassionately, these are very *queer* questions, and this seems to be a very *queer* way of dealing with issues of this kind. One would expect there to be debate, with appropriate considerations being adduced and weighed. And except for the fact that we may be starting to become acclimatized to such questions, one suspects that, from a dispassionate point of view, the question and the manner of dealing with the issue are just as queer in the environmental case too. One reason for such a reaction would no doubt be the fact that the issue of women priests, or of hanging, is regarded as an issue of principle. And to be asked to trade one's principles, even hypothetically, is likely to seem inappropriate and even morally disreputable.[3] Yet the environmental case may equally be viewed as raising issues of principle – about cultural identity, for example, or rights – and therefore as giving rise to exactly the same grounds for disquiet. At any rate it *feels* more like the religious or moral issue than it does the street market transaction. Before proceeding to

---

[2] Factored by the 250,000 to 300,000 people on safari each year, this helped to suggest a 'viewing value' for elephants of around $25 million.

[3] In the case of accepting payment to give up one's principles this is fairly obvious. But the idea that willingness to pay is a measure of how much something matters to us is in general somewhat suspect. In the sphere of parent–child relations, for example, we might reflect that paying out large sums of money is precisely not the way for a parent to demonstrate how much their child matters to them.

explore the grounds for this disquiet further, a very rapid résumé is offered of how the demand for environmental valuation has arisen.

How Has It Come to This?

Our environmental sensibilities have come a long way since Daniel Defoe commented on the desolation and 'inhospitable terror' which he experienced when travelling through the area of England known locally as the 'three peaks', now part of the Yorkshire Dales National Park and judged an area of outstanding natural beauty (Defoe, 1928, 269). In fact, he expressed a distinct preference for the cheerful productiveness of the Yorkshire mill town of Halifax. In time, however, this cheerful productiveness (the industrial revolution) got out of hand, and slowly spawned its own kind of desolation – a humanly induced kind. People then began to ask themselves how this situation had come about, and economists came up with the answer that it was because we had not taken proper account of the cost of things. We had imagined that 'the things which nature provides' were free when they were not. The next question was: how do we take proper account of 'the things which nature provides'? Economists came up with the answer that we must bring them into relation with the things we *do* know the cost of, such as a bag of sugar and other such commodities. So we make out that the things which nature provides are commodities. However, we cannot introduce many of these things into real markets; therefore we make extrapolations from real markets where we can, using indicators such as travel costs and differential property prices. Where we cannot – the ozone layer, biodiversity, the species of elephants – we create the idea of a hypothetical market, and ask people what they *would* pay, if there was a market and they had to, for such a thing as the maintenance of the current elephant population. How much we are willing to pay is supposed to reflect the strength of our preferences; and social welfare is supposed to be optimized to the extent that our preferences are satisfied. Hence, if everyone pays the *true* cost of the things which nature provides, as measured by their willingness to pay, we achieve the most efficient allocation of resources and thereby, it is assumed, an optimum of social welfare. The whole situation has come about through imprudent accounting: the solution, therefore – prudent accounting – is obvious.

Two questions arise. First, what is involved in making the value of the things that nature provides commensurable with commodities that are bought and sold? Second, how likely is it that this procedure will help to resolve the problems it is designed to address?

Among the leading features of the first question as it is currently conceived, three in particular deserve to be singled out:

1. The itemizing of environmental goods. Just as marketed goods have to be itemized, wrapped and packed for consumption, so too are the goods that nature provides. The sea (bits of it, at any rate) are packaged as 'bathing water', or elephants (glimpses of them, at any rate) as items for viewing – 'spectacles', and so forth.

2. The homogenizing of value. The value of marketed goods is measured in terms of money. Because of this common measure the value of any such good can be compared with that of any other. If the value of environmental goods is to be brought into relation with that of marketed goods, then the same has to be true of them also. But not only must their value be comparable to that of any other environmental good; it must also be comparable to that of any marketed good.

3. The privatizing of decision making. What transpires at the checkout between the consumer and the person at the cash desk is a very private affair. The contents of the trolley are the issue of the consumer's own individual choices. So too, what transpires between you and the person conducting the cost–benefit survey is a private affair. The question is what you and you alone would pay to view the elephants. There is even a virtue made of this privacy – that it issues in unadulterated choices.

Each of these three elements would appear to be features of cost–benefit analysis (CBA) as it is currently practised. The question arises whether they are in principle essential to the project. This would certainly seem to be true of the first two. One cannot buy and sell what is not in some way itemized. And one cannot tell the cost of what nature provides without a measure that relates these items to others that are already costed. It is not so obvious, however, that the third element is essential; for it would seem to be contingent upon some theory of what constitutes an adequate basis for democratic policy making. All three elements are, however, equally problematic.

How likely is it that the above procedures will help to resolve the problems they are designed to address? This question is considered in terms of the effectiveness of the above features in cost–benefit analysis as applied in the environmental context, by looking at each of the features in turn.

Itemizing

Goods that are usually the subject of a market transaction are by and large *fit to be itemized,* i.e. they are by their nature suitable for itemizing. The reason is that most goods which are bought and sold in actual markets are artifacts. Those which are not artifacts are natural or semi-natural items which are artificially circumscribed in some way, by being categorized as, for example, a flower, a vegetable or a plot of land. Artifacts are fit to be itemized because they have a function. A screw or a nail is an item with a particular function; the only question is how many are needed for the particular job in hand. Although a plot of land does not have a function, it is artificially circumscribed to serve a particular purpose – to build a house on, for example. (And even if it is bought precisely to *prevent* its being built on, the price paid is that which it will fetch as building land.) Similarly, the parts of a plant by which it nourishes or reproduces itself are sold as vegetables or flowers. The goods that nature provides, on the other hand, before being assigned a function, are not by their nature fit to be itemized – or at least not fitted to be itemized.[4] Indeed, the very description of them as 'goods that nature provides' already compromises their status. Butter-cups and daisies, unlike nails and screws, are not *for* anything. There is nothing which dictates what function they should have.

A corollary of this point is that environmental goods of this kind can be assigned value, or lack of value, on any number of grounds. But since the price one puts on the value of a thing is presumably guided by the value one takes it to have, it becomes a crucial question how it is to be decided which value or values are appropriate in the case of natural goods. This in turn will be guided by how the natural items are identified and what functions they are assigned. In practice, such identifications are to a greater or lesser extent built into the particular questions which the subjects of a CBA study are asked, and are therefore determined by those who devise the questions. So a prejudge-ment affecting the valuation of the natural good is already built in to what purports to be a procedure for the *discovery* of value. The significance of the results which are obtained using the procedure is therefore called into question in a quite fundamental way.

The itemizing of goods further assumes that they can be given a value independently of their context.[5] This is largely true of goods that are the normal subjects of trade, and is connected with the fact that they have a standard use. However, this assumption is a quite unreasonable one to make in the case of environmental goods. Consider, for example, the quality of silence. In some contexts, it may be this very quality that makes a particular place special, a place of peace and tranquillity. In other contexts, this same quality may be disturbing, a source of unease – perhaps because it is an unnatural silence – and therefore detracts

[4] This is intended as a logical point, not as the moral objection which says that environmental goods *ought* not to be traded.
[5] Of course, they may have a different value to different people because of their different circumstances, but that is a separate point.

from the value of a place. Screws, on the other hand, make pretty well the same contribution to whatever structure they help to keep together.

In response to this point, economists can restrict their questions, and their interpretation of the validity of the answers, to a particular context. For example, they can focus upon the value of silence on Coniston Water – clearly a pertinent question if the discussion is about whether power boats are to be allowed on the Water. However, this does not quite meet the point. The reason *why* the silence cannot be valued independently of context and why, therefore, the 'value' obtained cannot be extrapolated to another context is that the value of Coniston as it is is not the sum of the value of two things, the Water and its silence.

The questionable status of the project of itemizing the goods which nature provides may have some bearing on a problem which has arisen in the conduct of contingent valuation surveys: the so-called 'embedding effect' (Kahneman and Knetsch, 1992, 58). People are apt to declare themselves willing to pay almost as much to preserve a single elephant or rhinoceros as they would pay to preserve the whole of African wildlife. Or again, they declare themselves willing to pay almost as much to provide decent watering for 2000 migratory birds as for 200,000 (Desvouges, 1993). Economists are puzzled by this phenomenon and have produced a variety of hypotheses to explain it. It has been suggested that those who give such responses are not rational, or have failed to understand the question; or that the question has not been clearly articulated (Arrow *et al.*, 1993). It has been suggested that the phenomenon is due to the operation of diminishing marginal utility: the satisfaction derived from helping 2000 birds quickly palls as the number helped increases. The ingenious suggestion put forward by Kahneman and Knetsch (1992, 64) to explain this anomaly is that what respondents are hypothetically purchasing is not an environmental good at all, but simply the moral satisfaction they derive from contributing to a good cause. It is notable that what all these hypotheses have in common is that they impugn the wits and/or self-knowledge of those involved while leaving the credentials of the methodology intact.

A simple alternative explanation is available, however, which is that 2000 migratory birds cannot sensibly be treated as an item subject to independent valuation and aggregation, and that what is at fault is not the rationality or self-knowledge of those questioned, but the assumptions and methodology which are built in to the cost–benefit exercise. Perhaps people simply do not see 2000 migratory birds in the way they might see a pound of butter, so that 100 of these 'items' somehow has to compute and be regarded as 100 times more valuable.

To reintroduce the analogies with which we began, let us suppose that someone declares themselves willing to pay a million pounds to ensure the ordination of women priests, but would also pay no more to ensure 20 being ordained than to ensure just one; or would pay no more to prevent 20 people being hanged than to prevent one. Should we question their rationality, or suggest the operation of diminishing marginal utility – so that once one has been ordained or hanged the increasing utility of subsequent ordinations or prevented hangings rapidly evaporates? Or should we suggest that they are not really interested in the priesthood, or the fate of those who are hanged, but are out to secure their own moral comfort? At least as likely an explanation is that a single ordination, or a single hanging, is not viewed as an item subject to independent evelation and aggregation. That way of measuring the importance and significance of these issues simply does not map onto the way it is perceived by those involved.

A lesson from this might be that more concerted attempts should be made to capture the integrated vision people often have of these issues rather than to refine the techniques based on an itemizing procedure, which really does seem a lost labour. As the embedding phenomenon seems to show, people's responses are highly dependent on the way in which the issues are presented. Moreover, the difference made by how the issue is conceived and presented for evaluation quite outweighs any difference made by refining the results gained under any particular conception, introducing a radical uncertainty into any results which are gained. This source of uncertainty matches and compounds that which also arises from (i) the aggregation process itself, which will magnify any 'errors',[6] and (ii) the choice of the population whose preferences are to count (Common *et al.*, 1993, 309). All of these are problems that attend the itemizing approach.

Homogenizing

One objection to making the value of the things that nature provides commensurable with commodities that are bought and sold, which at present has a certain 'currency', is that it effectively turns everything into money. Nature is not simply a supermarket, but a bank (wherein, presumably, natural capital is to be found). In response to this objection, economists insist that it simply rests on a conflation of the measure with what is measured, and that the use of money to calibrate people's preferences is an entirely contingent matter of convenience.

---

[6] Whether any procedure exists for the detection of 'errors' is a further troublesome issue (Common *et al.*, 1993, 306).

Indeed, what seems to confirm this as a justified response is that one can well imagine another measure, such as time, being used to serve exactly the same function at present served by money. Instead of being asked how much money they would pay to help protect species, people would be asked how much time they would be willing to give up (their WTST – their willingness to spend time). This would actually have a number of advantages over the money measure. For example, not everyone has the same amount of money, and some WTP studies are said to be unreliable because of this. Everyone, however, lives through the same number of hours in a day. Moreover, there are said to be doubts about whether people respond to WTP unrealistically in relation to their available budget. In the case of the time measure, it would at least be clear if a person were doing without any sleep, or living a 75 hour day.

There still remains the objection to the monetary measure, namely that acts of monetary evaluation have a very definite cultural significance (O'Neill, 1993, 118–120). Monetary transactions cannot be treated as if they take place in a social vacuum; unfavourable connotations cannot be ignored. It might be replied that, just as the use of this particular measure is contingent to the CBA exercise, so also is the cultural significance of money a contingent phenomenon, and therefore capable of modification: we could come to think differently about money. In other words, this objection to the use of the money measure cannot be regarded as revealing an inherent flaw in the CBA project. But what this reply shows is only that money could be divorced of a particular social meaning, not that it could be divorced of any; which means, at least, that its claim to 'neutrality' cannot be upheld.

Moreover, the claim that money is 'merely a measure' is, in a sense, too successful. Money is 'merely a measure' in ordinary markets as much as it is in hypothetical ones. This suggests that the 'monetary' objection to bringing environmental goods into the market place is partly aimed, not at the use of the monetary measure itself, but at what it signifies. What it signifies is transferability. In other words, we accept the idea of monetary exchange for items that are readily substitutable: one bag of sugar is much like another. To bring environmental goods into the market is effectively to pronounce them also substitutable; and this is an idea that meets some resistance. It seems to be true of certain environmental goods, as of whom and what we cherish generally, that their very irreplaceability is part of what we value, so that any value assigned as if they were substitutable is bound to be wide of the mark.

One reply would be to point out that we do accept the idea of monetary exchange for items which are irreplaceable. Financial damages are awarded, for example, in reparation for injury or injustice. However, what is wrong with this reply is that the question of compensation is one which arises *after* an event which has been *involuntarily* undergone; it is a concept which arises in the context of a system of justice. The question of willingness to pay, on the other hand, is raised *before* an event which is *voluntarily* entered into. Therefore, to suppose that the practice of compensation for injury in any way vindicates contingent valuation is to confuse a system of trade with a system of justice. It should be noted that the point holds just as firm if no money at all is involved, as when developers propose compensation in kind − for example the creation of a meadow on another site to compensate for one which is needed for a supermarket.

A second reply would be to instance the art world, where 'priceless' and irreplaceable works of art are regularly the subject of monetary transaction. The problem with this reply, however, is that the cases are far from analogous. What is bought and sold in the world of art is the right of exclusive possession, not, as often in the environmental case, the right of demolition. If environmental transaction really were about the transfer of 'stewardship' over some environmental good, then environmental concerns would no doubt be far less acute.

The beginnings of another troublesome objection are to be found in Mark Sagoff's insistence that there is a categorical distinction to be drawn between our preferences and our values, and that cost−benefit analysis mistakenly assimilates the two. He conceives of preferences as essentially self-regarding affairs, the sort of thing we indulge only when we are playing the role of consumer and are at leave to consult only our own interests (Sagoff, 1988b, chapter 1). Thus CBA encourages everyone to think of themselves as consumers and their relation to the environment to be that of consumption. In fact, however, many of our environmental concerns are idealistic in nature, expressing our commitments, principles and values, so that the human response to the environment is *mis*represented, when it is presented as lying entirely within the sphere of human preferences. It is as if one were to try to settle the question of what the speed limit should be by asking people at what speed they like to drive, rather than at what speed they think they ought to drive.

It seems certain that Sagoff's distinction is overdrawn. As the phenomenon of the 'green consumer' shows, consumption is rarely a matter of 'mere' preference. Even such an inoffensive object as a bar of soap may be objected to on aesthetic, moral and religious grounds − if, for example, it is frog-shaped and made of animal fats in a factory on the Protestant/Catholic side of town. Moreover, environmental economists appear increasingly loath to restrict their understanding of the concept of preference in the way that Sagoff imagines; and understandably so. Not only will they miss out on crucial elements of environmental valuation, recognition of which helped to inspire this branch of economics in the first place, but it lessens considerably the importance of economic valuation if economic value has to be ranged alongside too many other kinds of values before a policy decision can be reached. Hence one response of environmental economists has been to go for an enlarged notion of economic value embracing any contribution to human well-being, which is equated with anything for which a human being can be said to have a preference; this is taken to include aesthetic 'preference' and a 'preference' – say – for the protection of some species irrespective of its utility to humans, so-called 'existence value'. 'To the economist, economic value arises if someone is made to feel better off in terms of their wants and desires. The feeling of well-being from contemplating a beautiful view is therefore an economic value.' (Pearce, 1992, 6.) All that is excluded is value, if such there be, which is not somehow reducible to the preference of some human being somewhere; Pearce equates this with 'intrinsic' value.

According to this response, what economists are trying to get at is what is important to people's lives and to how they would like the world to be. They also believe that a social policy will be for the best to the extent that it manages to track what people consider important. So far, and with one qualification which we shall come to later, both these positions seem plausible. What is implausible, and has nothing whatever to commend it, is the addition of the thesis of psychological egoism: the claim that people are incapable of regarding as important anything other than their own interests. Economics has no need of this thesis. The development of the concept of 'existence value' would seem to confirm this. For the hopeful significance of the 'existence value' concept is precisely that it jettisons this bit of unnecessary flotsam. It recognizes that people's vision of how they would like the world to be extends far beyond the furthering of their personal interests (cf. Turner and Pearce, 1993, 183). If they care about species protection then they will consider themselves as living in a better world – it is closer to how they would like the world to be – if species are protected.[7] Back comes the well-worn response: 'Better for whom? And if "for them", then this is psychological egoism vindicated after all!'. But this response simply confuses human *perspective* and human *interest*. It is better only *from their point of view*: it is something they would work to bring about and – yes – pay to bring about also, if that is what it takes. This does nothing whatever to show that they perceive it to be 'in their interest', and

---

[7] It may be objected: if a person's well-being is enhanced as a result of species being protected, and they realize this, then they will protect species in pursuit of their well-being; hence the wider and the narrower conception of economic value will be identical after all. However, species protection carried out for the sake of one's own well-being may well not yield the well-being which results from species protection carried out for the sake of the species.

certainly not that they do it *because* it is in their interest. And, to repeat, social policy should be seeking to track what is important in people's lives which is not at all the same thing as seeking to track their self-regarding interests. To suppose otherwise is to make the quite gratuitous assumption that the only thing which people are capable of working for or paying for is their own self-regarding interest. The point is that there are other ways of achieving personal well-being than by pursuing it; and the pursuit of well-being is not always the best way of achieving it. The corollary is that a policy maker will be a long way off achieving well-being across a population if he or she simply aggregates the results of studies designed to elicit where people perceive their own personal interests to lie.

It seems, then, that economists can respond to Sagoff's critique by denying that they are assimilating values to preferences narrowly understood, and insisting that the notion of preference with which they operate is an enlarged 'technical' notion embracing anything towards which a human being may be said to be favourably disposed. But this still leaves a substantial objection, which is that all favourable attitudes are being treated as *the same in kind*, as homogeneous.

The view of the human psyche as a 'bundle of preferences', each one having as much right to be satisfied as any other, was pilloried long ago by Plato in his famous treatment of the 'democratic soul' (Plato, 1945, 561a–e). In this account, the human soul is pictured as operating in a totally egalitarian fashion, with preferences being satisfied turn and turn about. The disastrous consequences of such an arrangement are revealed when, for example, 'decent desires' such as self-esteem cannot survive the satisfaction of a shameful desire and are destroyed (573a). Plato favours a conception of the human psyche as a hierarchical structure – the 'tripartite soul' – composed of the elements of 'reason', 'spirit' and 'appetite', each having a distinctive role to play in the construction and maintenance of a well-ordered psyche. In some ways this foreshadows contemporary discussion of the idea of 'lexical ordering' among people's preferences, by which is meant, roughly, that people have different *kinds* of preferences; and whereas 'trading off' is permitted *within* kinds, it is not permitted *between* kinds. Plato's point, however, is more subtle than this. His model of the human psyche is more like that of an ecosystem, with different species of desires, ideals and concerns bound together in subtle interdependencies. Thus, it is reason and spirit which together, for example, determine the proper limits to be placed upon the satisfaction of appetite. Plato's idea of a well-ordered psyche as the foundation of well-being appears to find echos in Etzioni's notion of a 'balance' of purposes underlying human behaviour – moral commitment and the pursuit of well-being (Etzioni, 1988, 83), while his concept of the 'spirited' element finds a modern resonance in the 'heroic ethic' which Boulding (1969, 10) postulates as necessary to explain certain features of human behaviour (see Common *et al.*, 1993, 312–13). Like Plato, both thinkers find it necessary to postulate a *heterogeneous* self.

The claim being advanced here is not that the homogenized model of the human psyche is necessarily wrong and the ecosystem model right. In particular, I am not supposing that there is an empirically discoverable 'fact-of-the-matter' about the human psyche;[8] the capacities which self-reflexivity makes possible precludes our thinking of the human psyche in this way. On the contrary, the danger is precisely that we probably could learn to see ourselves in the way that CBA requires us to see ourselves. The question is whether that is what we want.

Although many variations on Plato's threefold structure of appetite, spirit and reason are possible, the basic idea is surely a helpful one and has a degree of contemporary support. Our 'preferences' (understood here in the wide sense) are not all of the same order. Nor is the relative contribution of their 'satisfaction' to the well-being of the individual by any means a straightforward matter. For example, there are some – call them 'appetites' – whose satisfaction seems to contribute to well-being only if they are well-ordered.[9] There are others which might be thought of as 'second order' preferences, in that they express some attitude towards our appetites – for example, as to when and under what conditions it is appropriate to satisfy them. These second order preferences key into our values and the ideals that we try to live up to. To take health as an example: this is something everyone wants, but it may also be an ideal we have. And the attempt to live up to that ideal might involve curbing certain appetites.[10] Thus, the satisfaction of these preferences also keys in to notions of self-respect. Moreover, Sagoff seems correct in his assertion that much of the concern we feel over environmental issues is expressive of our ideals rather than of our appetites. CBA, on the other hand, proposes to treat all the preferences we may have concerning environmental goods as if they were on a single level and can be traded off, one against the other.[11] This completely ignores the fact that some of these 'preferences' may be ones we would prefer we didn't have. Should the former be weighed

---

[8] Common *et al.* (1993) cite empirical evidence for the fact that people actually do find difficulty in assimilating questions about – say – species preservation to questions about commodities. And it seems a step in the right direction to raise and investigate this empirical question. Nevertheless, it seems far from satisfactory to treat this phenomenon as a 'given', requiring only empirical investigation, because this fails to take account of the human capacity for self-creation.

[9] cf. Sagoff 1994, 137: 'Contentment depends more on the quality of one's desires and on one's ability to overcome them, than on the extent to which they are satisfied.'

[10] A symptom of the logical distinction involved here is that failure to act on 'ideal' preferences typically gives rise to guilt, whereas failure to satisfy an appetite is simply cause for regret.

[11] This would make guilt unintelligible and eradicate the distinction between guilt and regret (see previous note).

in the scale and allowed collectively to *out*weigh the latter? Arguably, it is just this process (which CBA seems to commend) that has generated the transport chaos affecting major cities across the world and constitutes one of the environmental problems that CBA is supposed to be enlisted to combat. There is no doubt that many of us enjoy the freedom that individual car ownership brings. And it is precisely the unconstrained expression of this (strong) preference that causes the problem. The situation is unlikely to be changed by a procedure which in effect protects the unconstrained status of such a preference and which does not somewhere and somehow register the view that this is a preference which should not count (so much) in the first place.

What is true, of course, and what economists will no doubt keep reminding us of, is that, ultimately, decisions have to be reached. But the question is: given the understanding of the human psyche just sketched, are they best reached by the process of disassembling and aggregating which seems to be part and parcel of the cost–benefit analysis method? This leads us to the third problematic aspect of the CBA approach.

Privatizing

Associated with his distinction between values and preferences Sagoff introduces the idea of two distinct roles which we all occupy in our capacity as human agents, that of citizen and that of consumer (1988b, chapter 1). As consumers we are concerned with our private interests and the satisfaction of our preferences. As citizens, on the other hand, our concern is for the public interest, about which we may come to form judgements, often consequent upon a process of reflective debate with others about matters of value. A crucial distinction between the two is that our values call for discussion and justification in a way that our preferences do not. Accordingly, so far as Sagoff is concerned: 'The contingent valuation method ... insofar as it tries to make respondents express preferences rather than form judgements, denies their status both as thinking and political beings' (1988a, 74). There is more than one reason, therefore, why environmental matters may require *another form of discourse* than that provided for by the procedures of cost–benefit analysis. One is, to risk oversimplification, that public goods require public discussion. The other is that the environment raises questions of value which require our engagement as citizens, that is, as people playing a certain sort of role in a community and contributing to its culture in a certain sort of way, including the making of considered judgements. And what is seen to be important here, perhaps indeed to be an *obligation*, concerns not so much the content of the judgement as the way it is formed; this should not be casual, but should involve such processes of trying and testing as are available.[12] CBA is seen to short-circuit these processes; it is charged, in a word, with the cuckolding of judgement.

One reply that economists might make is that discovering how people feel about the environment by the method of cost–benefit analysis is in some ways a particularly 'democratic' procedure; or, at any rate, that it 'gives results that better reflect the welfare of society as a whole' than alternatives which are on offer, such as pressure group politics, because it 'takes into account not only large effects on small groups ... but small effects on large groups' (Robert Laslett, Chapter 2 this volume). But the force of this point does seem to depend upon taking a somewhat one-sided view of the matter, and perhaps focusing on a narrow range of cases. For first, a number of different criteria can be offered for deciding what best reflects the 'welfare of society as a whole'. On some views, for example, the level of welfare of a society is to be judged precisely by how well it caters for minority interests. Second, although there may well be occasions when sounder decisions emerge from heeding the silent majority rather than the vociferous minority, this can hardly be claimed as a general rule. For example, some may think that unwise decisions in the sphere of the EC's common agricultural policy emerge as a result, say, of pressure from French farmers. But the other side of this coin is the possible justification of gang rape, in which the victim may be cast as representing only a sectional, if vociferous, interest. It is true that special interest lobbying can be corrosive of the democratic process, but only if it exerts *undue* influence; there are many occasions when vociferous representation is only too appropriate.

Another reply to the charge is that the procedure of cost–benefit analysis in itself lays down absolutely no stipulation about how the answers to a particular survey of attitudes should be arrived at. Thus, any amount of citizen deliberation may have preceded the CBA exercise. Indeed, briefing sessions may be introduced before the exercise to counter the problem which sometimes arises, that the results of the exercise may be deemed unreliable because the participants lack information. However, the substance of Sagoff's objection will remain as long as the CBA exercise requires answers to questions, and thus the delivery of a judgement rather than its formation. For once delivered it is then taken away to be used in ways over which the participant has no control. To answer the objection CBA procedures

---

[12] The solemnity of this obligation is a favourite theme of 19th century writers; see J.S. Mill's essay 'On Liberty' (in Mill, 1962) and W.K. Clifford's essay *The Ethics of Belief* (Clifford, 1947).

need to be adapted, or new procedures adopted, which allow human subjects to become reunited with their judgements and which both allow and facilitate the expression of an integrated vision of a preferred world.

Conclusion

The laudable aim of environmental economics is to identify and calibrate the *true* environmental cost of a project or policy, motivated by the belief of its practitioners that the neglect of such costs is largely responsible for our present environmental predicament. Its more specific objectives are:

1. to discover how people feel about and value environmental goods,
2. to aid the process of decision making, and
3. to deliver good policy and good decisions – in particular, ones which better recognize the value and the role of the goods that nature provides in human economic activity.

The tenor of this critique has been to suggest that cost–benefit analysis, as currently practised, is as likely to frustrate as it is to forward these objectives, and that it remains to be demonstrated whether it is in principle an adequate method for achieving such objectives. At the same time it is manifestly a resilient discipline showing hopeful signs of self-examination, and it would be nothing short of a tragedy if the existence of both internal and external critiques should lend strength to those economic forces, already virulent enough, which look set to continue the processes of environmental devastation. It seems clear that the threefold critique which has been offered cannot be addressed piecemeal; for the several strands of the critique are closely interrelated. There would be little point encouraging citizen deliberation, but restricting its subject matter to items presented solely as items for consumption; a citizen would want to raise the question whether they should be so presented. There would be equally little point asking people to make consumer type choices between items invested with idealistic significance. But the corollary is that steps to address one of these strands will also help to address the others. For example, dealing with the itemizing critique by introducing more participant control over how natural goods are described and itemized, could well involve sessions of public debate, and therefore go some way to address the 'privatizing' critique.

Among the positive points to have emerged are the potential for cost–benefit studies, or the descendants thereof, to play an educative and investigative role. Even the 'homogenizing' tendency which has been noted is capable of opening people's eyes to the extent to which their consumer choices constrain the attainment of states of affairs they would ideally like to obtain. Moreover, existing cost–benefit exercises are open to be used more creatively than they often are at present. It is well known that these exercises throw up anomalies of various kinds. There are people who refuse to engage with the questions at all, and there are others who give responses which are 'off the scale'. Usually, and in obedience to the axioms of neo-classical economics, these anomalous cases are 'written out' – regarded as so much 'noise' in the system and ignored. Increasingly, economists themselves appear unhappy about this response to the problem. An alternative response, suggested by the above critique, would be to heed this 'noise' and try to figure out what it signifies and how economics might try to take account of what is going on. Initially, this might be to accord the cost–benefit exercise a different kind of role – not the summarizing of some total 'benefit' which might accrue from the adoption of some project or policy, but the interactive discovery, articulation and refinement of the responses of participants, which will be an educative process both for the participants and for those who administer the exercise. It is important to recognize that this might be as much a creative exercise as a process of discovery. For cost–benefit exercises, by their nature, frame questions that participants may not have thought of before, and therefore are capable of creating new ways of looking at things. In short, what might function negatively as an appropriation of judgement may function positively as a two-way educative process.

Coda

Wider issues lurk in the wings. It is hard not to notice, for example, the massive *non sequitur* implied in our earlier story about 'how it has come to this'. The thing which brought on the *crise* was the environmental degradation; what is proposed as the solution is the efficient allocation of resources. Is there not a great deal of explaining to be done to show how there can be any connection at all between the two? The bold response is to insist that the problem of environmental degradation is after all an exclusively human problem. A more cautious response is to allow that scientific and ecological considerations must be taken into account *alongside* any of the deliverances of cost–benefit analysis (Turner and Pearce, 1993). A move of this latter kind can also serve to deflect objections to cost–benefit analysis which derive from its utilitarian ancestry – specifically its neglect of questions of justice and rights. Here again, economists seem increasingly to recognize that when it comes to making policy, their results will, and should, be moderated by considerations of equity, rather than function as the sole determinants of policy.

My claim, however, would be that some more radical departure from the utilitarian vision is needed. Received wisdom (albeit now a little long in the tooth) has it that it was the values associated with the Graeco-Christian world view which did most to fuel the practices which have wrought such environmental havoc (e.g. White, 1967), because it idealizes the status of humans and legitimizes their dominion over the rest of nature. But the truth is that environmental economics, as currently practised, with its anthropocentric outlook[13] and its emphasis on nature as a resource, would seem to accentuate those aspects of the Graeco-Christian view which most need to be discarded. Whether a fundamentally utilitarian approach really can contribute to turning this situation around, therefore, must be seriously questioned. A more hopeful move might be to tap into strands of the Graeco-Christian world view other than those which utilitarianism accentuates. Nowhere, for example, does the Bible suggest that it is the *maximizers* who will inherit the earth, and we have seen how Plato reserves a special scorn for the idea that a happy individual or a happy society might be built upon the 'democratic' satisfaction of desires. Most of all, in the domain of policy making at any rate, we seem to have completely lost sight of the central theme of Aristotelian ethics, which also pervades New Testament Christianity, that happiness is attained through the practice of the virtues and the moderation of desires. There is something just a little incredible about the fact that we should even now be attempting to build the castles of public policy upon sand which the ancients discarded.

Having begun with a religious analogy, this chapter ends with a political one, prompted by dissatisfaction at the thought that the discussion of environmental issues should settle down to be conducted in terms of the citizen/consumer dualism. For there is a sense in which the environment is an arena not only larger than the domain of consumer choice but larger than the domain of citizen choice also: in political terms, one might say that it is more like a *constitutional* matter. The idea is that the environment, like the constitution, is more like the framework within which we live our lives than a piece of scenery to be moved around at will. Regarding constitutional matters there is in many societies a sense, often upheld by constitutional safeguards, that these should not be too readily open to manipulation by citizens of the day in the light of concerns of the day. Regarding environmental issues, too, we need perhaps to cultivate the same sense that these are matters

---

[13] Paradoxically, neoclassical economists still, in the main, flinch from the full implications of the utilitarian philosophy, which would include taking account of the preferences of non-human as well as human subjects (Attfield and Dell, 1989).

of a particularly fundamental kind, whose significance reaches from the past and extends to the future, and concerning which, therefore, it is appropriate to 'consult' the citizens of the past and those of the future, as well as those of today.

References

Arrow, K., Solow, R., Portney, P., Learner, E., Radner, R. and Schuman, H. (1993) Report of the NOAA Panel on Contingent Valuation. *US Federal Register* 58(10), 4601–4614.

Attfield, R. and Dell, K. (eds) (1989) *Values, Conflict and the Environment: Report of the Environmental Ethics Working Party.* Ian Ramsey Centre, Oxford.

Boulding, K.E. (1969) Economics as a moral science. *The American Economic Review* 59, 1–12.

Brown, Gardner Jr (1993) The viewing value of elephants. In: Barbier, E.B. (ed.) *Economics and Ecology: New Frontiers and Sustainable Development.* Chapman and Hall, London.

Clifford, W.K. (1947) *The Ethics of Belief.* Watts, London.

Common, M.S., Blamey, R.K. and Norton, T.W. (1993) Sustainability and environmental valuation. *Environmental Values* 2(4), 299–334.

Defoe, Daniel (1928) *A Tour through England and Wales 1724–26.* Dent, London.

Desvouges, W.H. *et al.* (1993) Measuring natural resource damages with contingent valuation: tests of validity and reliability. In: Hausman, J.A. (ed.) *Contingent Valuation: A Critical Assessment.* North-Holland, Amsterdam.

Etzioni, A. (1988) *The Moral Dimension: Toward a New Economics.* The Free Press, New York.

Kahneman, D. and Knetsch, J.L. (1992) Valuing public goods: the purchase of moral satisfaction. *Journal of Environmental Economics and Management* 22, 57–70.

Mill, J.S. (1962) *Utilitarianism.* Collins, London.

O'Neill, J. (1993) *Ecology, Policy and Politics.* Routledge, London.

Pearce, D. (1992) Green economics. *Environmental Values* 1(1), 3–13.

Plato (1945) *The Republic.* Lindsay, A.D. (tr). Dent, London.

Sagoff, M. (1988a) Some problems with environmental economics. *Environmental Ethics* 10(1), 55–74.

Sagoff, M. (1988b) *The Economy of the Earth.* Cambridge University Press, Cambridge.

Sagoff, M. (1994) Should Preferences Count? *Land Economics* 70(2), 127–144.

Turner, R.K. and Pearce, D.W. (1993) Sustainable economic development: economic and ethical principles. In: Barbier, E.B. (ed.) *Economics and Ecology: New Frontiers and Sustainable Development.* Chapman and Hall, London.

White, L. Jr (1967) The historical roots of our ecological crisis. *Science* 155(37), 1203–1207.

4

The Role of Environmental Valuation in Cost–Benefit Analysis

Nick Hanley

University of Stirling

Introduction

The application of cost–benefit analysis (CBA) to decisions over projects or policies having environmental impacts clearly involves the use of environmental valuation for the CBA analysis to be comprehensive in scope. Such valuation may be crucial to the decision over whether to go ahead with the policy/project. Examples of such policies/projects include the provision of planting grants (and formerly tax breaks) for afforestation, such as in the Flow Country of Caithness and Sutherland; marine conservation policies, such as restrictions on fishing grounds, timing, mesh size, and marine aggregate extraction; improving water quality in rivers and estuaries, possibly through the setting of national water quality standards; the development of new downhill ski sites in Scotland; and the levying of charges on the disposal of solid wastes at landfill sites.

While environmental valuation makes decision making through cost–benefit analysis more efficient, it does not in any way guarantee that environmental quality in a country will be improved or even maintained and is thus not in any way necessarily the best option for conservationists. While Randall's (1986) argument that including environmental values in CBA elevates these to the same importance as more conventional costs and benefits (such as labour costs and the value of electricity), valuation might instead be argued to *reduce* environmental values to this common metric. No special treatment is thus necessarily accorded to the environment, which becomes treated equally with labour hours, kilowatts and bags of cement. Listing environmental impacts as intangibles in the past may have led to these

39

impacts being ignored or down-graded in the eyes of policy makers, but the effect could have been the opposite: namely, that by keeping environmental impacts out of the cost–benefit calculus, they retain a special status which makes their safeguarding more likely. Whether this is so, and whether this is deemed desirable, is entirely determined by the nature of the policy-making process and the cultural values held in a country: very little of a general nature can be said here. However, the point is worth making before we become lost in a technical debate about how best to value the environment within the CBA paradigm.

Notwithstanding the above, environmental valuation has increasingly become a part of policy making in the West over the last 20 years, and this is true in the UK in particular. This wider adoption has been partly brought about by arguments from academic economists that such valuation was an important feature of policy making (Pearce *et al.*, 1989), making it more efficient, and recent UK government statements have confirmed the new importance given to environmental valuation in official policy making (Department of the Environment, 1991).

Because of this, many UK government departments and public bodies are now funding valuation studies; these include the Forestry Commision (recreation, biodiversity, landscape); MAFF (Environmentally Sensitive Areas (ESAs), marine conservation, coastal defences); English Nature (Sites of Special Scientific Interest); the Scottish Office (urban regeneration, downhill ski sites, amenity woodlands); and the Department of Transport (value of life/accident savings; time savings). A brief review of UK environmental valuation studies is now provided, although a more comprehensive account is provided in Hanley and Knight (1992).

Economists at the University of Newcastle have been involved in extensive work on environmental valuation, including measuring the value of forest recreation (principally through travel cost studies) (Willis, 1991); hedonic price estimates of the amenity value of woods and canals (Garrod and Willis, 1992; Willis and Garrod, 1993); and contingent valuation estimates of preserving landscape quality in the Yorkshire Dales (Willis and Garrod, 1991a) and in two ESAs (Willis *et al.*, 1994). The contingent valuation method (CVM) has also been applied extensively at the University of Stirling, to air pollution from agriculture (Hanley, 1988); drinking water quality (Hanley, 1989); wildlife reserves (Hanley and Harley, 1989); protection of Sites of Special Scientific Interest (Hanley and Spash, 1993); the preservation of biodiversity (Spash and Hanley, 1994; Hanley *et al.*, 1994); urban landscape improvements and amenity forests (Hanley, 1992a); the preservation of the Flow Country (Hanley and Craig, 1991) and the valuation of forest characteristics (Hanley and Ruffell, 1993a). CVM has been utilized at the University of Middlesex to value river water quality (Green and Tunstall, 1991, 1992), beach recreation (Green *et al.*, 1990) and coastal protection. The value of coastal protection was estimated for sites on the East Anglian coast line by Turner *et al.* (1992) using CVM, while Bateman and colleagues (Bateman *et al.*, 1993) used CVM to value landscape preservation in the Norfolk Broads. Ecotec (1993) report CVM estimates of the benefits of reduced acid deposition in the UK, while MacMillan *et al.* (1994) give CVM measures of acid-reduction benefits for the Scottish Highlands. Finally, Bishop and Stabler (1991) used CVM to value amenity woodland at two community forests. Travel cost models for forest recreation in the UK have been estimated by several authors, including Willis (1991), Willis and Garrod (1991b), Price (1986, 1991) and Hanley and Ruffell (1993b).

Problems in Environmental Valuation: The Case of CVM

Environmental values are pivotal to many policy/project decisions. An early example of this is the work by Krutilla and Fisher on the Hells Canyon hydroelectric schemes in the late 1960s and early 1970s (Krutilla and Fisher, 1985). Hells Canyon divides Idaho from Oregon, and is a wilderness mountain area of great beauty. The Snake River, which flows through the canyon, was used for informal recreational purposes (such as backpacking and fishing), but was also the target of several hydroelectric power schemes proposed by the Pacific Northwest Power Company. The US Supreme Court, in passing judgement on these proposals, specifically endorsed the idea of off-setting the benefits from development (cheaper power, in this case) against foregone environmental benefits, which at that point in time (1967) were not included in economic appraisals of such schemes.

Krutilla and Fisher were able to show that, even if these environmental costs (loss of wilderness quality, damages to recreational fishing for salmon and steelhead) remained excluded, the first of the proposed dams (Mountain Sheep-Pleasant Valley) failed the cost–benefit test. A second proposal at High Mountain Sheep, however, passed the cost–benefit test if environmental costs were excluded. Krutilla and Fisher then demonstrated that given some very reasonable assumptions about the value of recreational benefits and the growth rate of these over time, the environmental costs of development outweighed the net market-valued benefits of development. The minimum value of preservation benefits for this to be so was calculated as $150,000 (in 1976 $s) for preservation to be preferred to development. The authors' estimate of actual benefits was $900,000, and this figure did not include any non-use benefits for wilderness preservation.

Since important (and sometimes irreversible) decisions over projects/policies having environmental impacts may hinge on environmental valuation, care needs to be taken given the problems in applying valuation methods. Some of the more important problems related to one valuation method, CVM, are reviewed in other chapters of this book. CVM is chosen as an example of the problems involved in environmental valuation because it is the most widely applicable of the valuation methods, and since it has come to the fore in policy making on the environment (and in litigation over environmental damages) in both the US and the UK. Problems with other valuation methods, and a more detailed account of problems involved in CVM, may be found in Hanley and Spash (1993) and Braden and Kolstad (1991). The more general problems in applying CBA to the environment are reviewed later in this chapter.

Among the difficulties of applying CVM are: (i) lexicographic preferences and protest bids; (ii) information: how much? what sort?; and (iii) uncertainty over the status quo and/or *ex post* level of environmental quality.

Lexicographic preferences

Lexicographic preferences are derived from an ethical system which refuses environmental quality (Q) money (M) trade-offs. Individuals holding such preferences always prioritize Q over M, in the sense that they always prefer more Q to any change in M. This means indifference curves between Q and M are undefined, and that willingness to accept compensation (WTAC) for any change in Q is infinite, while willingness to pay (WTP) is one's maximum wealth. Clearly, this extreme position describes few individuals: people, after all, need some minimum level of income to support themselves and their families. However, as Stevens *et al.* (1991) show, this may lead them to state the same WTP amount ($Y_{max} - Y_{min}$, where Y_{max} is their maximal income and Y_{min} is their 'subsistence' level of income) to avoid *any* decrease in Q. WTP is thus invariant with the level of Q provided. What is more, these individuals may still have infinite WTAC amounts for any decrease in Q, in that no amount of money (that is, no extra income) would offset the utility loss resulting from even a small decrease in Q.

If individuals holding such preferences indeed exist, then such individuals invalidate the Kaldor–Hicks Potential Compensation Test basis of CBA, since they are refusing any money compensation for environmental losses. The Kaldor–Hicks test, after all, is based on the *possibility* of compensating losers for any loss. However, if these individuals are treated as having an infinite WTAC to avoid environmental losses, then this will mean that no project involving such losses will pass the CBA test: this effectively disenfranchises all other citizens. More usually, therefore, such responses in CVM exercises are treated as protest bids, and ignored in the CBA process. Yet this disenfranchises the lexicographic individuals!

Evidence of individuals holding such preferences within CVM is confined to two studies, both of which looked at WTP to avoid an environmental loss. Both Stevens *et al.* (1991) and Spash and Hanley (1994) found that approximately a quarter of the sample of respondents refused to state a WTP amount, on the grounds that the environment had an absolute right to be protected. Future research in CVM on this area will need to be directed at testing whether this proportion increases when WTAC, as opposed to WTP, measures are sought; and whether hypothetical infinite WTAC sums are reduced when respondents can receive actual compensation in an experimental market.

Information effects

Consumer sovereignty is a basic principle of CBA. That is, the preferences of consumers, as revealed through markets (whether actual, hypothetical or experimental), are deemed to be the sole indicators of economic value. This value is expressed in terms of efffective demand, measured either as WTP or WTAC. This raises an awkward issue, however. In formulating their preferences, consumers clearly rely both on their tastes (I prefer beer to gin) and the information they hold on the choice possibilities (I know that beer is good for me and gin is not). But what if consumers are poorly informed about these choice possibilities? In choosing between, say, a programme that cuts air pollution and another which lowers taxes, consumers may know relatively little about the health effects of air pollution. Their WTP to pay for such a programme may therefore be small, if they underestimate the health damages of air pollution. Telling these individuals more about the adverse health effects of pollution might increase their WTP. Given that in a CVM study some information must be given to respondents, the awkward question that thus arises is 'how much'?[1]

The effects of information in CVM have been investigated by many authors (for a survey, see Hanley and Munro, 1994). The 'types' of information that have been argued to be important include information

---

[1] The value of a decrease in air pollution may also be measured indirectly through dose–response relationships. For example, higher sulphur dioxide emissions result in increased acid deposition which reduces fish catches. Consumers may be quite well informed about the characteristics of fish as a food commodity; thus the lack of information on the part of consumers about the dose–response relationship is not a problem, since the analyst calculates this and obtains an economic value from the final effect, changes in fish catch in this case. The problem being discussed here relates to *direct* valuation methods.

about the characteristics of the good; information about substitutes/
complements; information on relative expenditures; information on the
behaviour of others; and the provision rule (that is, on what criteria will
the goods be supplied?). Changes in any of these types of information
may effect true and/or revealed WTP (to use Hoehn and Randall's
terminology: Hoehn and Randall, 1987).

Empirical investigations of the magnitudes of information effects
have been quite common in the literature. One example is that carried
out by Hanley and Munro (1994), which considered the impacts on
WTP to preserve lowland heathland sites of changing information on
the characteristics of an individual site (Avon Forest), in particular the
types of flora and fauna that could be found there, and information on
threats to heathland from development (relative scarcity information).

Table 4.1 summarizes these results. 'Basic information' was information on the payment vehicle (entrance fees in the site specific case,
and payments to a trust fund in the 'all heathland' case) and the reason
for payment. 'Full information' means respondents received the basic,
characteristics and relative scarcity information. Each individual
received one set of information only. As may be seen, increasing
information in general leads to increasing WTP (in this case, this was
in line with a priori expectations). Thus the awkward question remains:
how much information should be provided to respondents? And
which is the correct measure of the non-market value of heathland to
our respondents? The recent National Oceanic and Atmospheric
Administration draft rules for the use of CVM in natural resource
damages assessment offer limited guidance on information provision[2]
(Federal Register, 1994), while the Arrow–Solow 'Blue Ribbon'
panel whose work preceded these draft rules recommended that full,
unbiased information should be provided to respondents, since otherwise they could not form a reasoned opinion; but that checks should be

Table 4.1. Effects of more information on WTP to preserve lowland heaths.

Scenario	Basic information	Relative scarcity	Characteristics	Full information
WTPs	6.77	11.49	10.39	10.32
WTPg	21.54	20.64	21.52	38.49

WTPs = site specific WTP: Avon Forest only; WTPg = all heaths in southern England. All values in £ per
person per year, 1991 £.

[2] That respondents should be told (in the context of natural resource damages) about the
programme for restoring the natural resource, about the 'natural resource context of the injured
resource', and about substitutes for the resource. Respondents should also be asked if they
understood and found credible this information.

made on how well respondents were able to understand the inform-ation provided, and whether they accepted it as being true.

Uncertainty

For some environmental changes, uncertainty exists over both the 'do nothing' case (the status quo) and the effects of policy change (the *ex post* case). Acidification damages to upland ecosystems are an example of this, since scientific uncertainty surrounds the level of damage, the level of recovery from damage should deposition be reduced, and the speed of any such recovery. MacMillan *et al.* (1994) report results from a CVM study of uncertain damages and recovery from damage in the Scottish highlands.

Economic theory suggests that:

1. the higher is the status quo level of damages, the higher should be WTP for a damage-reduction programme;
2. the greater is the level of recovery, the higher should WTP be;
3. faster recovery should attract higher WTP bids;
4. if three possible levels of recovery are possible: a (high recovery), c (no recovery) and b (a point mid-way between a and c), and respon-dents are offered a package which has a or c with 50% chance of each, or b for sure, then if they are risk-averse they will choose b;
5. respondents may also be uncertain as to the status quo. Again, define three possible levels of damage; x (high), z (minimal) and y (mid-way between x and z). Kahneman and Tversky (1979) argued that people who are risk-averse with regard to gains may be risk-seeking with regard to losses. In this case we would expect WTP for y to be less than WTP for a 50% chance of x and a 50% chance of z.

Empirical results showed that WTPa > WTPb, but that WTPc > WTPa. In the c scenario, losses are essentially irreversible, so loss aversion may explain this result. Macmillan *et al.* (1994) found that WTP across different recovery times was not significantly different, possibly caused by strong bequest motives. They also found that higher status quo damages give higher WTP; but did not find any statistically significant proof that propositions (4) and (5) were true.

Where environmental damages are such that individuals can, through their own actions, reduce the probability of these undesirable events occurring, then an important message from the work of Shogren and Crocker (1990) is that such self-protection expenditures must be allowed for in valuing any programme to reduce environmental risk.

Environmental Problems in CBA

In this section, several general problems facing the application of CBA to environmental management are reviewed. These are ecosystem complexity and the co-evolution of economic–ecological systems; whether the discount rate should be different for environmental as compared with non-environmental goods; the institutional capture of CBA; irreversibility; and CBA's compatibility with sustainable development.

Ecosystem complexity

The application of CBA to environmental management is complicated in many cases by uncertainty over the long-term environmental effects of current actions. Examples include pesticide leaching from farmlands to water courses, the health effects of low-level radiation from nuclear power stations, the effects of depleting biological diversity on ecosystem resilience (and thus on sustainability), and the environmental impacts of dumping at sea. Frequently this uncertainty is of a non-probabilistic nature, in that we do not know all states of the world that could occur, nor the probability with which each state will occur. Scientific uncertainty is made more likely if threshold effects or discontinuities occur. Examples here include some dose–response functions, such as critical loads for acid deposition, or dissolved oxygen levels in a river. In the absence of probabilistic information, CBA analysts are reduced to sensitivity and scenario analysis (for example, looking at best and worst cases), which clearly reduces the extent to which CBA can inform decisions.

What is more, several authors in the ecological economics field (Norgaard, 1984; Perrings, 1987; Common and Perrings, 1992) have argued that dynamic interdependencies between economic and ecological systems imply that strict economic optimizing may lead to a decrease in the stability of ecosystems, producing undesirable feedbacks on the economic system. This world view sees the parameters of both systems (economic and ecological) co-evolving, so that decision making based on one system only (the economic, if CBA used) is unlikely to be a sufficient stand-alone decision mechanism.

Indeed, the sheer complexity of ecosystems has led some economists to the view that CBA is inappropriate as a decision tool for projects/policies impacting on such systems. This point has perhaps been most forcibly made by the Swedish institutional economist, Peter Soderbaum, who comments that:

> For those who consider evolutionary processes and the paths that
> ecosystems take over time, the idea that non-monetary impacts

at different periods of time can somehow be pressed together into one
value … is absurd

(Soderbaum, 1987)

Discount rates and discounting

A large literature exists on the choice of discount rate for CBA (for a
summary, see Hanley, 1992b). An outrageous simplification of the
majority view evolving from this literature is that discounting can be
justified on grounds of intertemporal efficiency but not on grounds of
intertemporal equity (Howarth and Norgaard, 1993). Given the long-
term nature of many environmental costs and benefits (such as the
costs of global warming, benefits from deciduous forest planting, or
irreversible species losses), the outcome of CBA analyses of projects
with environmental impacts can often be highly sensitive to the choice
of discount rate.

But at what rate should the discount rate be set for environmental
projects, assuming for the present that efficiency is our sole criterion?
Jungermann and Fleischer (1988) show that discount rates for an
individual can vary (from positive to negative) according to whether a
pleasure or a pain is in prospect, implying that different discount rates
should be used for environmental gains or losses. Luckert and Adamowicz (1993) showed that on average individuals hold lower discount
rates for environmental goods than other goods, implying that the
government should reduce the discount rate on projects having
environmental impacts relative to all other projects. Much controversy
also exists over whether the Arrow–Lind theorem (that risk-spreading
across taxpayers means that the public sector disount rate should be
less than the private sector rate by an amount equal to the average risk
premium in the private sector; in other words, that the public sector
discount rate should be a risk-free rate) should hold for the social
discounting of environmental effects. This depends on the extent to
which environmental risk-spreading is possible; for Fisher (1973) it is
not, implying that the Arrow–Lind theorem does not hold for environmental costs. In fact Brown (1983) argues that, for environmental costs,
the discount rate should be less than the risk-free rate, which increases
the present value of future environmental damages.

Discounting has traditionally been partly defended on the grounds
that capital is productive. Natural capital is not always capable of
reproduction, however. While fisheries and forests can grow, and can
be re-invested in, in terms of increasing growth rates and/or stock
sizes, non-renewable resource deposits cannot grow (although additional resources can be expended to increase the economically-
available portion of a non-renewable deposit). Finally, the social rate of

discount for environmental effects may be lower than private rates due to the weight attached by individuals to 'citizenship' motives regarding the environment. Individuals may have lower time preference rates in their roles as 'citizens' as compared with their roles as consumers, to use the distinction put forward by Sagoff (1988).

Irreversibility

The environmental effects of certain policies or projects are irreversible. This means that such effects cannot be undone, and the initial condition returned to, either at all, or within a time frame thought relevant to individuals (say less than 1000 years). Draining wetlands for forestry, felling rainforests so that soils are eroded, and species extinction, are all examples of irreversibilities. The principal approach in CBA to irreversibilities involves the Krutilla–Fisher (KF) model (1985). This model treats irreversible costs as a financial perpetuity. As is well known, the present value of such a perpetuity is found by multiplying it by the inverse of the discount rate. Thus preservation benefits foregone into perpetuity are included in the net present value expression, alongside development benefits (such as the value of timber) and any initial development costs.

The net present value of an irreversible development NPV_d with initial costs C, development benefits D_t and preservation benefits foregone of P_t is given as:

$$NPV_d = -C + \frac{D_t}{(i-g)} - \frac{P_t}{(i-r)} \tag{1}$$

where i is the discount rate, g is the growth (decay) rate of development benefits and r is the growth (decay) rate of preservation benefits foregone.

However, the KF model requires two pieces of information which are impossible to know for sure. These are:

1. The preferences of future generations for environmental goods relative to other goods. These are needed in order to value the infinite stream of foregone preservation benefits. In practice, the preferences of the present generation (or some sub-set of it) are used instead, since only these preferences are capable of current valuation.
2. The rates of change for the real values of both the development and preservation alternatives. A possible asymmetry between the real rate of change in preservation versus development benefits was explicitly recognized by Krutilla and Fisher, who include estimates of these growth (or decay) rates in their empirical applications of the technique.

Such estimates may also be found, for example, in Hanley and Craig (1991). Yet forecasting the rate of change of the relative prices of preservation and development into the infinite future is a far from simple task!

Irreversible environmental effects may also give rise to a quasi-option value. Quasi-option value is an insurance premium (cost), and is most easily understood in a two-period model, where in period one a decision is taken either to develop, for example, a wilderness area entirely or else leave it untouched.[3] If new information is received at the start of period two about preservation benefits, then this information has value only if the area has been preserved in period one. Based on the new information, a decision is then taken in period two over how much (if any) of the wilderness to develop. Such information might be, for example, that a forest contains the last remnants of some rare species or is home to a plant with important medicinal properties. So long as there is a non-zero probability of such information becoming available, then a positive quasi-option value arises for the alternative of avoiding an irreversible development. This raises the opportunity costs of development. Development is therefore less likely to be preferred, *ceteris paribus*, when the existence of quasi-option value is admitted. However, while this is a helpful caution, the concept is of little empirical use in CBA because of the difficulty of actually estimating quasi-option value. Quasi-option value for avoiding irreversible developments cautions against sanctioning such developments, but is essentially unquantifiable *ex ante*.

Institutional capture

Can the 'institution' of CBA be captured by self-interest groups? Public choice theory suggests that if the use of CBA creates potential rents, then the answer must be 'yes'. Such rents must be broadly interpreted as applying to both public and private bodies/individuals, since the outcome of a CBA process could be viewed as favouring, for example, a particular quango in terms of its budget or public image, or a government in terms of future votes. Possible examples of such capture are listed in Hanley and Spash (1993), and include land drainage projects in England before water privatization, the Cardiff Bay barrage scheme, and US Corps of Engineers dam projects in the 1960s. To take the first of these as illustrative, Internal Drainage Boards were responsible in England for proposing large scale land drainage projects. The

---

[3] Hanemann (1989) considers the case of intermediate levels of development, but admitting this possibility complicates the analysis.

principal beneficiaries of such projects were farmers, who also comprised the membership of the Drainage Boards. The Boards, through the local Water Authority, had to demonstrate that projects passed a CBA test before public spending on them was authorized. However, Bowers (1988) alleges that the outcomes of such appraisals were basically fixed, in that those assumptions most likely to yield a positive NPV for the drainage project were employed. Examples include ignoring farmers' capital costs and assuming high productivity and take-up rates. Environmental costs of drainage schemes (such as landscape degradation and wildlife losses) were also ignored.

The possibility of institutional capture in CBA is a worrying one. Three possible solutions might be (i) to adopt an adversarial system of CBA, with gainers and losers presenting their own CBAs at a public inquiry; (ii) only permitting CBAs to be carried out by a body with no pecuniary interest in their outcome; and (iii) achieving much higher levels of public transparency of the CBA process than is frequently the case at present.

Sustainable development and CBA

To say anything useful about CBA and sustainable development, it is necessary to adopt a working definition of the latter concept. Such a definition is as follows:

> Sustainable development involves a non-declining stock of natural capital over time. 'Natural capital' includes all those assets which are gifts of nature: this includes renewable and non-renewable resources, all biota, hydrological, nutrient and carbon cycles, and the assimilative capacity of ecosystems for pollutants.

In adopting such a definition, the very obvious aggregation problems involved are passed over here. Since sustainable development is essentially an equity issue, it is unsurprising that passing the Kaldor–Hicks tests is *not* a sufficient condition for the sustainability of a project/policy. This is because CBA explicitly allows the environment to be traded off against other gains/losses, so that even if the environment has been correctly valued, CBA does not guarantee sustainable development on this definition.

To see this, assume that B_t represents the benefits from the investment portfolio, C_t represents the non-environmental costs, E_t the environmental costs (such as habitat loss), and δ_t the discount factor. The normal cost–benefit analysis criterion is that over the discrete time period $t = 1 \ldots T$:

$$\sum_{t=1}^{T} B_t \delta_t - \sum_{t=1}^{T} C_t \delta_t - \sum_{t=1}^{T} E_t \delta_t > 0 \qquad (2)$$

(that is, that the sum of discounted net benefits is positive). It can be seen that a positive E_t (that is, environmental costs are incurred) is quite compatible with a positive NPV.

CBA will therefore be consistent with a declining natural capital stock unless what Pearce and colleagues have called 'weak' or 'strong' sustainability constraints are introduced, using shadow projects. The weak constraint is that:

$$\sum_{t=1}^{T} \sum_{i=1}^{n} E_{it} \delta_t \le \sum_{t=1}^{T} \sum_{j=1}^{m} a_{jt} \delta_t \qquad (3)$$

where there are $i = 1 \dots n$ projects/policies in the portfolio and $j = 1 \dots m$ shadow projects each generating off-setting environmental benefits of value 'a_{jt}'. This only guarantees that the discounted sum of environmental damages is at minimum offset by the discounted sum of environmental benefits. The strong sustainability constraint is:

$$\sum_{t=1}^{n} E_t \le \sum_{j=1}^{m} a_j \quad \forall\, t = 1 \dots T \qquad (4)$$

In other words, that in each time period environmental costs and benefits cancel out. However, major problems exist with the concept of shadow projects; these include the valuation of their impacts, which in turn depends on the aggregation of the natural capital stock; and whether shadow projects themselves have undesirable environmental effects.

Conclusions

On any one of the grounds set out in the preceding section, CBA could be judged to be inappropriate as a decision tool for environmental management. It is certainly my view that CBA is unsuitable as a stand-alone decision mechanism; but that it does remain useful as one input to decisions over environmental management. At the very least, CBA offers a rigorous way of setting out the effects of commissioning an action, and acting as a framework for discussion. At best, it identifies how the allocation of resources can be made more efficient, in the sense of producing net gains in social welfare. Yet to do away entirely with CBA seems unjustified. No other stand-alone decision mechanism exists which is better in every respect to CBA. Environmental impact assessment merely informs us about the relative environmental effects of an action, but not whether the action itself is desirable. Multicriteria analysis is crucially dependent on the weights given to the different criteria, while cost-effectiveness analysis can only tell us about the most efficient way of meeting an objective, not whether the objective itself should be met. Finally, putting all our faith in the democratic process (and civil servants) to decide on every possible action with environmental impacts (as Sagoff suggests) presupposes that the government and its bureaucracy is a disinterested processor of citizens' wants, which is naive.

Thus CBA should retain a place in environmental decision making, and environmental valuation will clearly play a major role in determining the outcome of the CBA process in many cases. While it is true that many problems still exist both with environmental valuation and with the environmental application of CBA itself, it is the writer's opinion that at present the benefits of CBA outweigh the costs, provided that we bare these problems in mind at all times.

References

Bateman, I., Willis, K. and Garrod, G. (1993) *Consistency Between Contingent Valuation Estimates: A Comparison of Two Studies of UK National Parks.* Working Paper 40, Countryside Change Initiative, University of Newcastle upon Tyne.

Bishop, K. and Stabler, M. (1991) The concept of community forests in the UK: the assessment of their benefits. Paper to the European Association of Environmental and Resources Economists (Stockholm).

Bowers, J.K. (1988) Cost–benefit analysis in theory and practice: agricultural land drainage projects. In: Turner, R.K. (ed.) *Sustainable Environmental Management: Principles and Practice.* Belhaven Press, London.

Braden, J. and Kolstad, C. (1991) *Measuring the Demand for Environmental Quality.* Elsevier, Amsterdam.

Brown, S.P. (1983) A note of environmental risk and the rate of discount. *Journal of Environmental Economics and Management* 6(10), 282–286.

Common, M. and Perrings, C. (1992) Towards an ecological economics of sustainability. *Ecological Economics* 6, 7–34.

Department of the Environment (1991) *Policy Appraisal and the Environment.* HMSO, London.

Ecotec (1993) *A Contingent Valuation Study of Aquatic Ecosystems.* Ecotec Ltd, Birmingham.

Federal Register (1994) *Oil Pollution Act of 1990: Proposed Regulations for Natural Resource Damage Assessment.* Federal Register, US Government, 7 January.

Fisher, A.C. (1973) Environmental externalities and the Arrow–Lind public investment theorem. *American Economic Review* 63, 722–725.

Garrod, G.D. and Willis, K.G. (1992) The amenity value of woodland in Great Britain. *Environmental and Resource Economics* 2, 415–434.

Green, C. and Tunstall, S. (1991) The benefits of river water quality improvement. *Applied Economics* 23, 1135–1146.

Green, C. and Tunstall, S. (1992) The amenity and environmental value of river corridors in Britain. In: Boon, P.J., Calow, P. and Petts, G. (eds) *River Conservation and Management*. Wiley, Chichester.

Green, C., Tunstall, S., Penning-Rowsell, E. and Coker, A. (1990) *The Benefits of Coast Protection: Results from Testing the Contingent Valuation Method*. Discussion Paper 168. Flood Hazard Research Centre, Middlesex Polytechnic, Middlesex.

Hanemann, M. (1989) Information and the concept of option value. *Journal of Environmental Economics and Management* 16, 23–37.

Hanley, N. (1988) Using contingent valuation to value environmental improvements. *Applied Economics* 20, 541–549.

Hanley, N. (1989) *Problems in Valuing Environmental Improvements Resulting from Agricultural Policy Changes: The Case of Nitrate Pollution*. Discussion Papers in Economics No. 89/1. University of Stirling.

Hanley, N. (1992a) *The Valuation of Environmental Effects: Stage Two Report*. Scottish Office, Edinburgh.

Hanley, N. (1992b) Are there environmental limits to cost–benefit analysis? *Environmental and Resource Economics* 2, 33–59.

Hanley, N. and Craig, S. (1991) Wilderness preservation and the Krutilla–Fisher model: the case of Scotland's Flow Country. *Ecological Economics* 4, 145–164.

Hanley, N. and Harley, D. (1989) *Economic Benefit Estimates for Nature Reserves: Methods and Results*. Discussion Papers in Economics No. 89/6. Economics Department, University of Stirling.

Hanley, N. and Knight, J. (1992) Valuing the environment: recent UK experience and an application to greenbelt land. *Journal of Environmental Planning and Management* 35, 145–160.

Hanley, N. and Munro, A. (1994) *The Effects of Information in Contingent Markets for Environmental Goods*. Discussion Paper No. 94/5. Ecological Economics Series, University of Stirling.

Hanley, N.D. and Ruffell, R. (1993a) The contingent valuation of forest characteristics: two experiments. *Journal of Agricultural Economics* 44, 218–229.

Hanley, N. and Ruffell, R. (1993b) The valuation of forest characteristics. In: Adamowicz, W., Phillips, W. and White, W. (eds) *Forestry and the Environment: Economic Perspectives*. CAB International, Wallingford.

Hanley, N. and Spash, C. (1993) *Cost–Benefit Analysis and the Environment*. Edward Elgar, Cheltenham.

Hanley N, Spash, C. and Walker, L. (1994) *Problems in Valuing the Benefits of Biodiversity Protection*. Discussion Paper No. 94/8. Economics Department, University of Stirling.

Hoehn, J. and Randall, A. (1987) A satisfactory benefit–cost indicator from contingent valuation. *Journal of Environmental Economics and Management* 14(3), 226–247.

Howarth, R. and Norgaard, R. (1993) Intergenerational transfers and the social discount rate. *Environmental and Natural Resource Economics* 3(4), 337–358.

Jungermann, H. and Fleischer, F. (1988) As time goes by: psychological determinants of time preferences. In: Kirsch, G., Nijkamp, P. and Zimmerman, K. (eds) *The Formulation of Time Preferences in Multidisciplinary Perspective.* WZB Publications, Berlin.

Kahnemen, D. and Tversky, A. (1979) Prospect theory: an analysis of decision making under risk. *Econometrica* 47, 263–291.

Krutilla, J. and Fisher, A.C. (1985) *The Economics of Natural Environments.* Johns Hopkins University Press, Baltimore.

Luckert, M. and Adamowicz, W. (1993) Empirical measures of factors affecting social rates of discount. *Environmental and Resource Economics* 3, 1–22.

MacMillan, D., Hanley, N. and Buckland, S. (1994) Valuing the benefits of reduced acid deposition: an optimally designed contingent valuation study. Paper to the Agricultural Economics Society Conference, Exeter University.

Norgaard, R. (1984) Co-evolutionary development potential. *Land Economics* 60, 160–173.

Pearce, D., Markandya, A. and Barbier, E. (1989) *Blueprint for a Green Economy.* Earthscan, London.

Perrings, C. (1987) *Economy and Environment.* Cambridge University Press, Cambridge.

Price, C. (1986) Elasticities of demand for recreation site and for recreation experience. *Environmental and Planning A* 18, 1259–1263.

Price, C. (1991) Transformation and weighting in recreation demand regressions. *Journal of Environmental Management* 33, 91–104.

Randall, A. (1986) Valuation in a policy context. In: Bromley, D.W. (ed.) *Natural Resource Economics.* Kluwer–Nijhoff, Boston.

Sagoff, M. (1988) *The Economy of the Earth.* Cambridge University Press, Cambridge.

Shogren, J. and Crocker, T. (1990) Adaptation and the option value of uncertain environmental resources. *Ecological Economics* 2, 301–310.

Soderbaum, P. (1987) Environmental management. *Journal of Economic Issues* 21(1), 139–165.

Spash, C. and Hanley, N. (1994) *Preferences, Information and Biodiversity Preservation.* Discussion Papers in Ecological Economics No. 94/1, University of Stirling.

Stevens, T., Echeverria, J., Glass, R., Hager, T. and More, T. (1991) Measuring the existence value of wildlife. *Land Economics* 67, 390–400.

Turner, R.K., Bateman, I. and Brooke, J. (1992) Valuing the benefits of coastal defence. In: Coker, A. and Richards, C. (eds) *Valuing the Environment.* Belhaven Press, London.

Willis, K.G. (1991) The recreational value of the Forestry Commission estate in Great Britain: a Clawson–Knetsch travel cost analysis. *Scottish Journal of Political Economy* 38, 58–75.

Willis, K. and Garrod, G.D. (1991a) *Landscape Values: A Contingent Valuation Approach and Case Study of the Yorkshire Dales National Park.* Working Paper 21. Countryside Change Initiative, University of Newcastle upon Tyne.

Willis, K.G. and Garrod, G.D. (1991b) An individual travel cost method of evaluating forest recreation. *Journal of Agricultural Economics* 42, 33–42.

Willis, K.G. and Garrod G.D. (1993) Not from experience: a comparison of experts' opinions and hedonic price estimates of the incremental value of property attributable to an environmental feature. *Journal of Property Research* 10, 193–216.

Willis, K.G., Garrod, G.D. and Saunders C.M. (1994) *Valuation of the South Downs and Somerset Levels and Moors Environmentally Sensitive Area Landscapes by the General Public.* Research Report. Centre for Rural Economy, University of Newcastle upon Tyne.

5

Ecological and Economic Values

Charles Perrings

University of York

Introduction

It is an interesting characteristic of multidisciplinary discussions about the management of environmental resources that each discipline has a perception that the resource has a 'value' defined in terms of the concerns of that discipline, and that this 'value' is in some sense distinct from 'economic value'. In part this follows from the perception that economic value is the same as market price, and most scientists are acutely aware that market prices often capture very little of the 'value' that environmental resources have in supporting human activity. But it is also because they tend to have an implicit criterion of the relative importance of environmental resources defined by the objectives of the discipline in which they work. If one is interested in thermodynamics, for example, measures such as entropy and energy may seem to be natural candidates as standards of value. This characteristic is a source of both confusion and mutual suspicion between representatives of different disciplines. In extreme cases, each perceives themselves to be the guardian of a 'value system' that is not only distinct but often privileged over other 'value systems'; and common understanding is a casualty, as each hunts for the moral high ground.

In the case of ecology, the problem has been exacerbated by the often acrimonious relation between ecologists and economists. It has also been complicated by the emergence of the field of ecological economics which some, at least, perceive as an attempt to apply an ecological 'value system' to the analysis of the economic problem of the allocation of scarce resources between competing wants. The perception is mistaken, but it continues to obstruct dialogue between the two

56

disciplines. This chapter considers one way in which ecological 'values' relate to the concept of economic value and the methodology of economic valuation. More particularly, it focuses on one aspect of ecological 'value', discussing its importance for economic value, and the method by which it may be estimated.

It is worth making it clear that concern here is only with anthropocentric value. This is, in part, because interest is centred on the human management of environmental resources, and hence on those values which are relevant to the decision-making process. Non-anthropocentric values – the value placed on different resources by non-human species – are taken to be parametric, although they will naturally be weighted in the decision-making process according to human preferences. Note that concepts such as 'intrinsic' value are anthropocentric, since they describe a very well-defined preference based value. They may include, for example, the value placed by 'deep ecologists' on maintenance of the ecological system in an undisturbed state, or the weight given to the preferences of non-human species as a consequence of 'rights' assigned by humans to those species.

Ecological 'Value'

Human society derives value from ecological resources in two ways. First, individual organisms have properties which make them of direct value in satisfying human consumption or production needs. Second, the combination of organisms, and their role in the functioning of ecosystems from which human society derives services, makes them of indirect value. Demand for the services of ecosystems often derives from demand for a particular species. Individuals may be concerned about some habitat, for example, because they are concerned about a species whose existence is supported by that habitat. Value may also derive from the demand for some abiotic resource. Hence wetlands or watersheds may be valued because of their role in the hydrological cycle.

It is the second source of value that is generally at issue in the discussion of ecological 'value'. Ecology provides insights into the way in which organisms, populations, communities and ecosystems operate within biogeochemical cycles that underpin human activity. Hence it provides insights into the physical characteristics of structures and processes that are, in one way or another, tapped by human society. One example is the derived demand for habitat already mentioned. An understanding of food webs and nutrient cycles makes it possible to indicate the chain between some species targeted for conservation, and the species, communities or systems on which the target species

depends. Similarly, an understanding of the structure of metapopula-
tions makes it possible to identify colonization pathways between
individual populations that may be at risk. What is more interesting is
that it provides a means of distinguishing between substitutes and
complements within an ecosystem, and of ranking organisms, populations and communities on the basis of their relative contribution to the
'productivity' of the system.

There are a number of 'scarcity-relevant' concepts in ecology that
have significance for the allocation of ecological resources. These
include the concept of the keystone species or the keystone group,
being a species or group of species that makes an unusually pronounced contribution to community structure or processes (Paine,
1980). They also include the 'link' – mobile or critical – species which
link processes through pollination, seed dispersal or other material
transport (Westman, 1985). The notion that some habitats are more
productive than others is contained in the concept of source and sink
populations, which distinguish between populations that are net
exporters and those that are net importers of individuals. In addition,
there are several concepts of 'rarity': species being rare if they have a
highly restricted geographic range, high habitat specificity, small local
populations or some combination of these. Ecologists have not, as yet,
systematized their discussion of the relative importance of ecosystems
and the components of ecosystems: the ecological 'values' of each are
regarded as non-commensurable. It is clear that keystone species are
potentially more valuable than other species; the critical link species
derive value from the fact that they are complementary with other
species, and that the habitats supporting source populations are more
productive than the habitats supporting sink populations. But within
ecology there has been little attempt to rank, say, critical link species in
one ecosystem with keystone species in another.

Of particular interest is the role of biodiversity and its link with
'fitness': the ability of organisms, populations, communities and ecosystems to respond to changing environments. Biodiversity – including
intrapopulation diversity (heterozygosity), interpopulation diversity
(divergence), intraspecific diversity (phenotypic diversity), interspe-
cific diversity (genotypic diversity) and most importantly functional
diversity – is ecologically important primarily because it underpins the
ability to respond positively and creatively to environmental change.
Phenotypic diversity has ecological 'value' not because it provides
material for commercial exploitation by plant breeders and others, but
because it provides the means by which a single species can cope with
change in environmental conditions. In terms of Holling's (1987)
description of the four system function (exploitation, conservation,
creative destruction and reorganization), biodiversity assures the

effectiveness of the reorganization phase. At present, there is still no consensus on the link between diversity and the resilience of ecosystems (Orians and Kunin, 1990). Nor is there consensus on which ecosystem types or biomes are critical to the conservation of biodiversity, although there is some sense that what is important is the interactions between ecosystems (di Castri and Glaser, 1986). But there is consensus that a loss of diversity at any level implies a loss of fitness or ability to adapt to environmental changes at that level. The value of diversity in this respect is very closely related to the potential productivity of a system subject to external stress and shock.

Economic Value

It is now conventional to distinguish between two sources of the value of ecological resources: use value (the value of the services provided to the user) and non-use (Randall, 1991) or non-consumptive (Brown, 1990) value (the value accorded to the resource independently of whether it is put to use). Within these two, economists have at various times identified bequest and scientific value (Krutilla, 1967; Pearce and Turner, 1990); the value of the option to use it in the future (Weisbrod, 1964); and the 'quasi-option' value of the future information made available through its conservation (Arrow and Fisher, 1974; Henry, 1974). Formally, the distinction between the two is straightforward. Suppose there exists a preference relation in which the utility or welfare depends separately on two terms: one a function of the resource alone and the other a function which is not separable in the same resource and all other goods and services. Then non-use value is the value associated with the first term, and use value is the value associated with the second term (Maler, 1994).

For purposes of this discussion non-use value can be ignored. The questions to be asked here are (i) how ecological 'value' enters the function relating welfare to ecological resources, and (ii) how it may be estimated. It turns out that the answer to the second of these questions depends on the answer to the first. Although ecologists do know a good deal about the functioning of ecosystems, there is still enormous scientific uncertainty about how genotypes, species, and communities influence ecosystem function (Solbrig, 1991). There is also uncertainty about the degree of substitutability that exists for different functions. Plant species which are close substitutes as photosynthesizers, for example, may not be close substitutes in respect of other functions. At present, the degree of functional substitutability between species is still uncertain in most ecosystems. There do not yet exist adequate physical measures of the impact of disturbance on the size of ecosystem populations, or of the sensitivity of ecosystem functions to change in the size of populations, or the deletion of whole populations. And there are almost no price measures of the same phenomena.

It follows that economic demand for many ecological functions will not be directly observable. In the absence of markets for such ecological functions, all that may be observed is the change in the demand for market goods and services that accompanies a change in the provision of ecological functions. To address this, economists have either constructed hypothetical or simulated markets for ecological services, or have derived demand for those services from the observed demand for marketed goods and services. Both techniques have been widely used to evaluate non-marketed environmental resources and ecological services.

Two techniques dominate the constructed markets approach. The first relies on the contingent valuation of ecological resources in a hypothetical market. The second relies on the use of observed transactions in a simulated market. What these approaches look for are direct measures of human willingness to pay or willingness to accept compensation for some change in the availability of ecological resources (compensating or equivalent variation). The problem they share is that they rely on the subjective perceptions of respondents who (i) are operating under incomplete ecological and economic information, (ii) do not have the discipline of opportunity cost (face a hypothetical choice only), and (iii) have an incentive to respond differently depending on how the problem is communicated and whither it may confer strategic advantage.

The derived demand approach, on the other hand, depends on the specification of a functional relationship between the marketed goods and services for which demand may be observed and those unobserved ecological services which are to be valued (cf. Kolstad and Braden, 1991). The approach depends on the proposition that if output depends on a vector of marketed inputs and non-marketed inputs and non-marketed ecological services, the value that is placed on a unit change in the ecological services will bear a well-defined relationship to the income/ expenditure needed to compensate for that change. More particularly, it will reflect either the change in market income that would be needed to restore the original level of welfare (which is just compensating variation), or the change in market income that would produce the same final level as welfare as the change in the ecological service (which is just the equivalent variation).

Three relations between the ecological services and marketed goods have been considered: (i) where marketed goods and ecological services are perfect substitutes; (ii) where marketed goods and ecological services are perfect complements; and (iii) where marketed goods and ecological services are weak complements. The perfect substitutes case is least interesting, since if marketed goods and ecological resources are perfect substitutes in all their functions there is no problem. The perfect complements case implies that there is no level of defensive expenditure which can compensate for the loss of ecological services. It may very well be of interest in some cases, but it has not been explored in the literature. The weak complements case has been taken to mean either that the ecological service is weakly complementary with at least one marketed good (Maler, 1974) or that it is weakly complementary with all final service flows generated by the household (Bockstael and McConnel, 1983). In both cases, too, it is possible to recover the change in welfare (and hence the compensating variation in market income) associated with a change in the level of ecological services.

To this point, the generation of production functions that include ecological services has not rested on collaborative work between economists and ecologists. Indeed, it has been suggested that the reason why economists have not made more use of the technique is their inability to specify how environmental quality measures should enter the production function (Smith, 1991). Various options for proceeding in the absence of good ecological data have been suggested, including the use of the intercept term to measure the impact of some unrecorded ecological resource (Narain and Fisher, 1994). However, there seems little alternative to the proper specification of the production function. To this point, also, most work has focused on the household. Clearly, however, there is considerable scope for the development of appropriate functional forms both for production outside the household, and at more aggregated levels. (For an application to wetlands see Barbier, 1994.)

Biodiversity and the Production Function Approach

It is important to appreciate that the exercise involves more than just adding ecological factors to production functions of standard form. Collaboration between ecologists and economists in an attempt to uncover the value of biodiversity loss has in fact changed the general perception of the problem. Recent ecological research has switched the focus in biodiversity loss from the characteristics of particular organisms to the functions of the mix of organisms in ecosystems (Holling *et al.*, 1995), and this has had important implications both for the way we think about the social costs of biodiversity loss, and for the efficacy of policy instruments designed to deal with the problem. By changing our perception of the nature of the social costs of biodiversity depletion, the link that is now being emphasized between functional diversity and ecological resilience also changes our perception of the effectiveness with which the problem may be addressed at the global level. This is because it changes both the time path and the geographical distribution of the benefits of biodiversity conservation. In particular, it has shown that the main medium-term implications of biodiversity depletion lie not in the genetic information losses associated with species or population deletion, but in the loss of ecosystem resilience. This implies that the main benefits of biodiversity conservation lie not in the preservation of a global public good, but in the maintenance of ecosystem resilience at the local, national and regional level.

The change in perception of biodiversity by ecologists follows a shift in emphasis from the properties of system equilibria, to the resilience of systems far from equilibrium: their capacity to absorb shocks without losing stability (Walker and Noy-Meir, 1982 ; Schindler, 1990; Holling, 1992). Resilience is a measure of the magnitude of disturbance that can be absorbed before the system flips from one state to another. The role of biodiversity in this lies in its link with system resilience. Many systems ecologists now take the view that the dynamics of most terrestrial ecosystems are dominated by a small set of processes (Holling, 1992), and that the dynamics of species may be more sensitive to ecosystem stress than the dynamics of processes (Schindler, 1990). In other words, stressed ecosystems may maintain many of their functions even though the composition of the species comprising those ecosystems changes. However, the ability of the key structuring processes of a system to operate under a range of conditions depends on the number of alternative species that can take over functions when perturbation of an ecosystem causes the disappearance of the species currently supporting those functions. In short, it is the functional diversity of ecosystems that determines their resilience. Indeed, there is growing evidence that the least resilient components of food webs energy flows and biogeochemical cycles are those in which the number of species carrying out important functions is very small (Schindler, 1990). Biodiversity underpins the ability of far-from-equilibrium ecological systems to function under stress, and in so doing it underpins the predictability of those systems.

The valuation problem is, in one way, a standard one. Market prices which are the principle observers of the ecological–economic system are, in these circumstances, very poor indicators of the opportunity cost of committing particular classes of resource to some economic use. Moreover, allocation of ecological resources on the bases of market prices will be less efficient the closer the system is to critical thresholds. At the same time, estimation of the social opportunity cost of the allocation of ecological resources will be more difficult. The value of biodiversiy will show up in the change in the distribution of income associated with a change in the mix of organisms, populations, communities and ecosystems.

Consider the case of agriculture. The dominant characteristic of intensive agriculture is a reduction of biodiversity in order to focus on particular species with properties that include, *inter alia*, high rates of growth. That is, the crops selected in intensive agriculture are generally *r*-strategists with high rates of net primary productivity. This typically leads to an overall reduction in the resilience of the ecological systems on which intensive agriculture is based, and the growing dependence of agriculturists on intensive management regimes in which output is frequently maintained only by ever-increasing use of fertilizers, pesticides and irrigation. That is, agricultural systems have to be ever more tightly protected against perturbation (disease, drought and so on) precisely because their sensitivity to perturbation has increased with specialization.

Without external access to substitute plants and genetic material for engineering disease and pest resistance, and without the input of biocides the approach is extraordinarily susceptible to perturbation. The costs of the management regime needed to maintain a system of very low natural resilience provides a measure of the benefits of ecosystem resilience. That is, where intensive management has substituted for diversity of species as the primary insurance against collapse of the agricultural system, then the cost of the management regime may be thought of as the insurance 'premium' on system resilience.

Concluding Remarks

Those properties of environmental resources which make them of value from an ecological perspective are part of what make them of value from an economic perspective. That is, the role of species, populations and communities in the functioning of ecological systems is the source of what has been referred to earlier as the indirect value of such resources. This indirect value may be picked up by properly specifying the functions describing the relation between inputs and outputs in both consumption and production. This is the production function approach, and the challenge it poses to ecologists and economists is three-fold. First, specification of the appropriate functional form requires a joint effort between the two disciplines. Ecological processes, and economic–ecological feedbacks need to be incorporated into production functions in a way that makes the contribution of such processes transparent. This involves integration of important areas of methodologies of the two disciplines. Second, the nature and degree of uncertainty in the specification of functional forms needs to be made explicit, in order to establish the confidence which may be placed in the valuation of environmental resources generated by the approach. Economists and ecologists currently work with different concepts of uncertainty and stochasticity, and these need to be aligned. Third, since most production systems are non-linear, they are characterized by threshold effects and discontinuities. At the same time, many environmental resources subject to threshold effects are in the nature of public goods. These pose particular problems for both valuation and policy. Accordingly, they need to be clearly identified, and this depends not just on understanding the interactive dynamics of ecological and economic processes, but on understanding the degree to which environmental resources are exclusive and rival and in consumption. Once again, this relies on both socioeconomic and ecological data.

It is clear that there remain significant obstacles to interdisciplinary collaboration between ecologists and economists, not least because of the barriers to communications between them created by differences in methodology and the way in which the allocation problem is conventionally posed in each discipline. This is, however, one of most potentially productive areas for further work in the management of environmental resources, and is worthy of much more attention than it is currently receiving. The present efforts to explore the non-use value of environmental resources through contingent valuation methods (CVM) and related techniques beg the most important question that needs to be posed about our use of environmental resources: what is the value of the loss in output in production and consumption that is due to the degradation of environmental resources? This is a question that cannot be answered by considering the subjective evaluation of environmental resources by individuals with little understanding of ecosystem functions.

References

Arrow, K.J. and Fisher, A.C. (1974) Environmental preservation, uncertainty, and irreversibility. *Quarterly Journal of Economics* 88(2), 312–319.

Barbier, E.B. (1994) Tropical wetland values and environmental functions. In: Perrings C., Maler, K.G., Folke, C., Holling, C.S. and Janssen, B.O. (eds) *Biodiversity Conservation*. Kluwer Academic Press, Dordrecht.

Bockstael, N.E. and McConnell, K.E. (1983) Welfare measurement in the household production framework. *American Economic Review* 73, 806–814.

Brown, G.M. (1990) Valuation of genetic resources. In: Orians, G.H., Brown, G.M., Kunin, W.E. and Swierbinski, J.E. (eds) *The Preservation and Valuation of Biological Resources*. University of Washington Press, Seattle, pp. 203–228.

Di Castri, F. and Glaser, G. (1986) Interdisciplinary research for the ecological development of mountain and island areas. In: Polunin, N. (ed.) *Ecosystem Theory and Application.* John Wiley and Sons, New York.

Henry, C. (1974) Investment decision under uncertainty: the irreversibility effect. *American Economic Review* 64, 1006–1012.

Holling, C.S. (1987) Simplifying the complex: the paradigms of ecological function and structure. *European Journal of Operational Research* 30, 139–146.

Holling, C.S. (1992) Cross-scale morphology geometry and dynamics of ecosystems. *Ecological Monographs* 62, 447–502.

Holling, C.S., Schindler, D.W., Walker, B.W. and Roughgarden, J. (1995) Biodiversity in the function of ecosystems. In: Perrings, C., Maler, K.G., Folke, C., Hollings, C.S. and Janssen, B.O. (eds) *Biodiversity Loss: Ecological and Economic Issues.* Cambridge University Press, Cambridge, pp. 44–83.

Kolstad, C.D. and Braden, J.B. (1991) Environmental demand theory. In: Braden, J.B. and Kolstad, C.D. (eds) *Measuring The Demand for Environmental Quality.* North Holland, Amsterdam, pp. 17–40.

Krutilla, J.V. (1967) Conservation reconsidered. *American Economic Review* 57 (4), 778–786.

Maler, K.G. (1974) *Environmental Economics: A Theoretical Enquiry.* Blackwell, Oxford.

Maler, K.G. (1994) Sustainable development. In: Perrings, C., Maler, K.G., Folke, C., Holling, C.S. and Janssen, B.O. (eds) *Biodiversity Loss: Ecological and Economic Issues.* Cambridge University Press, Cambridge, pp. 213–224.

Narain, U. and Fisher, A. (1994) Modeling the value of biodiversity using a production function approach. In: Perrings, C., Maler, K.G., Folke, C., Holling, C.S. and Janssen, B.O. (eds) *Biodiversity Conservation.* Kluwer Academic Press, Dordrecht.

Orians, G.H. and Kunin, W.E. (1990) Ecological uniqueness and loss of species. In: Orians, G.H. *et al.* (eds) *The Preservation and Valuation of Biological Resources.* University of Washington Press, Seattle, pp. 146–184.

Paine, R.T. (1980) Food webs: linkage interaction strength and community infrastructure. *Journal of Animal Ecology* 49, 667–685.

Pearce, D.W. and Turner, R.K. (1990) *Economics of Natural Resources and the Environment.* Harvester-Wheatsheaf, London.

Randall, A. (1991) Total and nonuse values. In: Braden J.B. and Kolstad, C.D. (eds) *Measuring The Demand for Environmental Quality.* North Holland, Amsterdam, pp. 303–322.

Schindler D.W. (1990) Natural and anthropogenically imposed limitations to biotic richness in freshwaters. In: Woodwell, G. (ed.) *The Earth in Transition: Patterns and Processes of Biotic Impoverishment.* Cambridge University Press, Cambridge, pp. 425–462.

Smith, V.K. (1991) Household production functions and environmental benefit estimation. In: Braden, J.B. and Kolstad, C.D. (eds) *Measuring The Demand for Environmental Quality.* North Holland, Amsterdam, pp. 41–76.

Solbrig, O.T. (1991) The origin and function of biodiversity. *Environment* 33, 10.

Walker, B.H. and Noy-Meir, I. (1982) Aspects of the stability and resilience of savanna ecosystems. In: Huntley, B.J. and Walker, B.H. (eds) *Ecology of Tropical Savannas.* Springer, Berlin, pp. 577–590.

Weisbrod, B. (1964) Collective consumption services of individual consumption

goods. *Quarterly Journal of Economics* 77, 71–77.
Westman, W.E. (1985) *Ecology, Impact Assessment and Environmental Planning.*
    Wiley, New York.

6

Economic Valuation and Ecological Values

Martin Holdgate

The World Conservation Union

Perspectives and Propositions

The use of economic instruments in order to meet environmental standards has been debated in the UK and elsewhere for some considerable time, but it is still uncertain where these standards are coming from: the stable door is wide open, but the horse has yet to appear.

In the environmental field, the standards we now talk about are those for sustainability, for the universal catchphrase of the age is 'sustainable development'. There are many interpretations of this term. OECD finance ministers are said to have defined it as 'development which achieves the highest rate of economic growth without fuelling inflation'. In other words, if you are dealing entirely with models internal to the socioeconomic system, the concern is over the slope of a curve of continual growth. For ecologists on the other hand, sustainable development is the attainment of the optimum level of sustainable biological production from a system. It is a process of elevating the asymptote of a curve, with a sufficient safety margin to allow for the inevitable climatic and other seasonal variations. In this form, the concept is fairly easily understood, but the actual practice of its attainment is extremely difficult, and characterizing what form the optimum production of a system may take is in itself complex and controversial, and involves choice between alternatives that are likely not to have been defined with equal precision.

Another problem area in environmental policy concerns 'ecological values', for these are also ill-defined. Ecology is the interrelationship between living things and their environment. It encompasses all interactions among all living things, and as a consequence ecological values go far wider than nature conservation values. Accordingly, the term will be used here to mean 'those elements or attributes of environmental systems which are either essential to their functions or provide direct or indirect benefits to people or both'. The following discussion will therefore range from the large macro-scale systems like those governing atmospheric composition to the grassroots micro-scopic level like a nitrogen-fixing root nodule.

In the environmental world, there is a common perception that the socioeconomic system is not working properly. The argument commonly goes something like this:

1. all life, including human life, depends on the functioning of the natural systems of the biosphere – the habitable zone of crust, water, soil and air on the surface of the Earth;
2. the activities of society, and especially developed industrialized societies, are today impairing those functions at levels ranging from the microscopic to the global;
3. this is at least in part because of a failure to include the values such systems represent, and the costs of the damage to them, in economic models and equations on which, in turn, the major decisions of governments and industries are based;
4. as a result the market does not work properly, and fails to deter further damage (and ultimate cost);
5. the market also excludes environmental products which could be more useful, and more sustainable, than current uses because it gets their relative values wrong;
6. as a consequence, resource use patterns are inefficient, assets are wasted, and development is unsustainable.

It is important to try to test the hypothesis that development will become more sustainable if the natural capital represented by the components of the biosphere is correctly valued, and the revenues and services that capital provides are consequentially safeguarded. The hypothesis is that if we put better values into the models, they will work better. That is an evident truism. But can we – and will the results help? I can tell you my general conclusion now – that while better values are desirable they are not sufficient; that valuation in a complex system will inevitably be uneven, and that we must avoid the distortion that comes from providing figures of spurious precision, especially when the quality of those figures varies so much between one component of the system and another.

The problem is the immense complexity of the system, and the differences in the relationship of its components to human society. Some 'ecological values' are essential but almost infinite, like incident solar radiation which powers the whole biosphere. Some are support-ive but outside the systems used by people, like coral reefs as sea defences. Yet others are product-generating like soil, or products in the market like those from agriculture or fisheries, while some are potential, like genes in the wild relatives of crops.

This variation can be recognized in a hierarchical taxonomy of components of life-support systems. Such a classification might have three levels:

1. global life-support systems;
2. direct life-support systems;
3. ecological products.

These categories are briefly described.

Global life-support systems

Global life-support systems include those features of the biosphere which determine the habitability and productivity of the planet, operate across national frontiers, are not capable of direct regulation by human action, but may need protection against various products of human activity which are capable of inflicting damage. Examples include:

1. the exclusion, by the atmosphere and particularly by the ozone in the stratosphere, of solar radiation at wavelengths damaging to living organisms;
2. the maintenance of more or less stable concentrations of the various components of the atmosphere, and especially oxygen and the gases that determine radiation retention by the Earth (water vapour, carbon dioxide, and also methane and nitrous oxide – the 'greenhouse gases');
3. the cycling of the essential elements – carbon, nitrogen, oxygen, phosphorus and sulphur;
4. the photosynthetic fixing of carbon, using solar energy, as carbohy-drates, the base of all food chains;
5. the cycling of water, essential to life on land;
6. the maintenance of a sufficient diversity of life forms to allow evolution to adjust to changes as they occur, ensure that the various habitats and niches available for life are exploited, and maintain the functional integrity of ecological systems.

Direct life-support systems

Direct life-support systems include components of the environment that operate on a regional or local scale and are at the base of production of natural products used consumptively or non-consumptively by people. They all depend on the global life-support category and they generate specific products in the ecological products category. Examples include:

1. soil fertility, obviously essential to plant production whether in agriculture, plantations or wild habitats on land;
2. the flow characteristics and water quality of freshwater systems, in turn determining their productivity of fish and other useful products, their capacity to disperse effluents from human societies, and their aesthetic qualities (in turn a determinant of recreational use);
3. the quality of marine waters, as a base for ecosystems that in turn sustain fisheries and recreational uses;
4. the integrity of natural coast protection systems (coral reefs, mangroves, salt marshes, sea-grass beds) – which incidentally also support fisheries, are fish nursery grounds and can supply many other products as well as having major aesthetic and recreational importance;
5. the integrity and biological diversity of a range of natural and semi-natural 'wild' habitats and vegetation types on land, important as sources of an immense range of products.

Ecological products

Ecological products include both 'wild' living resources and those derived from agriculture, forestry or aquaculture. The two categories interlock: all aquaculture is of wild species, and some 'ranched' species (like crocodiles) are taken from wild breeding stock, while genetic material from the wild is used continually to develop new strains of crop plants. Moreover, many species are not currently used in agriculture or forestry but have considerable potential to be brought into more intensive human use. One sees this today with deer or wild boar farming in Britain or guanaco farming in Patagonia.

The subjects of valuation in this category are in fact of two kinds. First, there are some that are already within the conventional economy because they are harvested by fisheries, forestry or agriculture or by collection from 'wild' ecosystems, as are Brazil nuts, rattan canes and latex. Second, there are others that could be harvested and marketed, but are not, and so lie outside the formal economy (although many are used by local people). Some of these could in aggregate be as valuable, or more valuable, than the conventional harvested alternative.

A tropical forest, for example, can be used sustainably to provide a vast diversity of products including food (meat, fruits, nuts); other animal products (skins, horn, bone, teeth, etc.); medicines (many herbal remedies are the mainstay of local health care while some 40% of the pharmaceutical products traded in North America are said to be derived from substances first discovered in wild plants); genetic materials (for crop and livestock improvement, and now increasingly for biotechnology); wood, wood products, fibre, latex resin, and artefacts made from these; fuel, including wood and charcoal (non-commercial energy remains dominant in rural communities in most of the developing world); craft and culture objects, musical instruments, painting; research, enhancing understanding of the system; aesthetic enjoyment – often the foundation for tourism which is the biggest foreign exchange earner in a number of developing countries.

The issue for this sector is one of *relative value*, and then one of *choice*. It is a fact that many societies do use wild systems – whether forests or coastal marine ecocomplexes – sustainably, deriving many useful products from them, but that this multi-purpose use is often swept away in order to extract timber, or replace artisanal by larger scale commercial fisheries. Why? Is it a failure of valuation, or linked to aspects of social structure? This point will be discussed below. In this author's view it goes to the heart of the issue.

The Value of Global Life-support Systems

These global life-support systems, direct life-support systems and environmental products are linked by interactions which, in sum, are the processes of the biosphere. It may be important in some political and presentational context to stress the immense value of the upper levels of the hierarchy, but in practical terms it is almost impossible to attach meaningful values to these major systems. It is likely to be most useful to attach valuations as near to the human user or damager of the systems as possible. This is also most likely to give a prospect of comprehensiveness: at the big system level we are largely gathering anecdotal or illustrative examples, especially of the costs of damage.

It is fairly easy to demonstrate that at the macro level – that of global life-support systems – the changes being caused by human action, although marginal to those systems, could still have profound socioeconomic impacts. For example, if the damage to the stratospheric ozone layer admits more ultraviolet B radiation, and there is a consequent reduction in photosynthesis by the marine phytoplankton, knock-on effects will inevitably undermine the productivity of marine systems generally and reduce fisheries. The enhanced flux of radiation will also cause some increases in human skin cancer, including that of malignant melanoma, and may affect plant production on land. The costs involved are not easy to calculate but they certainly exceed the value to humanity of the chlorofluorocarbons which have been causing the problem and hence justify the action now in hand to remove these causative agents.

Similarly, the accumulation of greenhouse gases in the atmosphere, if it were to lead to significant temperature rises and alterations in rainfall patterns, would obviously have profound potential impacts on the distribution both of natural vegetation types and of agriculture. A 1°C rise in temperature displaces the zones of tolerance of trees and of other plants including crop plants about 100 km towards the Poles. Were temperatures to rise as much as 5°C (the upper limit of probability) major changes would be inevitable. The boreal conifer forest would move north over what is now tundra to the shores of the Arctic Ocean, oak woodlands would disappear from much of England, forests would be eliminated from southwest Australia, and energy use and settlement habitability patterns would alter as well. Where – as is predicted for central and eastern Australia – rainfall increases, it would probably fall on fewer days with implications for flooding and for the habitability of flood plains. Societies would be incapable of maintaining current land use patterns in the face of such changes and the adjustments would inevitably affect the relative wealth of nations and very possibly the integrity of their frontiers.

But while such analyses clearly indicate the potential costs of impacts on global life-support systems, and by deduction, say something about the values of those systems, the valuation clearly includes arbitrary elements and, as it deals with a global asset, is hard to incorporate in down-to-earth market systems. The analyses are likely to be most useful in comparisons of damage costs and control or protection costs, and hence in judgement of the importance of changes in *policy*. They do not feed easily into cost–benefit analysis.

The Value of Direct Life-support Systems

Much the same holds for impact on direct life-support systems. Again, the total values of these systems are effectively infinite, but the marginal costs of damage are calculable, and parts of the system are capable of valuation.

Soil erosion in many regions exceeds the rate of natural soil formation by one or two orders of magnitude. Worldwide, about 295 million hectares of land – an area only slightly less than that of India – has suffered severe degradation, and a much larger area – about 900 million hectares, or three Indias – is still capable of being farmed but has lost a considerable part of its productivity. Salinization, water-logging and alkalinization have affected large areas of irrigated land. These losses are calculable in terms of production foregone, and of remedial measures, and are clearly very large. World Bank analysis suggests that losses in productivity arising from soil depletion, gener-alized, amount to 0.5–1.5% of GDP annually: in Java on-site erosion costs in one year were put at US$323 million.

Natural sea defences, produced by mangroves, coral reefs or salt marshes have evident economic value. One calculation, for Boston Harbour in the USA, suggested that retention of natural, self-maintaining, wetland saved US$17 million a year in flood protection works. A hectare of intertidal marshland was estimated to be worth US$72,000 a year if its productivity as a nursery area for commercial fish species was taken into account. The damage costs when such resources are neglected are equally vast: last December I visited a resort on the east coast of the Chinese island of Hainan where destruction of an off-shore reef by dynamite fishing and quarrying for building stone and lime had led directly to the sea encroaching on the land by between 300 and 600 metres, with the loss of thousands of coconut palms, and the impending loss – for the process will continue – of a hotel complex.

Pollution from industry and agriculture has clearly damaged the quality and productivity of lakes, rivers, forests, farmlands and coastal seas. The Polish delegate at the UN Conference on Environment and Development in Rio said that air pollution was costing his country a sum equivalent to 16% of GNP. In the OECD as a whole, damage costs from pollution are put at around 3–5% – as against expenditure on controls of around 0.5–1.5%. Marine fisheries production is now at around the theoretical maximum, but is actually being reduced by overfishing. Clearance of forests in upland catchments may reduce the quality of water draining from them, and increase the irregularity of flow. The losses of biological diversity, largely as a result of the continuing destruction of wild habitats, through processes like defor-estation, mean that the genetic richness of the earth is being impaired, the capacity of living systems to adjust to changing climate and other processes is being reduced, the wild relatives crop breeders need to improve cultivated plants are being lost, and medicinal plants of great potential value are disappearing before their values have even been assessed. All these represent serious wastage of environmental assets, partly at least because the values involved have not been stated and taken into account by markets – or by governments.

The Value of Ecological Products

Valuation becomes more practical and more precise when one moves to the level of ecological products. However even here likes and unlikes clamour for comparison. Some directly used 'ecological products' include the yields of fisheries, agriculture and forestry (which all depend on the maintenance of ecological processes). These have of course been valued and are in the market – although this by itself has not deterred unsustainable use, for overfishing is a global problem and subsidy of intensive agriculture, with its heavy dependence on artificial fertilizers and pesticides, has created both economic distortions and ecological unsustainability. But these are real problems, to which real values can be attached. It is more difficult to carry the process forward when dealing with the other category of 'ecological product', lying outside the conventional economy. The problems arise in particular when we start trying to value the unknown or the inferred, and dealing with a wide spectrum of uncertainty.

For example, some 40% of pharmaceuticals traded across the counter in North America are said to be derived from wild plants, although the active ingredients are now very commonly synthesized in the laboratory. New ventures like INBio in Costa Rica, in partnership with the North American pharmaceutical firm Merck, are surveying and characterizing new potential. New industries like that marketing an ivory substitute made from tagua nuts in Ecuador are coming forward. Norman Myers calculated, as a generalization, that the sustainable harvesting of multiple products from tropical rain forests could have a value of US$200 per hectare per year against the US$150 per hectare from once-off logging that leaves a degraded landscape behind it. In practice there is a mosaic: the sustainable multiple product use of forests can actually provide anything from US$420 to as little as 75 US cents per hectare per year depending on forest type and situation! Tourism is also a variable asset – a lion in the Amboseli National Park in Kenya is said to be worth US$27,000 a year, and a group of elephants rather more – but obviously this is based on a rather arbitrary allocation of tourist revenues against stated tourist preferences. What is clear is that land use for such parks generates some 40 times the revenue it would produce under pastoral systems – but again like is not strictly being compared with like for the revenues would go to different people.

How precise can we be when we try to value an asset like a Site of Special Scientific Interest (SSSI)? Some queer questions and tacit assumptions can easily lead to funny answers. SSSIs are commonly chosen on criteria such as uniqueness, diversity, representativeness within the national frame of ecological variability, rarity of component species or importance for research. In the end a value judgement follows. This is inevitable for the products of such areas are intangible. Weighing the research papers would clearly be an extremely poor method. And many SSSIs in the United Kingdom are secondary – derived from human impact on preceding natural vegetation, often forests. People now cherish open, deforested and biologically impoverished uplands at the same time as they deplore the degradation caused by deforestation in the tropics. Again, how can we really value today's sacred cow – biological diversity? We can value parts of it like the marketed products derived from a rain forest or recreational use, or even the potential for both, and we can perhaps estimate the value of genetic potential that may be used in crop breeding in future, but we can really only make the wildest guess at the value of much of the diversity, because it is calculated that only between a tenth and a half of the species on Earth have been described by science, while the roles of many species, such as the beetles inhabiting the canopy of tropical rain forests, are unknown.

Valuation in Context

The deduction from the above is that while some parts of the environment can be valued others cannot. There is another conceptual gulf here in that there is an ecological view that there are intrinsic importances, if not values, that can be attached to components of environmental systems because they collectively constitute the global life-support system. This is the justification for seeking to conserve as much diversity as practicable regardless of its direct usefulness to people.

All of this has to be seen in a social context. There are fundamental divergencies between social groups. 'How can you buy or sell the sky, the warmth of the land' asks the famous speech attributed to Chief Seathl in 1855. The statement that every SSSI should be sacrosanct implies, for those who make it, an absolute value just as IUCN's demand that all primary rain forests should be protected is absolutist – and almost certainly unrealistic when tropical human populations are set to double in 20 years and will need land to cultivate. Other social group divergencies raise other difficulties. For example, on the face of it, the displacement of forest dwellers using multiple products by logging gangs, destroying the long-term biological productivity of the area makes little sense. But again, the issue needs analysing in rather greater depth.

Often such differences arise because of differing interests and freedoms of groups of people. For example, the use of forest to provide meat, fruit, nuts, wood, fibres, latex, medicines, musical instruments, or weapons by forest dwellers may be of high value to them, yet lie entirely outside the formal economy. They commonly lack ownership of the land they live on, which in many developing countries is vested in the State, and occupy a low status in the structure of their national societies. As small-scale, local sectors of the economy (or as resource users outside the formal economy) they tend to be overlooked, but where their resource use and output of products rises they tend to be taken over by new commercial enterprises, which have less stake in the land and more interest in short-term maximization of returns. Moreover, concessions to a timber company to log a forest for export bring revenues to central exchequers, may promote internal investment, and show in GNP statistics. The fact that multi-product cropping by local communities is almost certain to yield more useful products, sustainably, does not figure in the decision process. The same issues arise when investments are made centrally in offshore fishing fleets that compete with, and ultimately destroy, sustainable artisanal fisheries by coastal communities. Such conflicts within society are inevitable but they grow as human pressures on the environment increase. At the social level, such conflicts of interest demand not so much a valuation as a mediation process.

Intertemporal comparisons are also notoriously difficult. Ecologists start with an inverse perception to many short-term judgements in the political sphere. They recognize that 30 years from now world food production must be doubled, probably on no more cultivable land, and that the achievement of sustainable development sets prescriptive goals which may not be attainable by the unrestricted operation of the market. Hence they tend to treat tomorrow's environment as twice as valuable as today's – and question discounting practices that write the asset value down.

Conclusion

I conclude with the comment that while it is certainly useful to force a set of more explicit statements about the value of natural resources, and to seek a more consistent framework for the valuation process, because this can only enhance the use of cost–benefit analysis, that is only part of the process. For these values and the analysis are only inputs to social judgement, and alternative analyses based on deliberately different estimates, followed by a convergence test, may not be a bad thing. Perhaps ecologists should be challenged to produce their own systems of valuation to stand alongside the economic one. I suspect that such a valuation would seek to assess how far an area or environmental component contributed to *planetary life-support systems*, how far it supported an important *regulatory function*, for example in delivering pure water, shielding coasts from erosion or abstracting carbon dioxide; how far it contributed to *biological production* – both useful now and potentially useful; how far it sustained *genetic diversity* as a basis for the future; and just possibly how far it supported *cultural, scientific or aesthetic values* like research or tourism. But the ecologist would emphasize that in many cases we would be valuing alternatives, and that methodological imperfections make strict comparisons impossible.

Trends in human impact on the planet mean that we can no longer look on any resource (except solar radiation) as a traditional free good in the sense that it is endlessly available, limitless in scale and immune to disturbance by human action. We have expanded human impacts on the planet to cover virtually all components of the biosphere – the atmosphere, the oceans, the rocks, the soils and all species of life. Agriculturalists can no longer think of the wild reservoir of genetic resources as freely available when the habitats of those species are being destroyed as rapidly as they now are: conservation may become, or has already become, a priority for the crop breeder as well as the wildlife conservationist.

Similarly, the concept of commons is virtually outdated. Even in the atmosphere and on the high seas, property rights are being stated whether in terms of the extension of exclusive economic zones from the coastlines outward to 200 nautical miles or through the development of an increasing battery of international conventions to regulate the human management of the resources in question. It is true of course that those conventions do not base their allocation of resources on a conscious valuation system and it is also true that they do not work very well – the resources of the high seas are at present being devastated by uncontrolled fishing, with perhaps twice as many fishing boats as are required pursuing depleted stocks that could yield substantially more if the fishing effort were restrained. But whatever the inadequacies of the system, we are moving more and more toward internationally-agreed management systems for atmosphere and ocean that used to be thought of as global commons. Antarctica, likewise, is the subject of an international management regime.

The major issues confronting the world's community are of course much wider than environmental valuation. There is grave concern over the impact of modern trading patterns on environmental protection and over the conflict between environmental protection laws and Conventions and those seeking free trade, notably under GATT. South–North finance flows, debt, problems of investment, problems of feeding the world's mounting population overshadow the possibility of using resources sustainably, and this is a matter in which both economists and ecologists have a shared interest. We need a robust methodology as a means to that end. Cost–benefit analysis, used as one such tool, works best under systems of social governance that accept the rule of law, have codified property rights, and have groups that are willing to accept a judgemental process that may disadvantage individuals for what is perceived as the best that can be done to advantage the wider community. The process becomes meaningless where there is no consensus on social goals, or where there is gross inequity in ownership and the distribution of benefits, or where it is suspected that some group within society is using the process only to advantage themselves.

It is obvious that the process of social choice must be culturally sensitive as well as economically and scientifically sound. But we must recognize uncertainty and the need for adaptive capacity. Our knowledge of the workings of environmental systems is still gravely deficient. We can be sure that the values of today will seem strange tomorrow. No technique can be allowed to be a strait-jacket. Environmental valuation will be useful if it informs policy and social choice, but it needs to be taken into the wider context of techniques for dispute resolution, mediation, and the equitable use of the world's resources, bearing in mind the interests of tomorrow's as well as today's generation.

7

Contingent Valuation and Economics[1]

W. Michael Hanemann

University of California at Berkeley

Introduction

The question at issue is this: can we, as social scientists, measure in monetary terms the value that people place on the natural environment, or other public goods, when there is no other corroborating market behaviour that would allow measurement by revealed preference methods? Must we remain silent when methods such as travel cost or hedonic pricing (Freeman, 1993) are unavailable? Obviously, it would be simpler if we could restrict economic analysis to commodities where the conventional techniques of revealed preference can be applied. But, this would be a truly procrustean solution: it would put beyond the bounds of analysis many commodities that people value but do not purchase through a market or that they value in part for reasons unconnected with their own purchase and use.

One of the great errors of analysis is the fallacy of misplaced precision – measuring the wrong thing with exquisite precision, rather than the right thing with lesser accuracy. The need to avoid this error has been recognized since the very beginnings of cost–benefit analysis in the United States. In 1934, when a National Resources Board committee was appointed to consider cost-sharing for water resource projects, its report pointed out the need to study 'the part played by

[1] I alone am responsible for the views expressed here. Most of what I know about CV has been learned from working with Richard Carson, Robert Mitchell, and Kerry Smith. I have also gained much from conversations and collaboration with Richard Bishop, Gardner Brown, Michael Conaway, Barbara Kanninen, Ray Kopp, Bengt Kriström, Jon Krosnick, John Loomis, Stanley Presser, Alan Randall, and Paul Ruud. I am greatly indebted to them. I thank Nicholas Flores, Sandra Hoffmann and Jessica Wooley for their excellent assistance in preparing this paper.

intangible factors' in assessing public works programmes. There was similar consideration in the Flood Control Act of 1936, which permitted federal funding of flood control projects 'if the benefits to whomsoever they may accrue are in excess of the estimated costs, and if the lives and social security of people are otherwise adversely affected'. As this formula was applied over the next decade to other public investment programmes, there was a general recognition of the legitimate role of intangible factors such as national defence, saving human lives, and recreational or aesthetic impacts. This concern was endorsed in the first bible of cost–benefit analysis, the US Inter-Agency River Basin Committee's so-called Green Book, published in 1950. This explicitly recognized the category of intangibles and prescribed that these 'need to be described with care and should not be overlooked or minimized merely because they do not yield to dollar evaluation.'

When the Green Book was being written, economic valuation was generally perceived in terms of market prices. To value something, one had to ascertain an appropriate market price, adjust it for market imperfections, and then multiply this price by a quantity. There was no possibility of valuing items, such as intangibles, for which no market price existed. Two developments changed this view. The first was the recognition, prompted by the 'new welfare economics' of the 1940s and especially Hotelling's paper on public utility pricing, that the appropriate welfare criterion is maximization of aggregate consumers' plus producers' surplus (Hotelling, 1938). Hence, while market prices can safely be used to value marginal changes in the supply or demand for market commodities, the impact of non-marginal changes is measured by the change in areas under demand and supply curves. The second development was Samuelson's analysis of public goods and his finding that their valuation must be based on vertical aggregation of individual demand curves (Samuelson, 1938). Together, these developments led to an important paradigm shift during the 1950s – one that contributed directly to the emergence of non-market valuation and is still being felt in the current debate on contingent valuation (CV). This shift changed the focus of valuation away from market prices towards demand and supply functions as the underlying repositories of value. These functions are behavioural relations, and the implication of the paradigm shift was that economics is not just the study of markets but more generally the study of human preferences and behaviour.[2]

The conceptual link to non-market valuation is the recognition that, while a demand curve is not observable if there is no market for

[2] One might also say that, under the new view, the market interests economists because it generates choices rather than just prices. Economics owes its prestige among the social sciences to the fact that it has extended its focus beyond the market to other forms of human behaviour such as political society (Downs) and the family (Becker).

a commodity, there still exists a *latent* demand curve that perhaps can be teased out through other means. The classic example is a public bridge. Despite the absence of a charge, there still is a demand curve for the bridge and the bridge's value is given by the area under this curve. The measurement problem is to uncover the latent demand curve. The two main approaches to non-market valuation – the travel cost method and CV – represent alternative attempts at a solution.[3]

Remarkably, both approaches were first proposed in 1947. The travel cost method was suggested by Harold Hotelling in a letter to the National Park Service (NPS) responding to their request for advice on how to measure the economic benefits from the national parks when there were no revenues from entrance fees. Hotelling saw the similarity with valuing a bridge. Indeed, he felt that valuing a park was easier. Other inputs were involved in using the park, such as expenditures for travel, lodging and equipment; these expenditures were not captured by the NPS but, still, they set a price on visiting the park. Moreover, this price would vary among visitors coming from different origins. By measuring this price for visitors to a site one could estimate their demand curve, and then calculate the consumer's surplus in the usual manner. This was not followed up until Trice and Wood (1958) and Clawson (1959). Within five years, the travel cost method was well established in the literature.

Also in 1947, S.V. Ciriacy-Wantrup published a paper on the economics of soil conservation. He suggested the following solution to what he saw as a central problem, obtaining a demand schedule for benefits that did not involve conventional market commodities:

> [Individuals] may be asked how much money they are willing to pay for successive additional quantities of a collective extra-market good. The choices offered relate to quantities consumed by all members of a social group.... If every individual of the whole social group is interrogated, all individual values (not quantities) are aggregated. The results correspond to a market-demand schedule.[4]

While noting the possible objection that 'expectations of the incidence of costs in the form of taxes will bias the responses to interrogation', he felt that 'through proper education and proper design of questionnaires or interviews it would seem possible to keep this potential bias small.' As noted in Portney (1994), the first application of CV was by Davis

---

[3] The third approach – hedonic pricing – aims more at marginal valuation, since the underlying market demand function generally cannot be recovered from the hedonic price equation (Epple, 1987).

[4] This anticipates Samuelson's result about vertical instead of horizontal aggregation of individual demands for a collective good. The early history of CV and travel cost is described more fully in Hanemann (1992).

(1963) in his Harvard PhD dissertation on the economic value of recreation in the Maine woods.[5] Within ten years, CV studies were becoming commonplace, and CV was established as a technique for non-market valuation.

Travel cost was accepted more quickly than CV. One reason is that it was much closer to the standard paradigm of market commodities. Most economists not only believed in revealed preference but considered the purchase of market goods to be the only valid expression of preference. Voting, a paradigm Maler (1974) and Schelling (1968) linked with CV, was of interest to fewer economists. A second was that CV requires survey research expertise; it cannot be done well by economists alone. It took until the 1980s for adequate links to be forged with the other social sciences.[6] Like CV, the travel cost method was not accepted without debate. Eckstein (1958), for example, strongly opposed it as inaccurate and likely to harm the credibility of benefit–cost analysis in general.[7] Furthermore, there was a distinct learning curve in applying travel cost – the first studies in the 1960s were crude and unsophisticated, but the methodology was steadily refined over the next 15 years. The same was true of CV during the 1980s.

This history gives perspective to the current debate. The positions being staked out today on CV are not new – the contours of the debate have been known for some time. In 1958, Eckstein made the case against CV (which he liked no better than travel cost):

> To determine the price that consumers would be willing to pay if they could purchase national defense, they would have to be interviewed. Since they know perfectly well that the defense budget will not be influenced by their response, and in view of the unpleasant tax possibilities of giving a higher answer, they would have no reason to give truthful replies. And even if they were perfectly guileless ... their lack of experience in purchasing this 'commodity' would result in answers which might be far different from the answers they would give if actual purchases were involved.[8]

[5] Market researchers and others have long conducted what amount to CV surveys using what are sometimes known as 'stated preference' techniques. There is also a parallel with the techniques of multi-attribute utility assessment and conjoint analysis; when monetary cost is one of the attributes, these are a form of CV.

[6] The need for these links was first stressed in Cummings et al. (1986) and is a major theme of Mitchell and Carson (1989), now the standard work on CV, which places it in the broader context of social science research.

[7] From the beginning, practitioners were aware of certain problems with travel cost that are still studied now – e.g., measurement of price, site quality, time constraints, multiple destinations. Similarly with CV. In 1966, Knetsch and Davis catalogued and compared the problems with both methods. They compared empirical estimates of aggregate willingness to pay (WTP) for forest recreation in Maine using the two methods and found a difference of less than 3%.

[8] I certainly agree that it may be difficult to value national defence, or any other broad aggregate,

In 1968, Schelling framed the case for CV:

> There are two main ways of finding out whether some economic benefits
> are worth the costs. One is to use the price system as a test of what
> something is worth to people who have to pay for it.... Another way ... is
> to ask people. This can be done by election, interview or questionnaire ...
> Like the price system, these methods may be ambiguous. It is sometimes
> argued that asking people is a poor way to find out, because they have no
> incentive to tell the truth. That is an important point, but hardly decisive.
> It is also argued, and validly, that people are poor at answering
> hypothetical questions ... While this argument casts suspicion on what
> one finds out by asking questions, it casts suspicion too on those market
> decisions that involve remote and improbable events ... This problem of
> coping, as a consumer, with increments in the risk of unexpected death is
> very much the problem of coping with hypothetical questions, whether in
> response to survey research or to the man who sells lightning-rod
> attachments for the TV antenna.... In any case, relying exclusively on
> market valuations and denying the value of direct enquiry in the
> determination of government programs ... would depend on there being,
> for every potential government service, a close substitute available in the
> market at a comparable price. It would be hard to deduce from first
> principles that this is bound to be the case.

What, then, has changed since these words were written? Against
CV, very little has changed. Professors Diamond and Hausman (DH)
and their colleagues have conducted some experiments that they
contend support some of Eckstein's concerns.[9] However, their evidence
is less than convincing. For CV, there have been two changes. First,
there is now less concern about free-riding – the empirical evidence
shows that it is considerably less ubiquitous than feared in the 1960s
(Davis and Holt, 1993). Second, there was a steady improvement in CV
methods during the 1980s, making it more reliable and robust. The CV
literature now contains more than 1500 studies and papers from over
40 countries covering a wide range of topics – transportation, sanita-
tion, health, the arts, education, the environment (Carson *et al.*, 1993;
Navrud, 1992).

So, why all the *sturm und drang* about CV at this time? The answer,
as Portney (1994) explains, is its use in litigation over damages from oil

through CV. Just what does it mean to have zero national defence? Would respondents find this
credible? But, I believe one could use CV to value *specific* military programmes – just as the Swiss
sometimes hold referenda on them (Swiss Voters Approve $2.5B Order of McDonnell-Douglas
F/A-18 Fighters. *Wall Street Journal* 6/7/93).

[9] Cambridge Economics Associates Inc. (1992) is a set of papers funded by the Exxon Company
and presented at a conference in Washington, DC on 2–3 April 1992. These appear with minor
changes in Hausman (1993). Since I wrote most of this paper without having seen Diamond and
Hausman (1994), I relied heavily on those two sources for a statement of their position, especially their
chapter in Hausman (1993), to which I henceforth refer as DH.

spills, especially litigation arising from the *Exxon Valdez* oil spill in March, 1989.[10] In this chapter I focus on the general question of how one measures preferences for the environment. I will not discuss the *Valdez* litigation or other aspects of natural resource damages.

The rest of this chapter is organized as follows. The second section deals with the economic theory of non-use value and shows why it cannot be measured by revealed preference methods. The third section describes aspects of CV practice that enhance its reliability. The next two sections compare CV with public opinion polls and market research surveys. The sixth section reviews the empirical evidence marshalled by Hausman (1993), and the final section addresses economic theory and CV, including DH's theoretical arguments about CV.

The Economics of Non-use Value

People have long valued wildlife for many reasons besides wanting to shoot, eat, wear, or otherwise utilize it. The number who do so has grown steadily (Hoage, 1989). The first systematic attempts to account for this in economic terms were by Weisbrod (1964) and Krutilla (1967). Weisbrod focused on uncertainty and what became known as 'option value' – e.g., some people who do not now visit a wilderness area have a positive willingness to pay (WTP) to protect it in order to preserve their option of visiting it in the future. Krutilla focused on 'bequest value' – some people have a positive WTP for the wilderness area because they want to preserve it for future generations – and on what became known as 'existence', 'non-use' or, more recently, 'passive use' value – some people have a positive WTP for the area, even if neither they nor their children would ever visit it. As Krutilla put it, they may 'obtain satisfaction from mere knowledge that part of the wilderness in North America remains, even though they would be appalled by the prospect of being exposed to it'. These demands to protect the resource are not reflected in market prices but, Weisbrod and Krutilla contended, they do belong in a social benefit–cost analysis.

These arguments are now widely accepted. However, because they were expressed verbally rather than mathematically, an ambiguity remained concerning the definition of the concepts that was not resolved until the 1980s. I focus here on non-use value since this underlies the case for CV. A starting point is the welfare theory associated with the travel cost model. This was first articulated by Maler (1974), who sought to extend standard welfare theory of price

---

[10] I was one of a group of economists retained by the state of Alaska in connection with its suit for natural resource damages; our CV analysis is presented in Carson *et al.* (1992b).

changes to changes in the supply of a public good. His model is a generalization of Lancaster's (1966) model of demand with characteristics. In this model, the consumer has preferences over conventional market commodities, denoted by the vector x, and over a set of other items denoted by the vector q. Whether the elements of q are attributes of private market goods, supplies of public goods, or amenities, the key is that the consumer views them as exogenous. He can freely vary the x's, but not the q's. Preferences are represented by a utility function, $u(x, q)$, which is non-decreasing in x and q, and strictly quasi-concave in x but not necessarily q. The individual maximizes $u(x, q)$ with respect to x subject to the usual budget constraint, which yields ordinary demand functions for the market goods, $x_i = h^i(p, q, y)$, $i = 1, \ldots N$, and an indirect utility function, $v(p, q, y) \equiv u[h(p, q, y), q]$, where p represents prices of the x's and y is the consumer's income.[11] Dual to this are the compensated demand functions $x_i = g^i(p, q, u)$, $i = 1, \ldots, N$, and the expenditure function $m(p, q, u)$. Suppose, that q increases from q^0 to $q^1 > q^0$ while prices and income remain constant at (p, y). Accordingly, the individual's utility increases from $u^0 \equiv v(p, q^0, y)$ to $u^1 \equiv v(p, q^1, y)$. By analogy with the welfare theory of price changes, Maler defined compensating and equivalent variation measures for this utility change. The compensating variation, C, which corresponds to the individual's WTP for the change, satisfies

$$v(p, q^1, y - C) = v(p, q^0, y). \qquad (1)$$

The key question is how this quantity is measured. Maler developed a method based on what he called weak complementarity. This arises when there is some private market good, or group of goods, such that, when those goods are *not* being consumed, the marginal utility $\partial u/\partial q_k$ is zero for all the elements of q that change between q^0 and q^1. For example, if q is the availability of freeways, ownership of an automobile is a complementary good: without it, you don't care whether or not there are freeways. Or, q is water quality at some beach, the complementary good is visits to that beach, and you don't care whether the water is clean if you don't visit the beach. Whether this property holds is an empirical question. Suppose that x_1 is inessential and weakly complementary with the set of q's which change, so that $x_1 = 0 \Rightarrow \partial u/\partial q_k = 0$. Maler showed that the quantity C is related to the change in the area under the compensated demand curves for the weakly complementary commodity when evaluated at q^0 and q^1:

---

[11] This model includes the household production model as a special case when the **q**'s are production function parameters. It is discussed further and contrasted with the hedonic demand model in Hanemann (1982).

$$C = \int_{p_1}^{p_1^*} [g^1(p, q^1, u^0) - g^1(p, q^0, u^0)] \, dp_1, \tag{2}$$

where p_1^* is the cut-off price such that $g^1(p_1^*, p_2, \ldots, p_N, q^t, u^0) = 0$, $t = 0,1$.

In practice, the usefulness of this result is limited by the need to know the compensated demand functions, as opposed to the ordinary demand functions. As an approximation, one might consider using areas under ordinary demand functions – i.e., substituting $h^1(p, q^t, y)$ for $g^1(p, q^t, u)$ in (2) – but the resulting measure does not necessarily have the same sign as C, let alone the same magnitude. Instead, one can apply Hurwicz and Uzawa's (1971) integrability results and solve the fundamental system of partial differential equations

$$\partial m(p, q, u)/\partial p_i = h^i[p, q, m(p, q, u)] \; i = 1, \ldots, N, \tag{3}$$

for the expenditure function $m(p, q, u)$, from which compensated demand functions can be derived.[12] With this approach, moreover, one can bypass (2) and calculate C directly from the indirect utility function on the basis of (1). Weak complementarity *per se* is not needed.

With regard to non-use value, the definition due to McConnell (1983) and Hanemann (1988) rests on the particular structure of the utility function. Suppose that the direct utility function takes the form

$$u(x, q) = T[\bar{u}(x, q), q] \tag{4}$$

for some functions $T[\cdot]$ and $\bar{u}(\cdot)$, where $T[\cdot]$ is increasing in both arguments and $\bar{u}(\cdot)$ is non-decreasing in both sets of arguments and strictly quasiconcave in x. The key to (4) is that the marginal rate of substitution among the x's is independent of $T[\cdot]$; it depends on q to the extent that q enters into $\bar{u}(\cdot)$, but not to the extent that q enters into T $[\cdot]$. Let $\bar{v}(p, q, y)$ be the indirect utility function associated with $\bar{u}(x, q)$. Given (4), the compensating variation for the change in q, C from (1), can now be expressed as a sum

$$C = \bar{C} + C^T, \tag{5}$$

where $\bar{C}$ satisfies $\bar{v}(p, q^1, y - \bar{C}) = \bar{v}(p, q^0, y)$, and C^T satisfies $T[\bar{v}(p, q^1, y - \bar{C} - C^T), q^1] = T[\bar{v}(p, q^1, y - \bar{C}), q^0]$, $\bar{C}$ is the individual's WTP for the change in q based on $\bar{u}(x, q)$, while C^T is the balance of C once $T[\cdot]$ is taken into account. $\bar{C}$ is the natural candidate for use value – it reflects that part of preference for q associated with consumption of private

---

[12] Maler (1974) and Willig (1976a) pointed out that this system of differential equations provides a practical way of recovering the utility function; see also Hanemann (1980) and Hausman (1981). LaFrance and Hanemann (1989) provide a fuller account of what can and cannot be covered from (3). In this chapter, I use the term 'travel cost' generically for methods that recover $v(p,q,y)$ from (3) for *any* commodity, not just recreation.

market goods. C^T is the natural candidate for non-use value – it stems from that preference for q which is *separate* from preference for the x's. Non-use values arise, then, whenever the utility function can be factored into the form of (4). Hanemann (1988) showed that the absence of weak complementarity is neither necessary nor sufficient for this to occur.

Two consequences follow from this definition. Both $u(x, q)$ and $\bar{u}(x, q)$ lead to exactly the same ordinary demand functions, $h^i(p, q, y)$, even though they generate *different* compensated demand functions. It follows that the Hurwicz–Uzawa integrability approach based on (3) will recover $\bar{v}(p, q, y)$ but not $T[\cdot]$. As a result, revealed preference methods cannot be used to recover C^T. In contrast, contingent valuation does recover $C = \bar{C} + C^T$. Secondly, any q whose quantity the individual takes as fixed may generate non-use values; this depends on the structure of preferences, not on the type of change in q. It is an empirical question, therefore, whether non-use values arise or how large they are. Attempts to determine this a priori have no foundation in economic theory.

DH invoke economic theory repeatedly, claiming that it is not compatible with the empirical CV results in Hausman (1993). But, they are incorrect on the theory. Suppose that only one of the q's changes [e.g., $q^0 = (q_1^0, q_2, \dots, q_K)$ and $q^1 = (q_1^1, q_2, \dots, q_K)$]. From (1), the value of C depends on the remaining q's; from (4), so do the values of $\bar{C}$ and C^T. Madden (1991) shows that an increase in q_2, say, will *lower* C if q_1 and q_2 are what he calls R-substitutes, and *raise* it if they are R-complements. Likewise, C depends on y; while the income elasticity of C is related to the income elasticity of demand for q_1 and has the same *sign*, the two elasticities are not necessarily similar in magnitude, as DH (p. 42) assume. The income elasticity of C depends on not only the income elasticity of demand for q_1 but also the elasticity of substitution between q_1 and the x's. The latter is the more influential in determining the magnitude of C and could explain divergences between WTP and willingness to accept (WTA) (Hanemann, 1991a).

While DH consistently downplay substitution effects between q_1 and other q's or x's, these have important economic implications. For example, R-substitution explains the sub-additivity of WTP – if q_1 and q_2 are R-substitutes, the WTP for a change in both q_1 and q_2 is less than the sum of the WTPs for the changes taken separately. Far from being inconsistent with economic preferences (Diamond *et al.*, 1993, pp. 48–49), sub-additivity is likely to be the norm; while all goods cannot be R-complements, Madden shows they *can* all be R-substitutes. Similarly, R-substitution explains what Diamond *et al.* call sequence aggregation and Kahneman and Knetsch (1992) the embedding problem. If q's are substitutes, the WTP for a change in q_1 is *lower* when it comes at the *end* of a sequence of changes in q's than at the beginning, while the WTA for the change in q_1 is *higher* when it comes *later* in a sequence (Carson *et al.*, 1992a).[13] In short, it should come as no surprise that the value of one commodity changes when the quantity of another varies, i.e., that WTP depends on the economic context.

Survey Design and the Reliability of CV Responses

Likewise, it should come as no surprise that responses to CV surveys depend on the survey context. Surveys are an exercise in communication, and this is always sensitive to nuance and context. Moreover, *preferences* are inherently context-laden. A basic lesson of the cognitive revolution in psychology is that context determines meaning. Potter (1990) notes 'a central principle of encoding' that the same object is encoded differently in different contexts. It would be simpler if consumers disregarded context and had preferences for commodities in the abstract, as Platonic ideals. But, they don't.

I discuss the implications for economic theory later in this chapter; here I focus on the implications for CV design. Almost all data used in the social sciences are self-reported data obtained through surveys, such as household expenditure surveys, employment surveys, health surveys, and opinion polls. Like everything involving people, surveys are fallible. There is no magic formula for perfect measurement.[14] Procedures can be identified, however, that are likely to generate more reliable results. In the case of CV, certain aspects of study design enhance validity: avoiding self-administered surveys; using a probability sample; building quality control into the process of questionnaire development and testing; making the commodity to be valued realistic, and the payment credible; providing appropriate information; legitimizing a 'no' response; and using debriefing questions to probe respondents' perceptions and motives.

The survey must be formulated around a commodity that captures what one seeks to value. It must be consistent with economic theory. And, it also must be intelligible and meaningful to respondents in the field. A National Academy of Sciences Committee (1986) described how good researchers study human decision making:

[13] In natural resource damages where WTA is the relevant welfare measure, this implies that the usual practice of taking the injured resource as the first item in any possible valuation sequence is a conservative procedure.

[14] In all the social sciences, economics included, procedural invariance in measurement is an ideal, not the reality. It is even violated in the physical sciences for several reasons including the problem that no individual scientific hypothesis is conclusively falsifiable (the Duhem–Quine problem) (Cook and Campbell, 1979).

They question respondents about specific situations, rather than asking for generalizations. They are sensitive to the dependence of answers on the exact form of the questions. They are aware that behavior in an experimental situation may be different from behavior in real life, and they attempt to provide experimental settings and motivations that are as realistic as possible.

Exactly the same applies with CV. Respondents must be confronted with a commodity that is concrete and realistic, so they take it seriously. The more vague and less specific the scenario, the more likely they are to treat the valuation as merely a symbolic exercise. Likewise, the valuation question should not be overly counterfactual. For example, asking 'If it had been possible to prevent the accident, how much would you have paid?' requires people to deny an event that did occur. Rather than something in the *past*, one should try to value an action that can plausibly be taken *now* – e.g., a government programme to prevent future accidents. This programme can be described with sufficient detail and realism for people to believe in it.

This strategy does have drawbacks. Some respondents may regard preventing a future accident as less serious since the real damage was done in the earlier accident. Others may not believe there will be a future accident because people will now be careful. Yet others may believe that, while there is a chance of a future accident, the programme won't prevent it. They may value the environment but refuse to pay because they view the proposed programme as ineffectual. Hence, there can be a gap between what one wants to value and what respondents do value. But, this may not be a serious problem. First, one can try to ensure that the difference lies in a conservative direction. Second, one uses debriefing questions to quantify these effects. The debriefing comes at the end of the survey and asks respondents whether they had completely believed key parts of CV scenario (e.g., Was the damage as bad as described? Did you think you would *really* have to pay higher taxes if the programme went through?), and why they answered the WTP question as they had (e.g., What was it about the programme that made you decide to vote for it?). One can thus monitor for the presence of divergent or inappropriate beliefs, measure statistically how these affected respondents' WTP, and adjust accordingly.

Similarly, the payment description must meet three key requirements. First, the payment should be perceived as linked directly to provision of the commodity. Second, to make it plausible one should specify a particular context. Third, it is best if the payment is viewed as mandatory once a commitment has been made; e.g., if the programme is approved one can't avoid paying because firms will then raise prices or the government will raise taxes. One wants respondents to take the notion of payment very seriously.[15]

There has been much debate on the paradigm for CV: is it markets, voting, or charity? DH say the right paradigm is charity. But, most appeals for charity are not designed to elicit one's *maximum* WTP – they just ask for *some* donation. They usually focus on the symbolic aspects of the donation, without identifying a specific consequence or an outcome that would not occur without it. For these reasons, charity is generally a flawed paradigm for CV.[16] Markets will sometimes be the natural paradigm, depending upon the type of commodity. Environmental protection, however, is often a public good and this generally requires collective action. Therefore, as Schelling (1968) noted, voting is a natural paradigm. This was reaffirmed by the NOAA Panel: 'The simplest way to approach the problem is to consider an [environmental] CV survey as essentially a self-contained referendum in which respondents vote on whether to tax themselves for a particular purpose' (Arrow *et al.*, 1993).[17] It also set aside suggestions that CV be limited to commodities with which respondents have prior experience. As a California voter last November, I had no previous experience of voting on school vouchers but I made a decision and cast my vote. Prior experience, *per se*, was less important than adequate information.[18]

Another issue is whether the payment question should be asked as an open- or closed-ended question. Prior to 1985, most CV surveys used an open-ended WTP question, such as 'What is the most that you would be willing to pay for...?' Since then, most major CV surveys have used closed-ended questions like 'If it cost x, would you be willing to pay this amount (vote for it)?' I consider the latter far more reliable.[19] People do not know their WTP for most goods, private *or* public, in the way they know their shirt size. Nor can they discover it

[15] There may be 'protest zeroes' because respondents think it unfair that *they* should have to pay. This, too, can be detected through debriefing questions.

[16] The two studies DH cite as showing a lack of commitment in CV, Seip and Strand (1992) and Duffield and Patterson (1991), used payment to an environmental charity rather than voting on a government programme. Most of the subjects in Seip and Strand's study who were followed up afterwards said that they had been expressing a willingness to pay for environmental problems generally rather than to support the particular environmental group.

[17] DH refer many times to Andreoni's model which assumes a 'warm glow' from the act of giving to charity. However, I know of no empirical evidence that people get a warm glow from voting to raise their own taxes.

[18] A CV questionnaire should present adequate information, in an impartial and balanced manner, *before* the valuation question is asked. In the 'top-down' procedure of Kemp and Maxwell (1993) and Kahneman and Knetsch (1992), the information comes *after*. Subjects are asked to value some broad item, e.g., 'preparedness for disasters'. Then, they are told what things make up this item. They are asked their WTP for *one* of those components. Then, they are told what *it* comprises, etc. They also are not told at any stage just what is the *change* in the *quantity* of an item if they pay. All of this highlights the symbolic aspects of the valuation exercise at the expense of substance.

[19] Bishop and Heberlain (1979) first used this format for CV; the link with utility theory was developed in Hanemann (1984); see also Cameron (1988) and McConnell (1990).

by inspecting their utility function, as in the textbooks.[20] Rather, it is revealed to them as the consequence of acts of judgment when they face choices and make decisions. Whether in the market or in voting, these choices usually are discrete: here is an item, it costs x, will you take it? Therefore, the closed-ended format is more realistic. Further, there is abundant evidence that respondents find open-ended questions more difficult to answer than closed-ended ones.[21] Even if people have experience buying an item and can state *an* amount which they would be willing to pay, they may find it hard to state the *maximum* amount. As a result, open-ended responses can understate maximum WTP.[22] Since the maximum WTP is an extremum, errors of cognition tend to fall on the low side. This bias may be reinforced by strategic behaviour associated with open-ended questions which leads respondents to state less than their full value. Unlike free-riding, this is clearly supported by experimental evidence. With the closed-ended referendum format, in contrast, 'there is no strategic reason for the respondent to do other than answer truthfully' (Arrow *et al.*, 1993).[23] Experience also shows that, with open-ended questions, some respondents think about what the item could cost per household rather than what it is worth to them, which may be more. For all these reasons, the closed-ended format is to be preferred. The NOAA Panel agreed; it recommended using closed-ended questions set in a voting context.

The NOAA Panel also saw probability sampling as essential for CV surveys. With regard to survey mode, it considered mail surveys less reliable because of low response rates, difficulties with sample frames,

[20] DH seem to take literally the notion that an individual knows his utility function, e.g. in dismissing the responses by participants in Schkade and Payne's (1993) verbal protocol study. I find those responses thoughtful and reasonable; Professor Solow recently said 'they sound an awful lot like Bob Solow in the grocery store'. Kahneman *et al.* (1993) characterize responses to CV surveys as 'constructed values'. But, modern neuroscience suggests that *all* thought is a construct [see Rose (1992), who observes: 'brains do not work with *information* in the computer sense, but with *meaning* ... Our memories are recreated each time we remember'].

[21] Kriström (1990), Desvousges *et al.* (1992), and Söderkvist (1992) give evidence of lower participation rates and higher item non-response rates with open-ended questions. The difference in formats has a larger significance. It corresponds to the distinction in psychology between matching (open-ended) and choice (closed-ended) (Tversky *et al.*, 1988), and it underlies most of the evidence on preference reversal (Tversky *et al.*, 1990). The experiments switch between matching and choice, and the interpretation of the outcome as a reversal of preferences rests on the assumption that the two formats ought to produce identical results. This overlooks the cognitive differences and it treats the two formats as equally reliable. By letting the variance of WTP vary with format but keeping the mean the same, Alberini (1992) generates preference reversals like those observed.

[22] These arguments run in the opposite direction with WTA, and explain why open-ended WTA responses may *overstate* individuals' minimum WTA. Taken together, these arguments suggest that open-ended questions can exaggerate differences between WTP and WTA as compared to closed-ended questions.

[23] Responding to open-ended CV questions is analogous to participating in an oral auction or a first-price sealed bid auction. It is well documented that these generate lower prices than posted-price auctions (Plott, 1989).

and literacy problems among the general population.[24] It also saw lack of control over the interview process as a general problem with self-administered surveys – a respondent can look at all the questions before deciding which, if any, to answer. In-person interviews are expensive but offer practical advantages in permitting graphical aids, maintaining respondent motivation, and monitoring respondent performance.[25] Telephone surveys may be satisfactory if respondents are already adequately informed, or the issue can be conveyed briefly and without visual aids. The Panel concluded that in-person CV surveys would usually be preferable.[26]

CV and Voting

The analogy with voting is crucial to the debate on CV. The NOAA Panel saw the analogy as natural. DH disagree vehemently. They seek to bolster their case by citing Magleby's (1984) work on referenda. Magleby challenged the idea that direct legislation improves voter participation. He analysed voting on ballot propositions and concluded that voter turnout was neither increased nor made more representative by direct legislation. He found that ballot propositions were generally confusing, required advanced reading skills, and were poorly understood by most voters.[27] This actually strengthens the case for CV. Good

[24] Survey mode clearly affects response rates. For example, Infosino (1986) reports that, in AT&T's experience using telephone and mail to promote a new pricing option, three times as many customers exposed to the phone promotion purchased the product than those exposed to the mail promotion. A key factor with mail is whether people think the survey is junk mail and throw it out unopened. Seip and Strand (1992) made *no* allowance for the inherent non-response in mail surveys. Duffield and Patterson (1991) found a higher response rate with the University of Montana identified on the envelope as the sponsor than the Nature Conservancy. Apart from differences in response rates, the distributions of WTP responses were similar in their real and hypothetical payment experiments.

[25] After the interview, one debriefs the interviewer to ascertain how attentive the respondent was, whether he seemed to understand the questions, whether he appeared confident in his responses, etc.

[26] Most of the surveys in Hausman (1993) use open-ended questions, and none uses in-person interviews.

[27] In *his* book on referenda, Cronin (1989) had a very different view of voter rationality and rejected Magleby's position as exaggerated. Many others have seen a core of rationality in voter behaviour, including Downs (1957) and McKelvey and Ordeshook (1986) who emphasize how campaigners give out signals that overcome voters' limited knowledge. Lupia (1993) studied the insurance reform battle in the 1988 California ballot and concluded that the availability of informational 'short cuts' enabled poorly informed voters to act as though they were well-informed. Snyder (1993) studied California ballots between 1974 and 1990 and found that 'in the aggregate, preferences do not exhibit the instability that Converse and others have found at the individual level (so-called "non-attitudes").' Similarly, Page and Shapiro (1992) reviewed 50 years' of national opinion polls and concluded that 'at the *collective* level, public opinion displays impressive characteristics of stability, rational responsiveness to concrete political situations, and the capacity to adapt as new issues become available and change the contours of these situations.' DH do not mention any of the other literature on California referenda.

CV studies go to great lengths to ensure that questionnaires are clearly worded, intelligible, informative, and impartial, and use probability samples to ensure a representative sample. Hence, a well-conducted CV study offers advantages over an election as a means of discovering people's preferences because one can control for bias in the information set and overcome the vagaries of voter turnout.[28]

DH also attempt to exploit another of Magleby's findings: public support changes over the course of an election. He found that 53% of the elections on propositions in California from 1960 to 1982 involved a reversal (i.e., the side that had once been losing ultimately won) compared with only 14% of the elections on candidates. He attributed this difference to the fact that, in propositions, voters were less knowledgeable about the issues, less sure of their voting intentions, and more susceptible to campaign advertising. Going a step further, DH claim that these reversals prove opinion polls inaccurately predict election outcomes and CV surveys are not an expression of individual preferences. Neither claim can withstand scrutiny.

Magleby himself identified advertising as a major cause of reversals on propositions. He found that negative advertising (unlike positive advertising) frequently determines ballot outcomes: opponents of a proposition 'can virtually guarantee [its] defeat if they significantly outspent the proponents' (p. 147). This is illustrated by the case of 'Big Green' – Proposition 128 on the 1990 California ballot – to which DH devote much attention. A poll in June showed 46% in favour and 38% opposed, with the rest undecided. In the November election, it lost by 36% to 64%. How did this happen? Opponents spent $11.9 million, while supporters spent $4.5 million. The positive advertising stressed the general need to protect the environment. The negative advertising stressed several points: Big Green would cause economic havoc; it was too complex and the regulatory provisions in the fine print could be damaging; and it was supported by Tom Hayden who would become pollution czar if it passed (the ads called it the 'Hayden initiative'). Does this prove that the California voters didn't have stable preferences? Were the voters well-disposed to Tom Hayden in June, and ill-disposed in November? Surely not. It is more likely that, as the campaign unfolded, voters changed from seeing Proposition 128 as a single-attribute commodity to seeing it as a more complex, multi-attribute commodity. One attribute, evident from the beginning, was

[28] This has not escaped the attention of political scientists. Fishkin (1991) has proposed using 'deliberative opinion polls', in which a random sample of population is selected, given extensive information on an issue, and then polled – in effect, an extended CV survey. 'Instead of a public opinion that is formed by inattention and the shrinking sound bites, it's a public opinion formed by debate, by thought, by face-to-face engagement' ['American in London to test "Deliberative" Polling' *New York Times* 9/12/93].

environmental protection. The opponents successfully added various other attributes unfavourable to the proposition. This provided voters with new information and forced them to make a trade-off among the attributes.[29]

Opinion pollsters have long known that attitudes change during an election. For this reason, they avoid asking people about future intentions – they ask 'if the election were held tomorrow, how would you vote?' rather than 'how will you vote in November?' There is considerable evidence that polls reliably indicate public sentiment at the time they are taken, and that polls close to an election are generally accurate predictors of the outcome. DH cite an *L.A. Times* poll on Big Green to challenge the reliability of opinion polls. They claim the poll taken a week before the election found voters evenly divided. Their analysis is seriously incomplete. The *Times* article did state that Big Green trailed by only 2% among registered voters – 44% were against, 42% for and 14% undecided, with a 3% margin of error. But, it also stated that, *among voters considered the most likely to actually cast ballots*, it trailed by roughly 12%. Assuming that most of the undecided would vote against the proposition, as is commonly done by political experts, the poll implied that voters would reject the proposition by a margin close to the actual outcome.

Similar results were found in a CV study of Proposition 25, the Clean Water Bond Law, just before the 1984 California election. This received little media attention and passed in November with 73% of the vote. Carson *et al.* (1987) purchased questions on the Field California Poll a month before the election to conduct a CV survey. Respondents were given a brief description of the proposition, told what it would cost their household, and asked how they intended to vote. The proposition was estimated to cost about $4 per year per household. At this amount, 24% were undecided or did not intend to vote, 63% said they would vote yes, and 13% would vote no. If one assumed that between 50% and 70% of the undecided would ultimately vote no, this would have given a close prediction of the election outcome.

DH say that CV responses are more like opinion polls than a scientific evaluation of damages (p. 30). This misses the point. The goal, as the NOAA Panel defined it, is to elicit people's preferences as if they were voting in a referendum. The experience with real elections shows that advertising and turnout affect the outcome. CV deals with these by attempting to provide impartial information and using a random

---

[29] DH actually admit this but draw a strange conclusion: 'Proposition 128 demonstrates that individuals do react to the level of information they have and the context of the situation in which they make decisions. Thus, the referendum claim for the use of CV has no foundation in individual economic preferences' (p. 17). Apparently DH believe that economic choices ought *not* to be based on information or context.

sample of the population. The other lesson from real elections is the need to be sensitive to 'don't know' responses and, generally, to treat them as votes against.[30] This already is quite standard in CV studies. Beyond that, the available evidence suggests that the voting format needs little further calibration.

CV and Market Research

In market research, in contrast, calibration procedures are regularly applied to survey data on purchase intentions because of divergences between intended and actual purchases. Yet the NOAA Panel observed that these surveys must convey some useful information since firms continue to pay for them. But, more needs to be said. First, the degree of divergence, and therefore calibration, varies with circumstances, including the type of product and the investment in marketing effort. Urban and Hauser (1980) observe that 'if the product is well-positioned and an aggressive marketing strategy is planned', a conservative estimate would be that 90% of those who say they definitely will buy the product actually do so. Second, as Juster (1964) pointed out, the reason why actual purchases are liable to differ from intended purchases is the intervention of unforeseen events and new information. This cuts both ways: some fraction of those who say they don't intend to buy the item *will* end up buying it. If you discount the 'yeses' but not the 'nos', you typically underestimate total purchases.

However, this experience with market research might not apply to CV surveys.[31] First market research surveys usually provide considerably less information than a standard CV survey. For example, in a transportation study conducted at the University of Miami just before the opening of the Miami Metrorail (Sheskin, 1991), respondents were asked, 'Suppose Metrorail opens January 1, 1984; the price of gas remains as it is now; Metrorail costs $2.00 round trip, plus 25 cents for transfers to and from the bus; parking at a Metrorail station is $1.00 per day. Would you use Metrorail to go to and from this campus?' While this specifies some economic variables in admirable detail, it is incomplete in other respects. There is no mention of whether it would

---

[30] Indeed, Mosteller *et al.* (1949) identified ignoring 'don't knows' as a major reason for the pollsters' failure to predict the 1948 Presidential election, along with using quota samples and stopping their polls too soon.

[31] It should be noted that, where there are parallel CV and revealed preference estimates of use value, the results are often fairly close. There have been 78 studies since Knetsch and Davis (1966) which provide over 500 comparisons between CV and revealed preference; on average, the CV estimates of WTP in these studies are about 10% lower than the revealed preference estimates (Carson *et al.*, 1994). For morbidity risks, Magat *et al.* (1988) find that conventional CV gives a lower value than stated preference using conjoint analysis.

be hard to find a parking space at the station, whether the trains would run on time, the risk of getting mugged at night, or other attributes that could matter to users. Differences between the commodity described in the survey and the commodity subsequently experienced undoubtedly account for some of the divergence between intended and actual purchases. Second, people generally have control over the timing of their purchase of private goods, but not the timing of their voting on public goods. As an individual, you decide when your Ford gets replaced, but not your President. Some of the divergence between intended and actual purchases arises from changes in timing, which matters to market researchers in a way that doesn't apply to CV. For example, in Juster's study many respondents who said that they would definitely buy an air conditioner or a car during the next six months, and then didn't, *did* buy the product at a later date, as opposed to losing interest and never buying it.

In addition, cognitive errors in consumers' perception of the duration of time may affect reports of purchase intentions, just as they affect consumer recall of past expenditures. There is abundant evidence of 'telescoping' in the household expenditure survey literature, i.e., the tendency of respondents to allocate expenditures either to an earlier period than when they actually occurred or to a later period (Neter and Waksberg, 1964). The latter has often been found the more serious problem, causing overstatement of past activity (Loftus *et al.*, 1990), and increasing in severity with the length of the recall period (Westat, 1989). While not a factor in CV, this certainly can affect travel cost analysis. An example occurs in Hausman *et al.* (1993) (HLM), a travel cost study of the recreation losses from the *Exxon Valdez* oil spill. HLM used data from a 1990 telephone survey conducted for Exxon in which 8888 Alaskans were asked how many trips they had taken in Alaska for sportfishing and other recreation during 1989 and 1988. The Alaska Department of Fish & Game (ADFG) has conducted a survey of sportfishing each fall since 1977, in which a fishing log is mailed to a random sample of fishing licence holders. In 1989, it conducted a survey as usual and received responses from 14,517 anglers (Mills, 1990). Here, then, are two surveys intended to measure the same thing – one done for litigation, the other done to generate economic data for fisheries managers. The Exxon survey, conducted in the spring of 1990, produced an estimate of 2,464,000 fishing trips by Alaskan residents in 1989 and 2,480,000 trips in 1988. The ADFG survey, conducted in the fall of 1989, covered both resident Alaskan and non-resident anglers and produced an estimate of 1,731,000 fishing trips in 1989, 30% less than estimated from the Exxon survey. The 1988 ADFG survey showed 1,919,000 trips in 1988, 23% less than estimated from the Exxon survey. This significantly affects the interpretation of the two surveys. HLM intended to use their 1990 survey of fishing activity in 1988 as a control for the effects of the oil spill. Based on this control, HLM found that the spill caused a decline of 16,000 sportfishing trips, while the ADFG data showed a decline of 188,000 trips. In relative terms, this is a decline of 0.65% versus 9.8%.[32]

With CV, DH apply the criterion that 'because two ways measure the same quantity, they should yield approximately the same answer' (p. 47). This is clearly violated with the two sportfishing surveys. Should all recreation surveys therefore be discontinued? Should we give up on the travel cost method? Surely not. We should, however, recognize that surveys are fallible and that careful design and implementation are just as necessary for surveys used in revealed preference as in CV. Admitting these limitations should not cause us to abandon the effort in either case.

CV Studies Commissioned by Exxon

In the summer of 1989 Exxon retained a distinguished group of economists to investigate the CV method. One might have thought their empirical work would focus on the *Exxon Valdez* oil spill and CV's ability to measure its damages. Not so. The principal surveys reported in Hausman (1993) deal with *other* issues – preventing logging in wilderness areas in the Rockies, covering waste-oil holding ponds in Texas, and improving the capability for handling small oil spills that occur routinely each year in US coastal waters. These items could have been studied at any time before 1991. But, the surveys were all initiated in March 1991, just after plans were announced to settle state and federal suits against Exxon, and at a time when two federal agencies were gearing up to issue new regulations for natural resource damage assessment. The surveys went into the field in June. The entire process of instrument development, testing, and field preparation was compressed into the period March–June, 1991.[33]

DH justify their conclusion that responses to CV surveys are not an expression of underlying preferences by demonstrating inconsistencies between the responses to these surveys and what they claim are predictions of economic theory. This begs many questions. How do DH know the respondents' true preferences? Could the responses be

[32] HLMs only reference to the ADFG data is a footnote saying that it 'finds a larger decline in number of trips than does our survey' (p. 360). This is a masterpiece of understatement.

[33] Despite promises made at the Exxon Conference in April 1992 and repeated in Hausman (1993), the raw data from these surveys had still not been made available to outside researchers as of February 1994. Hausman (1993) provides summary statistics on WTP responses. In some cases, it has been possible to apply techniques for grouped data (Haitovsky, 1973) to reconstruct what the regression equations must have been (Carson and Flores, 1993).

affected by ambiguities or flaws in the surveys? Is DH's interpretation
of economic theory correct? These possibilities must all be eliminated
before one may conclude that CV is a defective measurement tool. In
this section I focus on issues concerning the survey design and data
analysis. In the next section I take up the arguments about economic
theory.

One group of surveys dealt with WTP to protect some of the 57
federal wilderness areas established in Colorado, Idaho, Montana, and
Wyoming under the 1964 Wilderness Act from being leased for
commercial development to reduce the federal deficit. The survey was
read over the phone to a random sample of households in the four
states. Respondents were told that the development would involve
harvesting mature timber at a rate of 1% per year, which would require
building roads and bringing in heavy equipment. Of the 57 areas, seven
had already been proposed for leasing. Respondents were asked their
WTP to preserve another area that might be considered for a similar
timber harvest, the Selway-Bitterroot Wilderness (1.3 million acres in
northern Idaho). Other versions of the survey proposed logging in two
other wilderness areas, individually or in combination: the Bob Marshall Wilderness (1 million acres in Montana), and the Washakie Wilderness (700,000 acres in Wyoming).

The lack of detail in this survey instrument is striking. Standard
practice would be to list the wilderness areas by name and provide a
map.[34] The survey should at least name the seven areas already
proposed for leasing. The questionnaire doesn't explain how the *named*
wilderness area differs from these other areas, nor why it is being
singled out for attention. Nor does it say what would happen to these
seven areas if the named area were preserved, or what would become
of the 49 *other* wilderness areas – if the Wilderness Act can be set aside,
don't these areas need protection, too? Failure to specify such details is
harmful in two respects.[35] First, the quantity of wilderness protection
that respondents are 'buying' is ill-defined. Since people's default
assumptions about this may vary, respondents may be valuing different commodities. DH lost control of their valuation exercise at the very
start. Second, the lack of detail creates an air of unreality which may
deflect respondents from taking the survey seriously.

[34] Without a map, names can be a problem in this area. For example, many guidebooks don't list
the Washakie Wilderness by that name; and there are several Roadless Areas that are called Selway-
Bitterroot. Although DH don't cite it, there *was* an earlier CV study of the Washakie Wilderness and
it *did* use a map (Barrick and Beazley, 1990).

[35] A colleague has remarked that this is like testing the accuracy of public opinion polls by
conducting surveys in which people are asked: 'If the Presidential election were being held today and
Bill Clinton were running against a tall guy from Maine and a short guy from Texas, who would you
vote for?' and 'If the Presidential election were being held today and Bill Clinton were running against
two tall guys from Maine....' Why would anyone do this?

This is exacerbated by incongruities between the scenario and events in the area's recent history. When the areas featured in the survey were first designated there had been considerable controversy over the possibility of *mining* development. The 1964 Wilderness Act permitted new *mining* claims in designated wilderness areas through 1983. There was a public outcry in 1981–1982 over applications to lease two-thirds of the wilderness acreage in Washakie for oil and gas exploration, with potentially serious adverse impacts on elk, moose, bighorn sheep and grizzly bears. This was opposed by the Wyoming Congressional delegation, not normally known as tree-huggers, and was quashed. Respondents might have taken the survey's mention of 'commercial development' to refer to something like this. Also, there was some public discussion of wilderness issues in 1991 due to an approaching deadline for adding areas to the National Wilderness System. But, this debate concerned proposals to designate *new* areas as wilderness, not to remove existing designated areas. For the scenario in the survey to be feasible, it would have been necessary to revoke the Wilderness Act, which would have been front-page news in the region.

Diamond *et al.* (1993) use these survey responses to test four sets of hypotheses which, they claim, expose incongruities between the CV responses and economic theory – hypotheses about the effects of size on WTP, substitution effects, embedding, and the additivity of WTP. The data do not appear to support their claims. Diamond *et al.* test the null hypothesis that WTP does not vary with size for the three featured wilderness areas and find that it cannot be rejected. However, they use a non-parametric test which has very low power in this case (Carson and Flores, 1993). A more natural approach is to regress WTP on size. When this is done, the null hypothesis is strongly rejected. The test for the absence of substitution effects takes the form of comparing the WTP for a featured site when respondents are told that *seven* other unnamed sites have been opened to logging versus *eight* other sites. Diamond *et al.* argue that the WTPs should differ if substitution effects are present. They test the null hypothesis of no difference in WTP for Washakie and Bob Marshall, again using non-parametric tests of low power, and find it cannot be rejected. For Washakie, however, if one employs a simple *t*-test instead of Diamond *et al.*'s non-parametric test, the null hypothesis is rejected and their conclusion is reversed.

Their embedding test focuses on whether WTP increases as one switches from a less to a more inclusive commodity. They approach this by testing a single null hypothesis that WTP is the same across surveys involving one, two and three featured wilderness areas, and find it cannot be rejected. However, if one compares WTP for individual sites taken alone versus in larger groups, the null hypothesis is rejected in about half the cases, as it is if one compares WTP for one site versus for all sites. They test for additivity – e.g., whether WTP to save both Washakie and Bob Marshall equals the sum of the WTPs to save each site taken separately – and find it can be rejected in favour of sub-additivity. However, as noted earlier, the sub-additivity of WTP is simply Madden's (1991) property of R-substitutability and should have come as no surprise.

McFadden and Leonard (1993) (ML) used data from other versions of the wilderness survey, including versions with a closed-ended WTP question. Their paper has some useful innovations including a Box–Cox formulation for the utility function generalizing the linear and logarithmic models in Hanemann (1984). ML raise many of the same issues as Diamond *et al.* (e.g., repeating their erroneous claim that sub-additivity is 'inconsistent with classical preferences'), while adding new ones concerning the effects of elicitation format and the income elasticity of WTP. ML make much of their finding that open-ended questions yield lower WTP estimates than closed-ended questions (p. 166). However, this has been documented in the CV literature for a decade.[36] It is explained by the factors I listed in the section on page 87, and is not *per se* inconsistent with economic theory. Likewise ML's finding that single- and double-bounded versions of the closed-ended format produce different results has already been noticed and discussed (Hanemann *et al.*, 1991). In Hanemann (1991b), I showed further that there can be an inconsistency between the first and second responses in the double-bounded format. But, the evidence is that the double-bounded format generates *lower* WTP values and this difference arises from an increased tendency to say 'no' to the second bid rather than 'yes'. Respondents having been told that the item can be provided at one price, now resist when told that the price might be higher. In statistical terms, the double-bounded format provides more information for a given sample size and greatly shrinks the confidence interval; in using it, one is trading off a large reduction in variance for some downward bias.

ML make much of the income elasticity of WTP for wilderness. They equate this with the Box–Cox parameter λ, which they estimate at 0.269. They consider this value is so low that it casts doubt on CV's validity (pp. 185–186). Yet ML have erred in calculating the income elasticity. It is *not* the same as λ and, indeed, varies *inversely* with λ.[37]

[36] ML don't mention this literature, which includes Bishop *et al.* (1983), Seller *et al.* (1985), Hoehn and Randall (1987), Kealy *et al.* (1988), Milton (1989), Walsh *et al.* (1992), Johnson *et al.* (1990), Söderkvist (1992), and Kriström (1993).

[37] Let η be the income elasticity of median WTP. Then, $\eta = 0$ when $\lambda = 1$, $\eta = 1$ when $\lambda = 0$, and $\eta > 1$ only when $\lambda < 0$. To a first approximation $\eta = 1 - \lambda$. An alternative to Box–Cox is Kriström's (1990) flexible utility model.

The correct estimate in their case is 0.731. This aside, it is hard to see how ML can make any statement about the correct value for an elasticity of WTP without knowing people's true preferences. In the literature on the demand for state and local government services, the income elasticities are usually well below unity; they generally range from 0.3 to 0.6 (Cutler *et al.*, 1993).

Another survey conducted for Exxon has received considerable attention, the 'bird' survey by Research Triangle Institute (RTI). This survey provides considerably more detail than the wilderness survey. It tells respondents that migratory waterfowl spend the summer in the northern parts of North America and fly south for the winter using four flyways, as shown in a map. The largest is the Central Flyway, used by 8.5 million waterfowl. Along the route, in parts of Texas, Oklahoma and New Mexico, there are over 250,000 waste-oil holding ponds ranging in diameter from 10 to 100 feet. Migratory waterfowl are attracted to these ponds because there are so few wetlands along the flyway and drown when they land on the ponds. To prevent this, the federal government is considering requiring owners to cover the ponds with fine wire mesh nets that would keep waterfowl safe. If the regulation is approved, consumers will face higher prices for petroleum products. Respondents are then asked their annual household WTP for this programme in an open-ended question. There are three different versions of the survey. The first version says that about 2000 migratory waterfowl die in the ponds; the second says about 20,000; and the third about 200,000. The programme would prevent these birds' death. The three versions were implemented as self-administered interviews with three separate samples of shoppers at two malls in the Atlanta area, averaging 10–12 minutes per interview.

While closer to standard CV practice than the wilderness surveys, the bird survey has some critical flaws. For example, Desvousges *et al.* (1992) mention that some people in the pre-tests worried that the waste-oil ponds might be harmful to children; therefore they added to the text that the ponds were located in 'remote and sparsely populated areas'. But, no evidence is presented that this wording eliminated human safety as a perceived benefit from the programme. There is also the credibility issue: did respondents believe that, with 8.5 million birds flying over one quarter of a million ponds, and with a federal programme in the works, there could be only 2000 bird deaths per year?

What is the real variation in scale? In terms of the absolute number of bird deaths, the three versions of the questionnaire differ by two orders of magnitude. But, the contrast perceived by respondents to the three versions may have been much smaller. Desvousges *et al.* (1992, p. 36) note that people often want injuries expressed as percentages – they want to know the relative rather than absolute impact on a population. This information was incorporated in the survey. In the 2000 bird version, the text said this was *'much less than 1 percent'* of the waterfowl in the Central Flyway; in the 20,000 bird version, it said *'less than 1 percent'*; and, in the 200,000 bird version, it said *'about 2 percent'*. If respondents focused on the relative impact, it is hard to believe that they would have perceived any significant difference in this tiny range of percentages. Moreover, there were no other cues, visual or verbal, to highlight the contrast among the three versions, apart from changing a few words in a text running to a dozen pages.

The lack of contrast was almost certainly exacerbated by the survey mode – intercepting shoppers as they walk around a mall, promising them a fee if they participated, and having them sit down with their bags for ten minutes to fill out a self-administered questionnaire. In a well-designed CV study, one wants respondents to reflect on the issue at hand and give a considered opinion. Unless the study deals with consumer products, shopping mall intercepts are a very poor way to accomplish this.[38]

All of this casts doubt on the ability of the bird survey to provide a meaningful test of the responsiveness of WTP to variation in the scale of the item being valued. This is compounded by statistical problems arising from the survey format and mode. It is an object lesson in why one should avoid an open-ended format: 17% of respondents could not give a numerical answer to the WTP question compared, for example, with 2% with a closed-ended format in another CV study by RTI. Of the rest, about 6.5% gave WTP amounts of $1000 or more, and 1.8% gave amounts over $12,000 or that exceeded a quarter of their annual income. Thus, the data are noisy and show signs of gross contamination unusual for a high quality CV survey.[39] With such data, the results depend crucially on how one treats the right tail. Desvousges *et al.* (1992) provide three treatments. The treatment reported in Hausman (1993) removes about three quarters of the responses of $1000 or more, leaving the rest; while the mean WTP does differ among the three bird

---

[38] In addition to distracted shoppers, another hazard of small intercepts is infiltration by teenagers. RTI's protocol for the bird surveys called for screening to exclude participants under 20. However, the lowest age group (20–29), where 'illegal' teenage participants would have been assigned if they had penetrated the study, accounts for 46% of the sample and for 73% of the respondents subsequently identified as outliers because they listed unusually high incomes and gave WTP responses of $1000 or more.

[39] Schkade and Payne (1993) provide evidence of a survey mode effect, since they use the same instrument but administer it differently. In their study, respondents recruited by phone came to a central location, responded to the questionnaire individually in the presence of an interviewer, and were asked to think aloud as they answered. Compared with RTI's self-administered mall intercepts, this procedure slowed respondents down and forced them to think. While RTI's respondents took about 10 minutes to complete the questionnaire, these respondents took about 30 minutes. This shows in the distribution of responses: only 9% could not give numerical answers to the WTP question and, of the remainder, only 2% gave amount of $1000 or more, the maximum response being $1200.

scenarios, the differences are not statistically significant. The second treatment trims 5% of the responses from each tail, which is roughly equivalent to the first treatment and yields similar results. The third treatment trims 10% from each tail. Then, differences in mean WTP *are* statistically significant: Carson and Flores (1993) find that, if one regresses WTP on the percent of birds killed, the slope coefficient is significant at the 95% level.[40]

To summarize, the Exxon CV surveys have some serious flaws. To regard them as examples of good practice in CV or a crucial test of the CV method is justified only if one believes that measurement results are invariant with respect to measurement practice. This is not true in economics or any other science.

CV and Economic Theory

DH argue that CV is incompatible with economic theory because CV responses are inconsistent with what economic theory says about people's preferences and CV violates economists' inclination towards revealed preference. Both issues are worth discussing even apart from the debate on CV.

As noted above, DH's assertion that CV responses don't vary with the scope of the commodity is not supported by Exxon's CV studies. Nor is it supported by the empirical literature on CV, to which DH makes no reference. In one of the early CV studies, Cicchetti and Smith (1973) looked at how WTP varied with commodity characteristics. They asked hikers in a Montana wilderness area about their WTP for trips involving different levels of solitude in terms of the number of encounters with other hikers on the trail during the day or in camp at night. These attributes had a statistically significant effect on WTP. For trips where other hikers were encountered on *two* nights the WTP was 34% lower than for trips with *no* such encounters. Many similar findings have been reported using both internal and external tests of scope.[41]

How much should WTP vary with scope? Diamond (1993) asserts

[40] If the WTP distributions for the three scenarios were the same, as Desvousges *et al.* (1992) maintain, trimming would have no effect on the outcome of tests for the equality of moments, as happens here. Hampel *et al.* (1986, pp. 401–2) conclude that, in the presence of gross contamination, applying procedures like trimming which are usually associated with symmetric distributions to *asymmetrically* distributed data is much preferable to making no adjustment at all.

[41] Kahneman's (1986) CV study is widely cited as showing that people are willing to pay the *same* amount to clean up fishing lakes in one region of Ontario as in all of Ontario. But, his graph actually shows a 50% difference in median WTP. For evidence of significant scope effects see the meta-analyses in Walsh *et al.* (1992) on outdoor recreation and Smith and Osborne (1994) on air quality. Carson and Mitchell (1995) focus on external tests and list over a dozen recent studies that show significant scope effects.

that the elasticity of WTP with respect to scope should exceed unity – people should value preventing 200,000 bird deaths *over a 100 times more* than they value preventing 2000 bird deaths. To prove this, he starts off with a model where people care about the number of birds originally in the population, q_0; the number at risk of dying, q_R; and the number of those that are saved, q_S. Letting z denote a Hicksian composite market good, the utility function $u(q_0, q_R, q_S, z)$ is decreasing in q_R and increasing in the other arguments. If u were quasiconvex in q_R, the elasticity of WTP would exceed one. Diamond imposes this restriction indirectly. He first assumes that u is quasiconcave in q_0 and then imposes the restriction that q_0, $-q_R$, and q_S are perfect substitutes, so that $u(q_0, q_R, q_S, z) = w(q_0 - q_R + q_S, z)$ for some function w. If u is to be quasiconcave in q_0, w must be quasiconcave in its first argument, which then makes w quasiconcave in q_R.

Arrow (1986) and Simon (1986) warned against the tendency in contemporary economics to make assertions about rational behaviour that depend primarily on auxiliary, factual assumptions. As Simon put it: 'Almost all the action, all the ability to reach nontrivial conclusions, come from the factual assumptions and very little from the assumptions of optimization. Hence it becomes critically important to submit the factual assumptions to careful empirical test.' Diamond's claim about the elasticity of WTP provides an excellent illustration. It follows not from rationality *per se* but, rather, from the assumption of perfect substitution, about which economic theory is silent. Let $q_1 \equiv q_0 - q_R + q_S$. Diamond asserts that $u(q_0, q_R, q_S, z) = w(q_1, z)$ – people should care only about the ultimate population size, not how many were in the original population, at risk, or saved. When CV data disconfirm this assumption, Diamond dismisses the method. Others might be more inclined to believe the data and reject the assumption.

Diamond's argument violates a foundational premise of economics. As Simon noted: 'neoclassical economics provides no theoretical basis for specifying the shape and content of the utility function'. Hausman (1993), too, abounds with prescriptions that violate this precept: people should care about outcomes, not about the process whereby they are generated; they should not care whether animals are killed by humans or die naturally; they should care only about the number of acres of wilderness; they should not care whether development takes the form of logging or mining; they should not be concerned about small or reversible injuries; they should value things only for selfish motives. In this torrent of 'economic correctness', consumer's sovereignty is swept away.[42]

[42] These prescriptions violate Hume's First Law, 'No normative conclusion, e.g., about what a private economic agent ... ought to do or not do, can validly be deduced from a set of solely positive premises' (Roy, 1989).

For welfare economics, DH adopt an extreme position. They follow Milgrom (1993) in contending that behaviour cannot be considered an acceptable expression of preference if it is motivated by ethical concerns. For non-use value to be validly included in benefit–cost analysis 'it would be necessary for people's individual existence values to reflect only their own personal economic motives and not altruistic motives, or sense of duty, or moral obligation' (p. 431). This is hardly consistent with the general practice in economics. We did not remove Catholics when estimating demand functions for fish before Vatican II. Nor do we adjust when childless couples vote for school bonds. The modern theory of social choice considers it immaterial whether preferences reflect selfish interest or moral judgment:

> It need not be assumed here that an individual's attitude toward different social states is determined exclusively by the commodity bundles which accrue to his lot under each. The individual may order all social states by whatever standards he deems relevant
>
> (Arrow, 1963, p. 17)[43]

DH are also at odds with the modern approach to demand analysis, due to Lancaster (1966). He rejected the 'puritanical view' that consumers should care just for the raw quantity of commodities and proposed instead a model in which they care for characteristics and how these are combined to form a consumption experience. It is characteristics, not commodities, that give rise to utility.[44] Any commodity possesses multiple characteristics. For example, 'a meal (treated as a single good) possesses nutritional characteristics but it also possesses aesthetic characteristics, and different meals will possess these characteristics in different relative proportions' (p. 133). This makes demand context dependent. Lancaster also noted that the units in which characteristics are measured may be arbitrary. They may be ordinal or cardinal. He emphasized that, while the characteristics of a commodity are an objective fact, people's *reaction* to them is subjective: e.g., some may find a shape beautiful, others not. Being subjective, the preference for characteristics is likely to vary among individuals: 'some [characteristics] may be relevant to one individual, others to a different

---

[43] Milgrom also claims that using CV to measure altruistic preferences creates double counting. His case is not convincing. First, it depends on the particular specification of the utility function, as Johansson (1992) notes: if the argument of the utility function is another's consumption rather than his utility, there is no double-counting. Second, it derives its force from the auxiliary assumption that the respondent *does not realize* that the other people for whom he cares will have to pay, too; this is not a problem in a referendum format. Third, in many CV studies the object of the altruism is often wildlife – sea otters, for example. Since the wildlife are *not* surveyed, the issue is moot.

[44] Cf. Adam Smith (1776): 'The whole industry of human life is employed not in procuring the supply of our three humble necessities ... but in procuring the conveniences of it according to the nicety and delicacy of our taste.'

individual. One person may scarcely notice the existence of properties which to him are of little account in his decisions but are important to someone else.' For this reason, aggregate behaviour cannot be expressed in terms of the traditional representative consumer. Above all, Lancaster stressed, 'goods are simply what consumers would like more of; and we must be neutral with respect to differences in consumer tastes' (p. 132). The same conclusion surely holds for CV, which applies Lancaster's model to environmental commodities specified in terms of characteristics.

Lancaster saw traditional demand theory as a 'coarse structure' theory appropriate to broad aggregates of goods such as 'automobiles', 'food', and 'clothing' rather than individual goods as strictly defined. There is necessarily less substitution among broad commodity aggregates than among the individual goods within a group. This should be borne in mind when one considers the embedding problem in CV. As noted above, this is a direct consequence of Madden's (1991) R-substitution. The greater the degree of substitution, the more extensive the sequencing effect that economic theory predicts for any one of a set of commodities. Substitution elasticities estimated for traditional commodity aggregates will understate the substitutability, and thus the sequencing effects, to be expected among individual commodities.

DH's ultimate argument against CV is that it violates economists' traditional commitment to revealed preference. Revealed preference has undoubtedly served economics well. But, this does not mean that it lacks shortcomings. As a profession we tend to be blind to them. Revealed preference is a reflection of the behaviourist movement that dominated Anglo-American psychology from the early 1920s to the mid-1950s. It was introduced into economics in 1938 by Paul Samuelson in his first published paper, which sought to eliminate from consumer demand theory 'any vestigial trace of the utility concept'.[45] Hutchison (1938), published the same year, introduced positivism and Popper to English-speaking economists. These two works were highly influential in establishing the position that inference and analysis in economics should be based solely on external observation of behaviour.

As both a logical principle and a methodological approach, behaviourism suffers from some severe problems that were exposed in the 1950s by the cognitive movement in psychology (Baars, 1986) and the linguistic movement in philosophy (Goldman, 1993). Much of the discussion in the debate centred on logical objections. But, in the view of my colleague John Searle, a leading authority on the philosophy of mind and language,

---

[45] Samuelson's subsequent retreat from this radical position is analysed by Wong (1978).

it is the commonsense objections that are the most embarrassing. The absurdity of behaviorism lies in the fact that it denies the existence of any inner mental states in addition to external behavior. And this, we know, runs dead counter to our ordinary experience of what it is like to be a human being

(Searle, 1992 p. 5).[46]

Forty years after it waned in the other social sciences, behaviourism continues to hold sway in economics. But, there has always been criticism, starting with Frank Knight's (1940) review of Hutchison. The subject matter of economics, Knight wrote, is human conduct and motivation, not the study of mechanical response.[47] Testing predictions is ultimately a social phenomenon. The fundamental propositions of economics are not inferred or verified in the same way as those of mathematics. The main source of knowledge about human conduct is interaction with humans. Economic behaviour involves intentions, which are not amenable to external observation; the imperfect link between motive and result is proof that one does not infer the former from the latter.

The difference between predicting human behavior and predicting the behavior of physical objects ... [is] that the latter neither behave irrationally or sentimentally, nor make mistakes, nor change their minds ... [This] is admittedly embarrassing to the economist as a scientist, but there does not seem to be anything that he can do about it

(p. 29).

The problem with revealed preference, as Sen (1973, 1993) and others have noted, is that like all induction it requires an act of faith to extrapolate from particular choices to general assertions about behaviour and preference. One needs a host of auxiliary assumptions to rule out factors that might invalidate the extrapolation.[48] Choice may have little to do with individual preference, perhaps because preferences are incomplete, or choice is a social act rather than an individual act. Tastes may vary among individuals; or, they may change over time. Since revealed preference compares the behaviour of different individuals, or the same individual at different times, in response to different prices,

---

[46] For this reason, Searle notes, behaviourists were accused of 'feigning anesthesia', as in the story of the two behaviourists. After making love, one turns to the other and says 'Well, it was great for you. But, how was it for me?'

[47] Knight noted the irony that, having waged a long struggle to escape from the idea that stones are like men, scientists now seemed intent on showing that men are like stones.

[48] This can also be an issue for experimental economics, though it has received scant attention. An experiment is a form of communication and, therefore, it is susceptible to context and interpretation. Whether the experiment was perceived by participants as the experimenter intended, and what was their motivation, are things that cannot simply be assumed but should be probed and tested, for example through debriefing questions.

how can we tell what part of the difference in behaviour is due to price and what part to a difference in preference? *Ceteris* may not be *paribus*. New goods may arise. For a Weak Axiom to hold over all market prices, one should observe the individual's choices under infinitely many price configurations. All these problems must be assumed away in order for revealed preference to work. But, that assumption is not verifiable if one is restricted to observed behaviour. This makes revealed preference a somewhat hypothetical undertaking.[49]

A crucial assumption of revealed preference as it is applied in practice is the 'universal choice set' – the consumer always chooses among the set of all possible alternatives, subject to a single budget constraint, and, in choosing any one item, has full regard for all his other consumption decisions. The reality is otherwise. From my work on the demand for beach recreation in Boston and sportfishing in Alaska, I concluded that few if any individuals were consciously choosing from all the sites that *I* knew to exist. Different individuals were choosing from different choice sets. One would have needed to model behaviour as a two-stage process, first the formation of a choice set and then a conventional maximizing choice within that set. Also, many people's recreation choices were separate from their other consumption decisions, in the manner not of a separable utility function but rather of piecemeal decision making: when going fishing, think of recreation alternatives; when buying a sofa, think of furniture alternatives; don't think of sofas when going fishing or vice versa. This form of satisficing where the choice set is edited so as to tailor it to the decision at hand can generate what look like large substitution effects. Also, we commonly assume a 'universal' attribute set – the same q's figure in everyone's utility function. But, this too is false. The q's differ among individuals and over choices. The earlier discussion of Big Green illustrates this – what initially was a question of protecting the environment later became a question of Tom Hayden's political standing.[50] In short, the Achilles' heel of revealed preference is that you

[49] The price at which demand falls to zero, needed to estimate consumer's surplus, may introduce another hypothetical element into revealed preference. This may be outside the range of the observed data (e.g., one knows travel cost only for participants, or one believes that participants and non-participants have different preferences). Thus, revealed preference can yield a less reliable estimate of use value WTP than contingent behaviour (Hanemann et al., 1993). Revealed preference estimates are sensitive to the measurement of price, which is often uncertain and precarious for disaggregated commodities (Pratt et al., 1990; Randall, 1994). With other variables there may be inadequate variation in the data (e.g. attributes are correlated across brands). Hence, revealed preference data alone may yield a less reliable estimate of demand functions than stated preference data, and one may need to combine both types of data for best results (Adamowicz et al., 1994).

[50] Political scientists are well aware that the q's can shift and this explains observed dynamics of behaviour. Riker (1990), for example, distinguishes two forms of political persuasion: rhetoric, which he defines as changing people's opinions about issues; and what he calls heresthetic, which is changing their conception of what issues are at stake.

have to know what the choice *is about*. Without asking, you may not be able to tell. As Sen (1973) put it, 'we have been too prone, on the one hand, to overstate the difficulties of introspection and communication and, on the other, to underestimate the problems of studying preferences revealed by observed behavior.'

These problems with revealed preference are counterparts to the problems raised about CV – context effects, framing effects, and embedding effects. The problems are not widely discussed in the demand literature because they are kept from sight through the imposition of maintained assumptions about the irrelevance of context, the nature of the choice set and the attribute set, and the homogeneity of preferences across individuals and choice situations. With individual CV responses, they are more readily apparent. But, these are general phenomena of human behaviour, not artifacts of the CV method.

Conclusions

Though much of the current controversy focuses on the assessment of non-use values for natural resource damages, CV is being used in many countries to measure both use and non-use values for many purposes involving market and non-market goods. The essential feature of CV is that it employs surveys to elicit respondents' value for a commodity. The scenario for providing the commodity is sometimes real; if not, the key is to make it real to respondents. However, the respondents are not actually making a payment during the interview; they are expressing their intention or predicting their decision to pay. Whether the responses are reliable, whether respondents are focusing on the intended commodity, whether they take the survey seriously, are empirical questions. The answer will vary with the type of commodity, the type of respondent, and the way the survey was conducted. Two things can be said. First, experience shows that certain practices generally tend to make the survey more reliable, including testing the instrument rigorously before going into the field, avoiding self-administered surveys, using a closed-ended response format and, where appropriate, setting the decision in a referendum or voting context. Second, there are techniques such as debriefing questions that can be used to monitor the interview, assess its effectiveness at conveying what was intended, and identify cases of divergence.

In the recent debate on CV, there has been some tendency to employ simplistic dichotomies. Surveys of attitudes are fallible and subject to the vagaries of context and interpretation; surveys of behaviour are unerring and immune from context or interpretation. Revealed preference is unambiguous and reliable; stated preference is equivocal and undependable. In the market place, people are informed, deliberate, and rational. Outside it, they are ignorant, confused, and illogical. As consumers, people can be taken seriously; as voters, they cannot. In particular instances these assertions may be correct. As generalizations, however, they are a caricature of reality.

All measurement in the social sciences is liable to error. It would be misleading for me to suggest that CV surveys can be made to work well in all circumstances. It is equally misleading to suggest that CV surveys can never be made to work reliably in any situation. This, however, is the position taken by DH. They assert (p. 29) that CV surveys never measure people's preferences and are never a suitable source of information on values in either benefit–cost analysis or damage assessment. The NOAA Panel saw these as 'extreme arguments', and rejected them (Arrow *et al.*, 1993, p. 41).

With use values, CV estimates can be checked against those obtained from revealed preference. When this has been done, there is generally considerable agreement, with the CV estimates typically a little lower than the revealed preference estimates (Carson *et al.*, 1994). For non-use values, revealed preference provides no alternative to CV. DH suggest that damages from oil spills be decided by experts, by 'people like you or me', as Hausman told the NOAA Panel (NOAA, 1992, p. 52). Experts clearly play a crucial role in determining the physical injuries. How they know the value that society places on the injured resources without resort to measurement involving some sort of survey is less clear.

Empirical demand analysis traditionally dealt with a representative consumer and broadly defined commodities. This was driven by the available data, which were usually highly aggregated over both individuals and commodities. Yet this obscures much of the reality of economic life. Over the last 30 years economic theory has developed a much richer view of individual behaviour in both market and non-market settings. This includes not only Lancaster's work on consumer demand but also all the work on the economics of the family since Becker and on the economics of public choice since Downs. CV provides one way in which the more realistic theory of individual behaviour can be given practical expression. It provides one way of tracing out the demand curve for a commodity that perhaps cannot be revealed through market data, but nevertheless exists and should count in an economic analysis.

References

Adamowicz, W., Louviere, J. and Williams, M. (1994) Combining revealed and stated preference methods for valuing environmental amenities. *Journal of Environmental Economics and Management* 26, 271–292.

Alberini, A. (1992) The Information Content of Binary Responses. PhD dissertation, Economics Department, University of California, San Diego.

Arrow, K.J. (1963) *Social Choice and Individual Values*. Cowles Foundation for Research in Economics at Yale University. John Wiley & Sons, New York.

Arrow, K.J. (1986) Rationality of self and others in an economic system. In: Hogarth, R. and Reder, M.W. (eds) *Rational Choice: The Contrast Between Economics and Psychology*. The University of Chicago Press, Chicago, pp. 201–216.

Arrow, K, Solow, R., Portney, P., Leamer, E., Radner, R. and Schuman, H. (1993) Report of the NOAA Panel on Contingent Valuation. *Federal Register* 58(10), 4601–4614.

Baars, B.J. (1986) *The Cognitive Revolution in Psychology*. The Guilford Press, New York.

Barrick, K. and Beazley, R. (1990) Magnitude and distribution of option value for Washakie Wilderness, Northwest Wyoming, USA. *Environmental Management* 14(3), 367–380.

Bishop, R.C. and Heberlein, T.A. (1979) Measuring values of extramarket goods: are indirect measures biased? *American Journal of Agricultural Economics* 61, 926–930.

Bishop, R.C., Heberlain, T.A. and Kealy, M.J. (1983) Hypothetical bias in contingent valuation: results from a simulated market. *Natural Resources Journal* 23(3), 619–633.

Cambridge Economics Associates, Inc. (1992) *Contingent Valuation: A Critical Assessment*. A Symposium, Cambridge Economics Associates, Washington DC, 2–3 April.

Cameron, T.A. (1988) A new paradigm for valuing non-market goods using referendum data: maximum likelihood estimation by censored logistic regression. *Journal of Environmental Economics and Management* 15, 355–379.

Carson, R.T. and Flores, N.E. (1993) *Another Look at 'Does Contingent Valuation Measure Preferences: Experimental Evidence' – How Compelling is the Evidence?* Economics Department, University of California, San Diego.

Carson, R.T. and Mitchell, R.C. (1995) Sequencing and nesting in contingent valuation surveys. *Journal of Environmental Economics and Management* (in press).

Carson, R.T., Hanemann, W.M. and Mitchell, R.C. (1987) *The Use of Simulated Political Markets to Value Public Goods*. Economics Department, University of California, San Diego.

Carson, R., Flores, N. and Hanemann, W.M. (1992a) *On the Creation and Destruction of Public Goods, The Matter of Sequencing*. Working Paper 690, Agr. & Resource Econ., UC, Berkeley.

Carson, R., Mitchell, R., Hanemann, W.M., Kopp, R., Presser, S. and Rudd, P. (1992b) *A Contingent Valuation Study of Lost Passive Use Values Resulting from the Exxon Valdez Oil Spill*, Report to the Attorney General of Alaska,

Natural Resource Damage Assessment, Inc. La Jolla, California, November, 1992.

Carson, R.T., Carson, N., Alberini, A., Flores, N. and Wright, J. (1993) *A Bibliography of Contingent Valuation Studies and Papers*. Natural Resource Damage Assessment, Inc., La Jolla, California.

Carson, R.T., Flores, N., Martin, K. and Wright, J. (1994) Contingent Valuation and Revealed Preference Methodologies: Comparing the Estimates for Quasi-Public Goods. Discussion paper 94-07, University of California, San Diego, 1994.

Cicchetti, C. and Smith, V.K. (1973) Congestion, quality deterioration, and optimal use: wilderness recreation in the Spanish Peaks primitive area. *Social Science Research* 2, 15–30.

Ciriacy-Wantrup, S.V. (1947) Capital returns from soil-conservation practices. *Journal of Farm Economics* 29, 1188–1190.

Clawson, M. (1959) *Methods of Measuring the Demand for and Value of Outdoor Recreation*. Reprint No. 10, Resources for the Future. Washington DC.

Cook, T.D. and Campbell D.T. (1979) *Quasi-Experimentation: Design and Analysis Issues for Field Setting*. Rand McNally College Publishing Company, Chicago, IL.

Cronin, T.E. (1989) *Direct Democracy: The Politics of Initiative, Referendum, and Recall*. Harvard University Press, Cambridge, Massachusetts.

Cummings, R.G., Brookshire, D.S. and Schulze, W.D. (1986) *Valuing Environmental Goods: An Assessment of the Contingent Valuation Method*. Rowman and Allanheld, Totowa, New Jersey.

Cutler, D., Elmendorf, D.W. and Zeckhauser, R.J. (1993) *Demographic Characteristics and the Public Bundle*. NEBR Working Paper No. 4283. National Bureau of Economic Research, Cambridge, Massachusetts.

Davis, D. and Holt, C. (1993) *Experimental Economics*. Princeton University Press, Princeton, New Jersey.

Davis, R. (1963) Recreation planning as an economic problem. *Natural Resources Journal* 3, 239–249.

Desvousges, W.H., Johnson, F.R., Dunford, R.W., Hudson, S.P., Wilson, K.N. and Boyle, K.J. (1992) *Measuring Nonuse Damages Using Contingent Valuation: An Experimental Evaluation of Accuracy*. Research Triangle Institute Monograph. RTI, North Carolina.

Diamond, P.A. (1993) *Testing the Internal Consistency of Contingent Valuation Surveys*. Working Paper, Department of Economics, MIT. MIT, Cambridge, Massachusetts.

Diamond, P.A. and Hausman, J. (1993) On contingent valuation measurement of nonuse values. In: Hausman, J. (ed.) *Contingent Valuation: A Critical Assessment*. North-Holland, New York, p. 30.

Diamond, P.A. and Hausman, J. (1994) Contingent valuation: is some number better than no number? *Journal of Economic Perspectives* 8(4), 45–64.

Diamond, P.A., Hausman, J., Leonard, G.K. and Denning, M.A. (1993) Does contingent valuation measure preferences? Experimental evidence. In: Hausman, J.A. (ed.) *Contingent Valuation: A Critical Assessment*. North-Holland, New York, pp. 41–89.

Downs, A. (1957) *An Economic Theory of Democracy*. Harper and Row, New York.

Duffield, J.W. and Patterson, D.A. (1991) Field testing existence values: an instream flow trust fund for Montana Rivers. Presented at the American Economics Association Annual Meeting, New Orleans, Louisiana, January 4. Mimeo, Department of Economics, Missoula, Montana, University of Montana.

Eckstein, O. (1958) *Water Resource Development: The Economics of Project Evaluation*. Harvard University Press, Cambridge, Massachusetts.

Epple, D. (1987) Hedonic prices and implicit markets: estimating demand and supply functions for differentiated products. *Journal of Political Economy* 95, 59–80.

Fiorina, M.P. (1981) *Retrospective Voting in American National Elections*. Yale University Press, New Haven.

Fishkin, J.S. (1991) *Democracy and Deliberation: New Directions for Democratic Reform*. Yale University Press, New Haven.

Freeman, A.M. (1993) *The Measurement of Environmental and Resource Values: Theory and Method*. Resources for the Future, Washington DC.

Goldman, A.I. (1993) *Philosophical Applications of Cognitive Science*. Westview Press, Boulder.

Haitovsky, Y. (1973) *Regression Estimation from Grouped Observations*. Griffin, London.

Hampel, F.R., Ronchetti, E.M., Rousseeuw, P.J. and Stahel, W.A. (1986) *Robust Statistics: The Approach Based on Influence Functions*. John Wiley & Sons, New York.

Hanemann, W.M. (1980) Measuring the worth of natural resource facilities. *Land Economics* 56, 482–490.

Hanemann, W.M. (1982) Quality and demand analysis. In: Rausser, G. (ed.) *New Directions in Economic Modeling and Forecasting in U.S. Agriculture*. Elsevier/North-Holland, New York, pp. 55–98.

Hanemann, W.M. (1984) Welfare evaluations in contingent valuation experiments with discrete responses. *American Journal of Agricultural Economics* 66, 332–341.

Hanemann, W.M. (1988) *Three Approaches to Defining 'Existence' or 'Non-Use' Value Under Certainty*. Working Paper No. 691, Giannini Foundation of Agricultural and Resource Economics, University of California, Berkeley.

Hanemann, W.M. (1991a) Willingness to pay and willingness to accept: how much can they differ? *American Economic Review* 81(3), 635–647.

Hanemann, W.M. (1991b) Comments. In: Imber, D., Stevenson, G. and Wilks, L. (eds) *A Contingent Valuation Survey of the Kakadu Conservation Zone*. RAC Research Paper No. 3. Resource Assessment Commission, Canberra, Australia.

Hanemann, W.M. (1992) Preface: notes on the history of environmental valuation in the USA. In: Navrud, S. (ed.) *Pricing the Environment: The European Experience*. Oxford University Press, New York.

Hanemann, W.M., Loomis, J. and Kanninen, B. (1991) Statistical efficiency of double-bounded dichotomous choice contingent valuation. *American Journal of Agricultural Economics* 73(4), 1255–1263.

Hanemann, W.M., Chapman, D. and Kanninen, B. (1993) Non-market valuation using contingent behavior: model specification and consistency tests. Presented at the American Economic Association Annual Meeting,

Anaheim, California, 6 January.

Hausman, J.A. (1981) 'Exact Consumer's Surplus and Deadweight Loss,' *American Economic Review* 71, 662–676.

Hausman, J.A. (ed.) (1993) *Contingent Valuation: A Critical Assessment*. North-Holland, New York, p. 462.

Hausman, J.A., Leonard, G.K. and McFadden, D. (1993) Assessing use value losses caused by natural resource injury. In: Hausman, J.A. (ed.) *Contingent Valuation: A Critical Assessment*. North-Holland, New York, pp. 341–368.

Hoage, R.J. (ed.) (1989) *Perceptions of Animals in American Culture*. Smithsonian Institution Press, Washington DC.

Hoehn, J.P. and Randall, A. (1987) A satisfactory benefit cost indicator from contingent valuation. *Journal of Environmental Economics and Management* 14, 226–247.

Hotelling, H. (1938) The general welfare in relation to problems of taxation and of railway and utility rates. *Econometrica* 6, 242–269.

Hurwicz, L. and Uzawa, H. (1971) On the integrability of demand functions. In: Chipman, J.S. (ed.) *Preferences, Utility and Demand*. Harcourt Brace Jovanovich, New York, pp. 114–148.

Hutchinson, T.W. (1938) *The Significance and Basic Postulates of Economic Theory*. Macmillan, London, p. 192.

Infosino, W.J. (1986) Forecasting new product sales from likelihood of purchase ratings. *Marketing Science* 5(4), 372–384.

Johansson, P.-O. (1992) Altruism in cost-benefit analysis. *Environmental and Resource Economics* 2, 605–613.

Johnson, R., Bregenzer, N. and Shelby, B. (1990) Contingent valuation question formats: dichotomous choice vs. open-ended responses. In: Johnson, R. and Johnson, G. (eds) *Economic Valuation of Natural Resources: Issues, Theory, and Applications*. Westview, Boulder.

Juster, F.T. (1964) *Anticipations and Purchases: An Analysis of Consumer Behavior*. Princeton University Press, Princeton, New Jersey.

Kahneman, D. (1986) Review panel assessment. In: Cummings, R.G., Brookshire, D.S. and Schulze, W.D. (eds) *Valuing Environmental Goods: An Assessment of the Contingent Valuation Method*. Rowman & Allanheld, Totowa, New Jersey.

Kahneman, D. and Knetsch, J.L. (1992) Valuing public goods: the purchase of moral satisfaction. *Journal of Environmental Economics and Management* 22, 57–70.

Kahneman, D., Ritov, I., Jacowitz, K.E. and Grant, P. (1993) Stated willingness to pay for public goods: a psychological perspective. *Psychological Science* 4(5), 310–315.

Kealy, M.J., Dovidio, J.F. and Rockel, M.L. (1988) Accuracy in valuation is a matter of degree. *Land Economics* 64 (2), 158–171.

Kemp, M.A. and Maxwell, C. (1993) Exploring a budget context for contingent valuation estimates. In: Hausman, J.A. (ed.) *Contingent Valuation: A Critical Assessment*. North-Holland, New York, pp. 217–269.

Knetsch, J.L. and Davis, R.K. (1966) Comparisons of methods for recreation evaluation. In: Kneese, A.V. and Smith, S.C. (eds) *Water Research*. Resources for the Future Inc., John Hopkins Press, Baltimore, pp. 125–142.

Knight, F.H. (1940) What is truth in economics? *Journal of Political Economy* 18(1), 1–32.

Kriström, B. (1990) A non-parametric approach to the estimation of welfare measures in discrete response valuation studies. *Land Economics* 66(2), 135–139.

Kriström, B. (1993) Comparing continuous and discrete contingent valuation questions. *Environmental and Resource Economics* 3, 63–71.

Krutilla, J.V. (1967) Conservation reconsidered. *American Economic Review* 57(4), 777–786.

LaFrance, J. and Hanemann, W.M. (1989) The dual structure of incomplete demand systems. *American Journal of Agricultural Economics* 71, 262–274.

Lancaster, K.J. (1966) A new approach to consumer theory. *Journal of Political Economy* 74, 132–157.

Loftus, E., Klinger, M.R., Smith, K.D. and Fiedler, J. (1990) A tale of two questions: benefits of asking more than one question. *Public Opinion Quarterly* 54, 330–345.

Lupia, A. (1993) *Short Cuts versus Encyclopedias: Information and Voting Behavior in California Insurance Reform Elections*. Working Paper, Department of Political Science, UC San Diego.

Madden, P. (1991) A generalization of Hicksian q substitutes and complements with application to demand rationing. *Econometrica* 59(5), 1497–1508.

Magat, W.A., Viscusi, W.K. and Huber, J. (1998) Paired comparison and contingent valuation approaches to morbidity risk valuation. *Journal of Environmental Economics and Management* 15, 295–411.

Magleby, D.B. (1984) *Direct Legislation: Voting on Ballot Propositions in the United States*. Johns Hopkins University Press, Baltimore, Maryland.

Maler, K.-G. (1974) *Environmental Economics: A Theoretical Inquiry*. The Johns Hopkins University Press for Resource for the Future, Baltimore.

McConnell, K. (1990) Models for referendum data: the structure of discrete choice models for contingent valuation. *Journal of Environmental Economics and Management* 18, 19–34.

McConnell, K. (1983) Existence and bequest values. In: Rowe, R. and Chestnut, L. (eds) *Managing Air Quality and Scenic Resources at National Parks and Wilderness Areas*. Westview, Boulder.

McFadden, D. and Leonard, G.K. (1993) Issues in the contingent valuation of environmental goods: methodologies for data collection and analysis. In: Hausman, J.A. (ed.) *Contingent Valuation: A Critical Assessment*. North-Holland, New York, pp. 165–215.

McKelvey, R.D. and Ordeshook, P.C. (1986) Information, electoral equilibria and the democratic ideal. *Journal of Politics* 48, 909–937.

Milgrom, P. (1993) Is sympathy an economic value? Philosophy, economics, and the contingent valuation method. In: Hausman, J.A. (ed.) *Contingent Valuation: A Critical Assessment*. North-Holland, New York, pp. 417–441.

Mills, M.J. (1990) Harvest participation in Alaska Sport Fisheries during 1989. *Alaska Department of Fish and Game Division of Sport Fishery Data Series* No. 90, 44.

Milton, J.W. (1989) Contingent valuation experiments for strategic behavior. *Journal of Environmental Economics and Management* 17(3), 293–308.

Mitchell, R.C. and Carson, R.T. (1989) *Using Surveys to Value Public Goods: The Contingent Valuation Method*. Resources for the Future, Washington, DC.

Mosteller, F., Hyman, H., McCarthy, P.J., Marks, E.S. and Truman, D.B. (1949) *The Pre-Election Polls of 1948: Report to the Committee on Analysis of Pre-election Polls and Forecasts.* Social Science Research Council, Bulletin 60. SSRC, New York.

National Academy of Sciences (1986) Decision Making Problem Solving. In: *Research Briefings 1986: Report of the Research Briefing Panel on Decision Making and Problem Solving.* National Academy Press, Washington DC.

National Oceanic and Atmospheric Administration (1992) Contingent Valuation Panel, Transcript of Public Meeting, Washington DC. 12 August.

Navrud, S. (1992) *Pricing the European Environment.* Oxford University Press, New York.

Neter, J. and Waksberg, J. (1964) A Study of response errors in expenditures data from household interviews. *Journal of the American Statistical Association 3,* 18–55.

Page, B.I. and Shapiro, R.Y. (1992) *The Rational Public: Fifty Years of Trends in Americans' Policy Preferences.* University of Chicago Press, Chicago.

Plott, C.R. (1989) An updated review of industrial organization: applications of experimental methods. In: Schmalensee, R. and Willig, R.D. (eds) *Handbook of Industrial Organization,* Volume II. Elsevier Science Publishers, New York, pp. 1111–1167.

Portney, P.R. (1994) The contingent valuation debate: why economists should care. *Journal of Economic Perspectives 8*(4), 3–17.

Potter, M.C. (1990) Remembering. In: Osherson, D.N. and Smith, E.E. *Thinking: An Invitation to Cognitive Science.* The MIT Press, Cambridge, Massachusetts.

Pratt, J.W., Wise, D.A. and Zeckhauser, R. (1990) Price differences in almost competitive markets. *Quarterly Journal of Economics 93,* 189–212.

Randall, A. (1994) A difficulty with the travel cost method. *Land Economics 70*(1), 88–96.

Riker, W. (1990) Heresthetic and rhetoric in the spatial model. In: Enelow, J.M. and Hinich, M.J. (eds) *Advances in the Spatial Theory of Voting.* Cambridge University Press, Cambridge, pp. 46–65.

Roy, S. (1989) *Philosophy of Economics: On the Scope of Reason in Economic Inquiry.* Routledge, New York.

Rose, S. (1992) *The Making of Memory: From Molecules to Mind.* Anchor Books, Doubleday, New York.

Samuelson, P.A. (1938) A note on the pure theory of consumer's behavior. *Economica* Feb., 61–71.

Schelling, T. (1968) The life you save may be your own. In: Chase, S. (ed.) *Problems in Public Expenditure Analysis.* Brookings Institution, Washington DC, pp. 143–144.

Schkade, D.A. and Payne, J.W. (1993) Where do the numbers come from? How people respond to contingent valuation questions. In: Hausman, J.A. (ed.) *Contingent Valuation: A Critical Assessment.* North-Holland, New York, pp. 271–303.

Searle, J.R. (1992) *The Rediscovery of the Mind.* MIT Press, Cambridge, Massachusetts.

Seller, C., Stoll, J.R. and Chavas, J.P. (1985) Validation of empirical measures of welfare change: a comparison of nonmarket techniques. *Land Economics* 61, 156–175.

Seip, K. and Strand, J. (1992) Willingness to pay for environmental goods in Norway: a contingent valuation study with real payment. *Environmental and Resource Economics* 2, 91–106.

Sen, A.K. (1973) Behavior and the concept of preference. *Economica* 40 (August), 241–259.

Sen, A.K. (1993) Internal consistency of choice. *Econometria* 61(3), 495–521.

Sheskin, I.M. (1991) Relationship between surveyed behavioral intent and actual behavior in transit usage. *Transportation Research Record* 1297, 106–115.

Simon, H.A. (1986) Rationality in psychology and economics. In: Hogarth, R. and Reder, M.W. (eds) *Rational Choice: The Contrast Between Economics and Psychology*. The University of Chicago Press, Chicago, pp. 25–40.

Smith, A. (1776) *Wealth of Nations*.

Smith, V.K. and Osborne, L. (1994) Do Contingent Valuation Estimates Pass a 'Scope' Test?: A Preliminary Meta Analysis. Presented at the American Economics Association Annual Meeting, Boston, Massachusetts, January 5.

Snyder, J.M. (1993) *The Dimensions of Constituency Preferences: Evidence from California Ballot Propositions, 1974–1990*. Working Paper, Department of Political Science, MIT Press, Cambridge, Massachusetts.

Söderkvist, T. (1992) *Estimating the Economic Value of Health Risk Reduction: A Background to Results of a Contingent Valuation Study*. Mimeo, Stockholm School of Economics.

Trice, A. and Wood, S. (1958) Measurement of recreation benefits. *Land Economics* 34, 195–207.

Tversky, A., Sattah, S. and Slovic, P. (1988) Contingent weighting in judgment and choice. *Psychological Review* 95, 371–384.

Tversky, A., Slovic, P. and Kahneman, D. (1990) The causes of preference reversal. *American Economic Review* 80, 204–217.

Urban, G. and Hauser, J. (1980) *Design and Marketing of New Products*. Prentice-Hall, New Jersey.

Walsh, R.G., Johnson, D.M. and McKean, J.R. (1992) Benefit transfer of outdoor recreation demand studies: 1968–1988, *Water Resources Research* 28(3), 707–713.

Weisbrod, B.A. (1964) Collective-consumption services of individual-consumption goods. *Quarterly Journal of Economics* 78, 471–477.

Westat, Inc. (1989) *Investigation of Possible Recall/Reference Period Bias in National Surveys of Fishing, Hunting and Wildlife-Associated Recreation*. Final report, US Department of Interior, Fish and Wildlife Service, Washington DC.

Willig, R. (1976a) Consumer's surplus without apology. *American Economic Review* 66, 589–597.

Willig, R. (1976b) Integrability implications for locally constant demand elasticities. *Journal of Economic Theory* 12, 391–401.

Wong, S. (1978) *The Foundations of Paul Samuelson's Revealed Preference Theory*. Routledge & Kegan Paul, London.

8

Contingent Valuation in a Policy Context: The National Oceanic and Atmospheric Administration Report and Its Implications for the Use of Contingent Valuation Methods in Policy Analysis in Britain

Ken Willis

University of Newcastle upon Tyne

Introduction

On 24 March 1989, the tanker *Exxon Valdez* grounded and spilled 11 million gallons of crude oil into the waters of Prince William Sound, Alaska. US Federal law allowed Exxon to be sued for:

1. losses of marketed goods, e.g. to fishermen;
2. restoration of the natural resource system, and loss of non-use values.

The loss of marketed goods is essentially a private action for damages. However, under the Comprehensive Environmental Responses and Compensation Liability Act (CERCLA) 1980, public trustees were allowed to sue polluters who damaged natural resources held in public trust. Exxon was thus sued for damages for both loss of use values and non-use values, as well as having to pay the clean up costs.

The estimation of non-use values by contingent valuation methods (CVM), for the state (Alaskan) and federal governments by environmental economists, ran into billions of dollars. Exxon attempted to challenge these resource damage estimates for the impending court case, and a number of environmental economists and non-environmental economists demonstrated how easy it was to discredit CVM as a technique when assessing non-use values.

The subsequent Oil Pollution Act 1990 in response to the *Exxon Valdez* case, required the President, acting through the Under Secretary of

Commerce for Oceans and Atmosphere, to issue regulations establishing procedures for assessing damages to or the destruction of natural resources resulting from a discharge of oil covered by the Act. These procedures are to ensure the recovery of restoration costs as well as the diminution in value of affected resources and the costs of damage assessment. Damage assessment for use values are well recognized, but the need to establish the value or satisfaction that individuals who make no active use of a particular natural resource such as a particular beach, river or wildlife species, derive from its mere existence, even if they never intend to use it (passive or non-use value) gave cause for concern. In response to this the National Oceanic and Atmospheric Administration (NOAA) commissioned a 'blue-ribbon' panel of eminent economists to report on the calculation of these non-use values.

The Panel was composed of members who both supported the use of CVM for non-use damage assessments, and who were sceptical or opposed to CVM. The Panel was jointly chaired by two Nobel Prizewinners in economics, Kenneth Arrow and Robert Solow. Generally the findings of the NOAA Report (Arrow *et al.*, 1993) gave qualified recognition to CVM, but with a series of recommendations about the implementation of the technique. The NOAA Panel's two principal conclusions were firstly that:

> CV studies convey useful information as reliable by standards that seem to be implicit in similar contexts, like market analysis for new and innovative products, and the assessment of other damages normally allowed in court proceedings
>
> (4610/c3)[1]

under the conditions recommended by NOAA Panel.

But that, 'hypothetical markets tend to over estimate WTP for private as well as public goods. The same bias must be expected to occur in CV studies.'

However, the Panel felt secondly that:

> the appropriate ... agencies should begin to accumulate standard damage assessments for a range oil spills ... that process should improve the reliability of CV studies in damage assessment. It should thus contribute to increasing accuracy and reducing the cost of subsequent damage assessment cases
>
> (4611/c1)

---

[1] It should not be thought, however, that conventional tort cases of damage assessments made by courts to determine compensation for accidents, using traditional economic concepts like opportunity costs (loss of earnings, etc.) and compensation for pain, suffering, distress, etc., necessarily produce more accurate or 'true' estimates of value. Parkman (1985) demonstrates that capitalized court estimates of such damages can often be inaccurate.

Detailed Conclusions of the NOAA Report

The two main conclusions of the NOAA Report were followed by a number of detailed recommendations. These were tabulated under three sections: general guide-lines, guide-lines for value elicitation surveys, goals for value elicitation surveys.

General guide-lines

The general guide-lines contained six recommendations on:

1. *Sample type and size*: that probability sampling is essential.
2. *Non-response*: this should be minimized otherwise survey results will be unreliable.
3. *Personal interview*: it is unlikely that reliable estimates of values can be elicited with mail surveys. Face-to-face surveys are preferable, although telephone interviews have some advantages in terms of cost and centralized supervision.
4. *Pretesting for interviewer effects*: interviewers may contribute to 'social desirability' bias, since preserving the environment is widely viewed as something positive. CV studies should incorporate experiments that assess interviewer effects.
5. *Reporting*: each CV study should define the population sampled, sampling frame used, sample size, non-response rates, present the questionnaire, and make the data availability to other researchers.
6. *Careful pretesting for CV questionnaire*: to ensure respondents have understood and accepted the main description and questioning reasonably well, and that answers of questionable meaningfulness be reduced by providing respondents with a 'no opinion' type of alternative when a key valuation question is posed.

Value elicitation surveys

The Panel argued that these guide-lines needed to be followed to assure reliability and usefulness of information:

1. *Conservative design*: increases the reliability by eliminating extreme responses that can enlarge estimated values. Thus, an option which tends to underestimate willingness to pay (WTP) is preferred.
2. *Elicitation format*: WTP should be used instead of willingness to accept (WTA), because the former is the conservative choice.
3. *Referendum format*: the valuation question should be posed as a vote on a referendum.
4. *Accurate description of programme or policy*: adequate information must be provided to respondents about the environmental programme being valued.

5. *Pretesting of photographs*: because photographs may have a great emotional impact.

6. *Reminder of undamaged substitute commodities.*

7. *Adequate time lapse from accident*: to avoid misunderstanding of restoration possibilities, and respondents reporting a substantial passive use loss even when informed full restoration will occur. Questionnaire should force respondents to consider the difference between interim and steady state passive use value.

8. *Temporal averaging*: to reduce measurement noise. A time trend in responses would cast doubt upon the reliability of the findings.

9. *No-answer option*: to allow for approximate indifference, inability to answer without more information, preference for another mechanism, and boredom with the survey.

10. *Yes/no follow ups*: to ascertain why respondents answered yes or no to a WTP question.

11. *Cross tabulations*: to interpret WTP responses in terms of prior visits, distance from site, attitudes towards environment.

12. *Cross-checks on understanding and acceptance*: the extent to which respondents accept as true the descriptions given and assertions made prior to the valuation question.

Goals for value elicitation surveys

The Panel considered that the following items were not adequately addressed by even the best CVM surveys; and that these needed to be convincingly dealt with in order to ensure the reliability of CV estimates.

1. *Alternative expenditure possibilities*: respondents should be reminded their WTP for the environmental good would reduce their expenditure on other private goods.

2. *Deflection of transaction value*: the survey should be designed to deflect warm-glow effect. Utility derived from charitable giving may come mainly from the act of giving rather than the material change that follows the gift. While both are real values, there may be close substitutes to cleaning up oil spills which would produce the same charitable 'warm-glow' effects.

3. *Steady state or interim losses*: respondents should be able to distinguish between these, since full restoration in the future greatly reduces passive use loss.

4. *Present value calculations of interim losses*: it should be demonstrated that respondents are sensitive to the timing of restoration.

5. *Advance approval*: the CV survey should be approved by both sides in the legal action.

6. *Burden of proof*: to rest with CV survey designers, to demonstrate that the CV survey is reliable.
7. *Reliable reference surveys*: government should create reliable reference surveys to interpret the Panel's guide-lines and calibrate surveys in meeting their conditions.

Recommendations Currently in Use

A number of recommendations of the NOAA Panel are or have already been included in CV studies in Britain. Practically all CV surveys in Britain are based on personal interviews,[2] and invariably CV questionnaires are pretested in pilot surveys. WTP was adopted in one of the first CVM studies in Britain on the value of safety (Jones-Lee, 1976) and since that date WTP has almost always been used in preference to WTA, whether to evaluate gains or losses with respect to compensating variation or equivalent variation measures.[3] Theoretical studies have shown the close approximation of compensating variation, consumer surplus and equivalent variation measures (Willig, 1976). Empirical studies have revealed considerable divergence between WTP and WTA (see Bateman and Turner, 1993), with WTA estimates typically two to six times WTP values.[4] Possible explanations for the apparent anomaly between WTP and WTA include questionnaire design and interviewing techniques; respondent's rejection of the property right implied in the WTP approach; prospect theory (Kahneman and Tversky, 1979) in which individuals have different values for losses and gains of the same magnitude; and lack of substitutes for the commodity being valued (Hanemann, 1991). Adamowicz *et al.* (1993) found some support for Hanemann's hypothesis: in one laboratory study the difference between WTP and WTA was 40% smaller when substitutes were included in the sub-sample than for the sub-sample without the availability of substitutes. But differences between WTP and WTA remained significant even with the inclusion of substitutes.

Most CV studies make strenuous attempts to provide an accurate description of the good, often by way of information in a brochure (see for example, Ecotec, 1993; Loomis and duVair, 1993; Willis *et al.*, 1993a). Photographs in CVM brochure information have also been tested in Britain (see Willis *et al.*, 1993a). The pretest involved a sample of 80

---

[2] However, Macmillan *et al.* (1994) reported good results from a mail survey of Scottish households.

[3] The CVM study of agricultural landscapes in the Yorkshire Dales by Willis and Garrod (1991, 1993a) used both Compensating Variation (CV(WTP)) and Equivalent Variation (EV(WTP)); while the study by Bateman *et al.* (1992, 1993) only assessed an EV(WTP) to-avoid-loss scenario.

[4] This was also demonstrated in a CVM study of the amenity benefits of green belt land in Britain, where WTA was three times WTP values both expressed through a compensation/payment vehicle of local house taxation payments (Willis and Whitby, 1985).

visitors to the Somerset Levels and Moors Environmentally Sensitive Area (ESA), who were shown larger photographs of positive ESA features than those eventually used in the main survey. Mean WTP for the ESA landscape with these photographs was estimated as £15.54 (s.d. £20.96) from a usable sample of 64 after illegitimate bids had been excluded from the analysis. Another sample of 85 respondents who were presented with photographs standardized in size, indicated a mean WTP of £11.30 (s.d. £15.38). Because of the small sample size the difference was only statistically significant at the 12% level. Such pretesting of photographs does not of course indicate what the correct size photographs should be. In addition there are questions of the impact on WTP estimates through variations in landscape backdrop, weather, etc. depicted in the photographs. In an attempt to standardize for these influences Willis and Garrod (1991, 1993a) used montages with the same landscape backdrop, of village, fields, clouds, etc., painted by the same artist, with only the effect being considered (i.e. agricultural policy) permitted to vary. The montage approach to evaluate different alternative policies was also used by Tunstall and Coker (1992) in a study of coastal erosion.

Yes/No follow-ups are increasingly being used in CVM studies to identify legitimate and illegitimate responses to WTP questions. CVM studies of flood protection in the Broads (Bateman *et al.*, 1992, 1993); landscape, wildlife and historical archaeological preservation benefits of landscapes through ESA prescriptions (Willis *et al.*, 1993a); benefits of low flow alleviation in the River Darent (Willis and Garrod, 1993c); and the protection of the aquatic environment from acid rain (Ecotec, 1993), all included questions on why respondents had indicated that their WTP was zero, or why they were WTP an excessive amount for the particular environmental good. Responses to such questions are used to eliminate illegitimate responses (e.g. strategic bids), and identify legitimate bids (e.g. genuine zero bids arising from low income, etc.).

Most CV studies include cross tabulations to assess the relationship of WTP with explanatory variables. Typically this extends to modelling WTP amounts to validate WTP estimates in terms of economic theory. This theoretical validity is usually examined through an estimation of the bid function, typically using a linear functional form. Values of r^2 are often extremely low. In the study by Cobbing and Slee (1993) of the Mar Lodge estate in the Cairngorms only 2% to 3% of the variance in WTP could be explained by independent variables. Good questionnaire design and interviewer training, however, permits a much greater proportion of the variance in WTP responses to be explained: Willis *et al.* (1993a) explained 44.8% in visitor's WTP bids for the Somerset Levels and Moors ESA. Dichotomous choice models tend to indicate high theoretical validity, with price (bid) being the most important explanatory variable explaining demand (probability of consuming the good) (Bateman *et al.*, 1993).

Recommendations Not Generally in Current Use

Sample sizes vary enormously in CV studies. Many, often eminent CV studies (see Cummings *et al.*, 1986), adopt a small sample size (160 or so), which is permissible with an open-ended WTP format and the acceptance of a level of statistical reliability only requiring estimated WTP to lie within 20% of the true WTP 90% of the time. The NOAA Panel recommend large random sample sizes of around 1000, although this mainly derives from their recommendation of the use of referendum type CV WTP formats which require much larger sample sizes than open-ended WTP formats.

The NOAA Panel give no consideration to the complexities involved with sampling strategies. For example, while most CV studies in theory aim at a random sample survey design, a purely random sample survey based on complete enumeration of the relevant population is impossible, because a complete list of the sampling units is rarely available. In such a situation a two-stage stratified sampling strategy is often adopted, e.g. visitors are interviewed only at some sites, with unknown visitor numbers to some or all sites.[5] For non-use values held by the general public (e.g. of ESAs), a number of areas across the country might typically be selected first, within which randomly selected households are then sampled.[6] Choe *et al.* (1994) have shown that increasing the number of sampling areas while maintaining a specified sample size in the second stage, is less efficient statistically than increasing the second stage sample size regardless of the number of areas selected at the first stage.

Another random sampling problem arises when some sample populations are subject to sample selection bias, although a correction can be made in the analysis to deal with this problem (see Willis *et al.*, 1993a; Willis and Garrod, 1993c).

Where referendum type formats have been employed in Britain, sample sizes consistent with or in excess of the recommendation of the NOAA Panel have been adopted. Bateman *et al.* (1992) in a study of the Norfolk Broads had a sample in excess of 3000, split between open-ended, iterative bidding and dichotomous choice formats; while Willis *et al.* (1993a) had a sample of 3000 in a similar study of ESAs.

---

[5] This is typical of surveys valuing landscape regions, see Bateman *et al.* (1992).
[6] This was the approach adopted by Willis and Garrod (1993b) in estimating the non-use values of ESAs.

To test for interviewer effects, the NOAA Panel suggested modifying the standard face-to-face survey to allow respondents to either: (i) write their vote on a ballot and deposit it in a sealed box; or (ii) mail their ballots back to the survey organization. Pretesting for interview effect clearly requires a larger pilot survey than normally employed. This may be impractical on cost grounds for many CV studies. Many surveys do test for interviewer effects in the main survey: it is relatively easy with modern statistical packages like SAS to assess variations in WTP by interviewer.

Reporting on the sample frame and assumptions used in the benefit estimation models occurs more often in USA. This is exemplified by the use of meta analysis to estimate the influence on consumer surplus of variables describing the good to be valued, activities undertaken, behavioural assumptions and specification of the model (see Walsh *et al.*, 1989; Smith and Kaoru, 1990); and also by the fact that one data set is often used by different researchers sometimes years later (see Hanemann, 1984; Cameron, 1988; for example[7]). In Britain it is becoming more commonplace to make CV questionnaires available to other researchers; although data sets still tend to remain the sole property of the original researcher, and not open to subsequent scrutiny and interpretation.

Averaging across independently drawn samples at different points in time, to reduce time dependent measurement 'noise' and assess the reliability of responses,[8] has not been undertaken in CV studies. If the project to be valued creates immediate emotional concern, and/or losses are likely to be interim, i.e. the environment will recover over time,[9] then temporal averaging should be undertaken.

CV studies vary in the weight they give within the CV questionnaire to reminding respondents of substitutes and alternative expenditure possibilities, and the respondent's budget constraint. The questionnaire survey of low flow alleviation in rivers (Willis and Garrod, 1993c) asked:

> What is the maximum sum in additional water rates, over and above that amount you currently pay, that your household would be WTP each year so that alternative water sources could be developed, to eliminate the need

---

[7] Hanemann (1984) reworked the data collected by Bishop and Heberlein (1979) to estimate compensating and equivalent surpluses from discrete choice reponses to WTP and willingness-to-sell (WTS) hunting permits. Cameron also employed previous CV referendum data used by Hanemann (1984); Bishop and Heberlein (1979); Bishop *et al.* (1983); and Seller *et al.* (1985); to show that a Hicksian demand function can be derived from a censored logistic regression. Cameron compares the results of her method with those of the original authors.

[8] A statistically significant time trend would cast doubt on the reliability of the findings.

[9] As happened in 1992 when the oil tanker *Braer* grounded on Shetland. Despite spilling more oil than in the *Exxon Valdez* disaster, within a few months the oil pollution had virtually disappeared.

to abstract more water and reduce flows below current levels in these 40 rivers?, bearing in mind that whatever additional sum you spend in water rates you will have less to spend on other things.

The degree to which budget constraints and substitute goods should be stressed in CV questionnaires is a matter of debate: the NOAA Report did not set specific guide-lines.

It is also rare in CV studies to have agreement on the questionnaire by two opposing parties having an interest in the analysis. Agencies with an interest in the results of a CV study invariably try to influence the framing, or the choice of elicitation method, or the choice of the payment vehicle,[10] in whatever way will produce a favourable outcome to them.

Referendum versus Alternative Elicitation Methods

One of the main recommendations of the NOAA Report was to advocate the use of a referendum format in preference to others in eliciting WTP. The Panel thought open-ended questions were unlikely to provide the most reliable valuations, for non-use estimates, because the scenario lacks realism: respondents are rarely asked in everyday life to put money values on a particular public good; and the fact that the approach invites strategic overstatement.

Nevertheless, in an earlier review of strategic behaviour and its impact on CV studies, Mitchell and Carson (1989) concluded, for a WTP framework, that strategic bias was unlikely to be a major problem, but that if strategic bias was present a slight overestimation of value may be expected. The general absence of revised bids in CV studies where respondents are presented with this opportunity; the analysis of outliers and tests for bimodal distribution; and tests of sub-samples in CV surveys subjected to incentives to under and overstate WTP; generally show either no or weak strategic behaviour. However, truthful demand revelation can only be guaranteed if cooperative behaviour is assumed, or if dishonest responses have positive costs.

The presence of free-riding will result in an under-estimate of WTP for an environmental good. However, studies comparing true payment conditions with those which encouraged free-riding suggest that under experimental conditions free-riding accounts for a modest downward

---

[10] In one CV study (see Willis *et al.*, 1993b), British Coal Opencast attempted to minimize the estimates of externalities of opencast coal mining by suggesting changes to the framing and payment vehicle, in very forcible terms. They suggested a WTP additional 'poll taxes', at a time when protests over this tax and refusals to pay the tax were at their height, rather than using impacts on house prices (British Coal, Opencast, 1991, personal communication).

bias in WTP amounts of 10–30%. Free-riding can be minimized by introducing the risk of potential exclusion from the provision of the good, which results in the convergence of expressed WTP and true WTP amounts; and by identifying those respondents under-bidding in subsequent attitudinal questions on reasons for expressed WTP amounts.

The NOAA Report failed to consider in detail arguments against the use of referendum formats. There is no definitive evidence that referendum models out-perform open-ended (OE), payment card (PC), and iterative bidding (IB) formats for public goods. There is simply no 24 carat gold standard against which results from different methods can be compared. Further, people in Britain are unfamiliar with voting on tax propositions, compared with people in the USA where they are a regular feature of State election processes.

In addition referendum models are expensive requiring a sample of around 1000 or more, compared with 160 to 385 completed

Table 8.1. Mean WTP estimates[1] (£ per annum) to preserve the Norfolk Broads.

(a)

| Truncation option[2] | Linear logistic models | | Log-logistic models | |
	Single variable (BID)	Full model	Single variable (LBID)	Full model
C*	240 (218–261)	238	143 (74–260)	139
C**	242 (225–258)	241	112 (68–168)	111
C***	256 (237–276)	253	144 (75–261)	140

[1] Numbers in parentheses represent 95% confidence intervals around the mean.
[2] Truncation options are as shown in (b).

(b)

Truncation type	Lower truncation point	Upper truncation point
C*	$-\infty$[3]	∞
C**	0	maximum bid amount (£500)
C***	0	∞

[3] Zero in log logistic form for which C* estimates median WTP.
Source: Bateman et al. (1993).

questionnaires in OE, PC, and IB methods to achieve comparable statistical reliability (see Mitchell and Carson, 1989).

Referendum models are sensitive to the functional form of the model and to the truncation points applied to the data. Incorrect choice of functional form can lead to significant error in the estimation of means. In a study of WTP to preserve the Norfolk Broads, a linear logistic form produced mean WTP estimates between 68% and 116% higher than those produced by a log-logistic form (see Table 8.1) (Bateman *et al.*, 1993). Moreover, in a study of devices (risk ladders and pie charts) to communicate risk levels from hazardous waste in CV questionnaires, Loomis and duVair (1993) found that different devices produced statistically different logit equations of the referendum results, and hence different estimates of WTP for reductions in exposure to hazardous waste.

Referendum models appear at first sight to produce better fits than OE models of WTP. However, they are actually modelling a different perspective: referendum models typically model the probability of acceptance at a given price:

$$\text{logit} (.) = f(\text{bid(WTP)}, Y, A, R, P, S, \text{etc.})$$

where

(.) = probability of saying no to a given WTP bid
Y = income
A = age
R = recreational activities undertaken

Table 8.2. Truncation effects: open ended WTP estimates to preserve the Nofolk Broads (£ per annum).

Upper tail truncated (%)	N	Mean WTP[1] (£)	Median WTP (£)	SD	Mean	Minimum bid (£)	Maximum bid (£)	Lower quartile (£)	Upper quartile (£)
0%	846[1]	67.19	30.00	113.85	3.91	0.00	1250.00	5.00	100.00
5%	804	46.76	25.00	55.19	1.95	0.00	250.00	5.00	60.00
10%	762	37.38	25.00	38.64	1.40	0.00	150.00	5.00	50.00
15%	720	32.57	20.00	33.69	1.26	0.00	100.00	2.13	50.00
20%	678	28.39	20.00	30.10	1.16	0.00	100.00	2.00	50.00
25%	635	25.54	12.00	24.41	0.97	0.00	100.00	1.00	50.00

[1] Includes, as zeros, those who refused to pay anything at all.
[2] Total sample of 862 interviews includes 16 incompleted questionnaires (omitted from calculation of mean).
Source: Bateman *et al.* (1993).
SD, standard deviation; SE, standard error.

P = preferences
S = substitutes

whereas OE, PC and IB models typically model WTP as a function of income:

$$\text{WTP(OE)} = f(Y, A, R, P, S, \text{etc.})$$

Of course OE WTP methods are also sensitive to truncation as *trimmed estimators* reveal (see Table 8.2) (Bateman *et al.*, 1993).

Given the limited research budgets of agencies, and the lack of definitive evidence on the superiority of referendum over OE, PC, and IB formats, it seems doubtful if CV studies in Britain will or should adopt only a referendum format.

Embedding Problems

Embedding effects were first observed by Kahneman and Knetsch in 1984 (see Kahneman, 1986, in Cummings *et al.*, 1986) when similar WTP estimates were obtained to clean up lakes in the Muskoka region of Ontario and for all the lakes in Ontario. Although attempts were made to address the problem of part–whole bias (see Willis and Garrod, 1991), the article by Kahneman and Knetsch (1992)[11] focused the attention of environmental economists on the issue. The controversy was further fuelled by the Kemp and Maxwell (1992) experiment in the *Exxon Valdez* case, in which the top-down disaggregation method resulted in estimates of WTP for a particular commodity that were approximately 300 times smaller than those obtained for the same commodity in a comparable single-focus CV survey.

The NOAA Report largely accepted that embedding effects were produced by careless questionnaire design, and that embedding also reflected the fact that different levels of provision of the good had not been clearly specified to respondents. The NOAA Panel also suggested increasing information and context would reduce self-reported warm glow/embedding effects.

---

[11] Kahneman and Knetsch report many pairs of public goods where mean WTP for the specific good was greater than the generic environmental good which encompassed it. For example, WTP for research on dengue fever, a tropical disease $52.42, for research on all tropical diseases $17.83; for protection for the peregrin falcon, an endangered bird $125.00, for all endangered birds $59.07; improve sports facilities in small communitites in British Columbia (BC) $209.75, improve sports facilities in small communitites in Canada $55.96; rehabilitate recently released young offenders $233.16, rehabilitate all recently released criminals $25.04; improve literacy for recent adult BC immigrants $190.53, improve literacy of adults in BC $56.61; replant trees in cutover areas in B.C. $151.70, replant trees in cutover areas in western Canada $54.74; increase research on toxic waste disposal $234.12, increase research on environmental protection $98.77; famine relief in Ethiopia $157.67, famine relief in Africa $72.68; research on breast cancer $243.14, research on all forms of cancer $162.09.

The argument that the value of a good is determined by the context or theatre in which the good is presented is not surprising. Ascertaining respondents' WTP for an additional conifer forest habitat like Kielder Forest in Northumberland, for example, is likely to be much lower than respondents' WTP for protecting the red squirrels in Kielder Forest, even though the conifer forest habitats are the same. Indeed, this is precisely what Willis and Garrod (1993d) found in a study of WTP for different additional habitat protection by members of the North-umberland Wildlife Trust. The change in the context has actually changed the nature of the good respondents are being asked to value. Hence it should not be expected that CVM will estimate similar WTP values in different contexts. The same contextual effects are present in the sale of private goods: respondents' value or utility of a good changes when a salesman or brochure informs a prospective purchaser that good X has some feature which is absent in an otherwise identical good Y. The manner in which goods are presented and described (contextual information) impacts on sales, and price differences. Indeed, if such effects were absent, they would violate Lancaster's (1966) theory of consumer behaviour.

As well as the problems of context and theatre in embedding, the presence or perceived presence of substitutes is also important: as more substitute goods are added to the choice set, the value of any one individual component decreases. Thus it can be argued that the valuation results derived from embedding studies are precisely what would be predicted from simple consumer theory: as the number of substitutes increases, so the consumer surplus on any one particular good declines.[12] Indeed, it has been suggested that the absence of the embedding phenomenon, not its presence, is an indictment of CVM. Loomis *et al.* (1993) found embedding was not always a pervasive feature of CVM, if the spatial context is clearly communicated to the respondent. Although some embedding effects remained, Loomis *et al.* believe CVM provides policy makers and courts with a reasonable indication of the value society places on public goods.

However, there is no exogenous criterion to specify how much information or context to provide to respondents. But if respondents

[12] The substitute problem of course does not explain the Kahneman and Knetsch results reported in footnote 11, where WTP for the specific good was more than that of the generic good of which it was part: these are explained by context and theatre above. But the absence of substitutes in the choice set can explain their other embedding results, where WTP for one specific good was only three to four times less than its generic good area which contained literally hundreds of other substitute goods. Examples in Kahneman and Knetsch include: WTP to reduce acid rain damage in Muskoka, Ontario $40.91, WTP to reduce acid rain damage in eastern Canada $214.55; restore rural BC museums $32.78, restore rural Canada and heritage museums $113.47; improve sport fishing stocks in BC fresh water $41.89, improve sport fishing stocks in Canada fresh water $147.16; protection for marmot, a small animal in BC $33.27, protection for small animals in BC $141.75.

have similar WTP values for different quantities of the same good; or have similar WTP for the same good valued in different scenarios; or in different hierarchical orderings, then the CV results violate the fundamentals economic theory. Thus the effect of different descriptions of the same ecological good, in terms of the number of attributes mentioned as being associated with the good, were found by Hoevenagel and van der Linden (1993) to produce significantly different WTP values, as economic theory predicts.

CV responses cannot be context free. The size and nature of the choice set does, in fact, matter and sequencing effects should be expected. Indeed Randall (1991) has argued that market prices are conditional: they depend on institutions, supply and demand conditions, and expectations about both. The rational markets hypothesis posits that the market price at any moment in time reflects all the available information at that moment.[13] Thus Randall argues that price is conditional, generated by conditions unique to that moment in time: a natural experiment which can never exactly be replicated. As well as observed market prices being conditional, contingent values are also conditional: responses are sensitive to the wording of questions, the inclusiveness of the choice set etc. For some issues there may be no basis for choosing among alternatives. But by deliberate experimentation in choosing alternatives and systematically reporting variations in valuations, it would be possible to map the relationship between reported WTP or WTA and the various conditions which influence value.

This brings us back to one of the main recommendations of the NOAA Panel, stated in the introduction to this chapter, that agencies should begin to accumulate standard damage assessments for a range of situations, in which the assumptions behind the CV estimates were explicitly mapped out. This would not only allow the accuracy of new CV results to be validated, but would also reveal the various conditions which influence CV estimates.

Warm Glow Effects

The NOAA Report argues that warm glow effects should be minimized. The Panel suggest that people only support one or two charitable organizations to the tune of $10 to $20 per year; and that 99.9% of charities receive no support from any individual. Thus, one of

---

[13] Randall cites the notorious sunflowers painting by Van Gogh, valued at $10 million in the early 1980s, purchased by Alan Bond for $50 million in the late 1980s, and sold for less than $30 million two years later.

the expected findings of CVM surveys of the general public is that for minor public goods, or a public good with large numbers of substitutes, 99.9% of the sample should state a zero WTP.

But to what extent is this true in a revealed sense: if someone knocks at your door and asks for a donation to X, even though you don't support X, a donation is often given. To make a donation avoids feelings of embarrassment and conveys a sense of social responsibility to family, friends and the community. Such values are created almost randomly, by someone knocking at your door. These values are WTP to avoid guilt, or to buy a warm glow, and as such would not normally have been paid unless the collector or interviewer had not created the social situation. Should such values be counted? Such values are clearly counted in a revealed sense as part of monies raised by charities, and reported in their annual returns to the Charity Commissioners. Is there any reason therefore to regard such expressed sums, these avoidance of embarrassment effects estimated in a CV survey, as illegitimate? Surely the ultimate test is whether someone would actually pay the stated WTP amount.

Some Framing Issues

Framing can affect the valuations derived for an environmental good through CVM, yet the NOAA Report does not consider to any great extent the issues involved in framing. The NOAA Panel considered that valuation questions should be framed in terms of WTP and not WTA. Yet no logical reason is presented why WTP rather than WTA should be adopted, other than the empirical one of providing a more conservative CV estimate.

Where there is a risk of irreversible or catastrophic environmental effects, some precautionary principle is often adopted, such as a safe minimum standard.[14] The application of such precautionary principles implies the need for better methods of risk assessment. But one of the areas in which the impact of framing on decisions is strongest occurs in risk evaluation. For example, most prefer a 0.25 chance to lose £200 (and a 0.75 chance of losing nothing), to the sure loss of £50. However, when that sure loss is called an insurance premium, people tend to reverse their preferences and forego the £50.

---

[14] This is the basis of the Endangered Species Act in the USA. For a species to be listed, a minimum safe reproductive standard must be defined. This requires scientists to determine the minimum number of individuals required to maintain a viable population (MVP). Typically one of two criteria are used (i) the population size necessary to ensure a given probability that a population will persist for a given duration, e.g. a 95% probability of persistence for 100 years, (ii) the size necessary to ensure that a population will continue to have the capacity to evolve (Hyman and Wernstedt, 1991).

The effect of framing, in terms of lives saved or in terms of lives lost, was graphically documented by Tversky and Kahneman (1982). They asked respondents to imagine 600 people will die unless something is done. Two options are available: option A saves 200 lives for certain; while option B offers a one-third chance of saving 600 and a two-thirds chance of saving nobody. In such a situation most people prefer option A. Another similar group of respondents was again asked to imagine 600 people will die unless something is done. Again two options are available: option C means 400 will die for certain; while option D offers a one-third chance that nobody will die and a two-thirds chance that all 600 will die. Presented with this scenario most people prefer option D. But options A and C are identical, as are options B and D: respondents have merely switched responses as a result of framing.

As with embedding and problems of information, context and theatre, there is no criterion in framing to dictate which questionnaire framework ought to be adopted. The results clearly depend upon the framing, and this should be reported to map the CV estimates in the light of other CV results.

It is clear in CV studies that people's ability to process small probability event changes is limited. Jones-Lee *et al.* (1985) found 47% of respondents had a preference for reducing the event in which the risk of death was 2 in 100,000 to a reduction in the probability of an event where the risk of death was 20 in 100,000; while 48% correctly chose the latter; and 5% were undecided. In the same study 42% of respondents gave the same WTP valuation response in one question for quite different reductions in the risk of death: from 8 to 4 in 100,000 as from 8 to 1 in 100,000. This pattern was repeated in another question where 47% of respondents reported the same WTP to reduce risk of death for 10 to 5 in 100,000 as from 10 to 8 in 100,000.

Many changes to policy in the environment typically result in small changes in the probability of a certain event occurring. In such cases great care is required in interpreting WTP estimates of the benefits of such policy changes.

Framing can affect results in a more traditional way: in terms of the distinction between *ex ante* appraisal and *ex post* evaluation. What is spent on protection *ex ante* is often quite distinct from what people regard as justifiable *ex post*.[15] Some of this difference is an information effect. Bernknopf *et al.* (1990) evaluated the changes in risk perceptions and values following the issuing of official hazard notices about the imminent threat of earthquakes in 1980 and volcanic activity in 1982 in the Mammoth Lakes area of California. These notices were

---

[15] Expenditure on house security after a burglary is a typical example.

subsequently withdrawn, allowing an analysis of risk perceptions, recreation participation, and investment behaviour in housing before, during, and after the issuance of notices. The introduction of natural hazard information into the market was found to alter individuals' perception of risk, and the value of housing, as estimated through a WTP hedonic price model. Hazard notices, however, had no effect on recreation visits.

Embedding problems are likely to be prominent in valuing large numbers of similar goods. For example, in 1992 MAFF initiated a study to value the benefits of two ESAs: the South Downs and Somerset Levels and Moors. How should these two ESAs be valued? A traditional economic approach would be to value these two ESAs conditional on the continued protection and preservation of the other eight. This could be done either by:

1. asking respondents their WTP for the first eight ESAs and then asking their WTP for all ten ESAs: the difference would be the value of the South Downs and Somerset Levels and Moors ESAs.
2. asking respondents to value eight ESAs and then asking respondents their added WTP for the South Downs and Somerset Levels and Moors, given that they are additional to the original eight areas.

Both these approaches essentially consider the ESAs as marginal to the original set, i.e. they are valued at the margin. If there are strong diminishing returns from additional landscape protection then the total value of ten ESAs might only be slightly higher than for eight. Clearly, as the number of ESAs increase, the increase in total WTP will decline given rational behaviour, reflecting the decline in marginal utility (marginal WTP) for each additional ESA landscape unit quantity.

However, since each ESA is not a perfect substitute for another[16] the utility of the South Downs and Somerset Levels and Moors might be greater than, equal to, or less than the utility attached to other ESAs. Hence it is quite possible that any large values attributed to these ESAs do not result from embedding but simply from the greater value of these areas because of their different attributes or location.

In other cases where large numbers of goods are to be valued which are perfect substitutes for each other, e.g. in the case of the non-use value of Sites of Special Scientific Interest (SSSIs) or low flow alleviation (LFA) in rivers, respondents may be quite unable to allocate utility to any one SSSI or to alleviating low flow in any one particular river.

---

[16] Despite each ESA preserving the landscape through supporting traditional farming practices, ESAs cover different landscape types. Moreover, the option price of access to ESAs varies depending upon the location of any one ESA and the residence of the current non-user and prospective visitor.

Nevertheless, such a value may be required if the benefits of LFA have to be compared with the costs in an economic appraisal. In such a situation respondents may allocate:

1. more than a proportionate amount of their total WTP to site X, because they know the site;
2. a zero value, because they don't value the site at all;
3. a strictly proportionate amount because they don't know the site and think LFA must be equally valuable in all rivers (a logical Laplace decision criterion approach);
4. by an 'according to need' criterion (i.e. they postulate that they – probably quite rightly – lack the information necessary to make a judgement and hence decide to let experts decide to allocate resources to protect the site 'according to need' within their overall WTP for LFA in general).

In many ways the last response is a rational reaction given the lack of information on all low flow rivers. Again there are similarities in private good arenas: in unit trusts and private voluntary pension schemes, individuals are explicitly allowing managers to make expenditure allocation for them, within their budget constraint, on the basis of the presumed superior knowledge of the unit trust or other manager.

Contingent values are contingent upon other things in the world being equal. Part of the embedding problem may simply reflect the fact that they are not. When an individual expresses a contingent value for a good, they assume they are not being asked to pay for a whole range of other environmental goods. If individuals are asked the maximum they would be willing to pay for one good while simultaneously being asked the maximum they would be willing to pay for hundreds of other environmental goods then, as economic theory predicts, their WTP for the specific good will be less, because of income effects.

The production of modified national resource accounts requires estimates of the benefits from national resources stocks and changes in stocks. Where modified national resource accounts have been produced this has usually taken the form of reporting sets of environmental indicators or physical quantities, rather than incorporating the value of environmental damage or the value of benefits from environmental improvements. Some organizations are sceptical of the latter approach because the value of environmental goods is not an unambiguous term, since it depends on how the damage is measured (replacement cost, preventative expenditure, compensating variation, etc.), and assessing how the rest of the economy will be affected (changes in relative prices, distribution of income, etc.), and hence have not recommended the preparation of an environmentally adjusted domestic product (Central Bureau of Statistics of Norway, 1992).

However, other economists have sought to modify national resource accounts by applying values of environmental costs and benefits. Adger and Whitby (1991) derived aggregate values of resources and resource changes by simply multiplying the land area of specific designated uses by CVM and other WTP estimates from studies that had evaluated one part of one environmental good, e.g. one green belt or one SSSI. This is justifiable in some instances, e.g. WTP for green belt preservation by residents in one green belt area can be applied to other green belt land, since a different set of residents are involved. But when the same respondents also have to pay for the use and non-use values of national parks, SSSIs, and a whole host of other environmental resources, then aggregating single focus CV WTP responses will overestimate the benefits of environmental resources and resource changes. For modified national resource accounting a national non-point CV survey is required in which all environmental goods of interest are valued simultaneously (see for example Drake, 1993).

Other Issues

The NOAA Report concentrated on only a few of the items of concern to economists, psychologists and statisticians in CV studies. Of course the literature is vast and only the main controversial issues were addressed in relation to the use of CVM to estimate non-use or passive use values of natural resources.

Despite the fact that the inquiry which led to the Report was stimulated by psychologists' concerns over contingent valuation methods (CVMs), the work of psychologists does not figure prominently in the Report except through the problem of embedding. Other issues of concern not addressed by the NOAA Report that ought be be given further attention in CV studies are:

1. Covariation misestimation: even with information respondents tend to consider only two alternatives; whereas judging the effectiveness of a policy prescription requires four positions to be considered.
2. Perceptions of environmental hazards are known to be affected by a number of characteristics: by magnitude of the event (a single large event or large number of small random dispersed events); familiarity with the event and knowledge about the risks involved; the degree of control which respondents believe they have over the event; immediacy of effect; severity of the consequences; newness; commonality or dread; voluntariness; and equity and ethical considerations. It is important to map CV estimates in relation to these factors if we are to understand their contingent nature.

3. Lack of awareness: people often have minimal awareness factors which influence their judgements (Kirwan *et al.*, 1984); hence it is important to understand the process by which respondents arrive at WTP values. Studies in the medical field have shown that feedback through policy capturing equations can lead to convergence in decision making and in the importance and weight which individual experts attached to factors which explain particular outcomes, e.g. disease diagnosis.

4. The effect of information on CV estimates, in terms of:

- overconfidence: people disregard or censor information which conflicts with or contradicts their current views, and conversely seek confirmatory evidence which supports their views. To what extent does this affect CV WTP estimates?

- the way in which respondents process information: studies have shown that individuals place too much emphasis on recent or new information or test results, and ignore prior probabilities of events: people do not in general think in Bayesian terms. Nor do they necessarily think in terms of expected utility, but may adopt some alternative decision making and valuation framework, e.g. regret theory (see Loomes and Sugden, 1982). In any contingency forecast or WTP estimate, the experimental outcome of a set task depends upon whether the respondent adopts an aleatory or an epistemic strategy. It would be helpful if the investigator knew which strategy was being adopted (Beach *et al.*, 1986).

Eliciting people's values is a pursuit central to CV. Most economists tend to work within a paradigm in which people are assumed to be able to articulate and express values on the most diverse range of topics. This paradigm leads to the concerns (e.g. strategic response, etc.), treatment (e.g. proper incentives, referendum models, etc.), theoretical base (e.g. demand analysis, etc.), and tests of success (e.g. sensible answers, etc.), discussed by the NOAA Panel.

But there are other paradigms against which elicited values and CV responses can be judged: paradigms of basic values, and partial perspectives. The perspective of basic values recognizes that people's time is limited, with the set of possible evaluative questions very large indeed. Consequently, people cannot be expected to have articulated values on more than a small number of issues of immediate concern. High rates of 'don't know' responses in CV studies, embedding, failure to express WTP in decreasing amounts for marginal increases in consumption of a good (e.g. days improvements in atmospheric visibility (Tolley *et al.*, 1986), or days of relief from tiredness or headaches (Dickie *et al.*, 1987)), are evidence that people have pertinent but inarticulate values for some goods. An intermediate position views people as working within a partial perspectives paradigm: of having stable but incoherent perspectives, causing divergent responses to formally equivalent forms. People lack well-differentiated values for all but the most familar evaluation questions, about which they have had the chance, by trial, error, and rumination to settle on stable values. In other cases, they must derive specific valuations from some basic values through an inferential process.

A broader consideration of the characteristics upon which elicited values are based than that contained in the NOAA Report might offer a fruitful avenue of research (Fischhoff, 1991); the identification of conditions favourable to the elicitation of articulated values; and more confidence in the results of CV studies, results which can have enormous policy consequences in terms of environmental investment and regulation.

CV and the Law

Both CV estimates and non-use values are recognized in law in the USA (see Loomis, 1996). Compensation for damages to non-use environmental values is remitted to the federal government's Superfund, to pay for environmental clean-ups where compensation cannot be claimed, perhaps because a firm is no longer in business.

Environmental damage in English law is regulated by both criminal law (e.g. under the Wildlife and Countryside Act 1981, and other Acts), and, to the extent that it affects individuals, tort law. In the latter case compensation for damage is assessed in terms of loss of use. The loss is determined by the market value of the lost resource, plus transactions costs. The term loss in English law only has clear meaning when things are valued objectively in the sense that there is a market in what has been lost. Non-pecuniary losses (e.g. in relation to health effects such as loss of limbs, etc.) are regarded as essentially arbitrary.

Perhaps the nearest non-use values come to be recognized is in exemplary damages. Exemplary damages are amounts awarded over and above the loss suffered as a result of tortious conduct. Exemplary damages were claimed by the plaintiffs in *Gibbons and others* v. *South West Water Services Ltd* when 20 tons of aluminium sulphate were accidently introduced into the defendant's drinking water system via the Company's treatment works in Camelford, Cornwall, in 1988. The plaintiffs drank the contaminated water and a variety of ill effects resulted. The defendant admitted liability, but the plaintiffs alleged they were also entitled to exemplary damages, for withholding accurate and consistent information about the water, failing to give proper information to health authorities, failing to advise on precautions to minimize the ill effects of drinking the water, and for failing to close down the water plant and supply fresh water.

Arguments against exemplary damages centre on their payment to individuals affected by the tort: the unjust enrichment (compensation exceeds losses) to the individual; and their apportionment between individuals (Cane, 1993). While exemplary damages serve as a deterrent over and above use value losses, they do not specifically reflect the magnitude of passive use values lost.

There is a clear economic case for counting passive use values. Enacting new legislation to create a Superfund along American lines would have a number of advantages. It would permit compensation for passive use losses to be entered into the public domain for environmental protection and clean-ups which benefit society as a whole; and would ensure both environmental improvement from the money while avoiding the unsatisfactory nature and allocation of the current legal framework encompassing exemplary damages.

Acknowledgements

An earlier version of this paper was delivered to a Department of the Environment GECB Environmental Valuation group meeting in July 1993, and this revised version is presented with the kind permission of DoE. The views expressed, however, are those of the author alone, and do not necessarily reflect the views of the Department of the Environment.

References

Adamowicz, W.L., Bhardwaj, V. and Macnab, B. (1993) Experiments on the difference between willingness to pay and willingness to accept. *Land Economics* 69, 416–427.

Adger, N. and Whitby, M.C. (1991) National accounting for the externalities of agriculture and forestry. *Countryside Change Working Paper Series, WP 16.* Countryside Change Unit, Department of Agricultural Economics and Food Marketing, University of Newcastle upon Tyne.

Arrow, K., Solow, R., Portney, P.R., Leamer, E.E., Radner, R. and Schuman, H. (1993) Report of the NOAA Panel on Contingent Valuation. *Federal Register* 58(10), 4601–4614.

Bateman, I.J. and Turner, R.K. (1993) Valuation of the environment, methods and techniques: the contingent valuation method. In: Turner R.K. (ed.) *Sustainable Environmental Economics and Management.* Belhaven, London.

Bateman, I.J., Willis, K.G., Garrod, G.D., Doktor, P., Langford, I.H. and Turner, R.K. (1992) Recreation and environment preservation in the Norfolk

Broads: a contingent valuation study. *Report to the National Rivers Authority.* Environmental Appraisal Group, University of East Anglia, Norwich.

Bateman, I.J., Langford, I.H., Willis, K.G., Turner, R.K. and Garrod, G.D. (1993) The impacts of changing willingness to pay question format in contingent valuation studies: an analysis of open-ended, iterative bidding and dichotomous choice formats. *CSERGE Working Paper GEC 93-05.* Centre for Social and Economic Research on the Global Environment, University of East Anglia, Norwich, and University College, London.

Beach, L.R., Barnes, V.E. and Christensen-Szalanski, J.J.J. (1986) Beyond heuristics and biases: a contingency model of judgemental forecasting. *Journal of Forecasting* 5, 143–157.

Bernknopf, R.L., Brookshire, D.S. and Thayer, M.A. (1990) Earthquake and volcano hazard notices: an economic evaluation of changes in risk perceptions. *Journal of Environmental Economics and Management* 18, 35–49.

Bishop, R.C. and Heberlein, T.A. (1979) Measuring values of extra market goods: are indirect measures biased? *American Journal of Agricultural Economics* 61(5), 926–930.

Bishop, R.C., Heberlein, T.A. and Kealy, M.J. (1983) Hypothetical bias in contingent valuation: results from a simulated market. *Natural Resources Journal* 23(3), 619–633.

Cameron, T.A. (1988) A new paradigm for valuing non-market goods using referendum data: maximum likelihood estimation by censored logistic regression. *Journal of Environmental Economics and Management* 15, 355–379.

Cane, P. (1993) The scope and justification of exemplary damages: the Camelford case. *Journal of Environmental Law* 5(1), 149–172.

Central Bureau of Statistics of Norway (1992) *Natural Resources and the Environment 1991.* Rapporter 92/1A. Central Bureau of Statistics of Norway, Oslo.

Choe, K.A., Parke, W.R. and Whittington, D. (1994) A Monte Carlo comparison of OLS estimation errors and design efficiencies in a two-stage stratified random sampling procedure for contingent valuation study. Mimeo. Department of City and Regional Planning, University of North Carolina at Chapel Hill. Chapel Hill, North Carolina.

Cobbing, P. and Slee, B. (1993) A contingent valuation of the Mar Lodge Estate, Cairngorm Mountains, Scotland. *Journal of Environmental Planning and Management* 36, 65–72.

Cummings, R.G., Brookshire, D.S. and Schulz, W.D. (1986) *Valuing Environmental Goods: An Assessment of the Contingent Valuation Method.* Rowman and Allenheld, Totowa, New Jersey.

Dickie, M., Greking, D., Brookshire, D., Coursey, D., Schulze, W., Coulson, A. and Tashkin, D. (1987) Reconciling averting behaviour and contingent valuation benefit estimates of reducing symptoms of ozone exposure, in US Environmental Protection Agency. *Improving Accuracy and Reducing Costs of Environmental Benefit Assessment.* US Environmental Protection Agency, Washington DC.

Drake, L. (1993) *Relations among Environmental Effects and Their Implications for Efficiency of Policy Instruments: An Economic Analysis Applied to Swedish*

Agriculture. Department of Economics, Swedish University of Agricultural Sciences, Uppsala, Sweden.

Ecotec (1993) *Contingent Valuation of Acquatic Ecosystems*. Ecotec, Birmingham.

Fischhoff, B. (1991) Value elicitation: is there anything in there? *American Psychologist* 46(8), 835–847.

Hanemann, W.M. (1984) Welfare evaluations in contingent valuation experiments with discrete responses. *American Journal of Agricultural Economics* 66, 332–341.

Hanemann, W.M. (1991) Willingness to pay and willingness to accept: how much can they differ? *American Economic Review* 81(3), 635–645.

Hovenagel, R. and van der Linden, J.W. (1993) Effects of different descriptions of the ecological good on willingness to pay values. *Ecological Economics* 7, 223–238.

Hyman, J.B. and Wernstedt, K. (1991) The role of biological and economic analyses in the listing of endangered species. *Resources* No. 104, 5–9. Recources for the Future, Spring 1995.

Jones-Lee, M.W. (1976) *The Value of Life: An Economic Analysis*. Martin Robertson, London.

Jones-Lee, M.W., Hammerton, M. and Philips, P.R. (1985) The value of safety: results of a national sample survey. *The Economic Journal* 95, 49–72.

Kahneman, D. (1986) Comments by Professor Daniel Kahneman. In: Cummings, R.G., Brookshire, D.S. and Schulze, W.D. (eds) *Valuing Environmental Goods: An Assessment of the Contingent Valuation Method*. Rowman & Allenheld, Totowa, New Jersey, pp. 185–197.

Kahneman, D. and Knetsch, J.L. (1992) Valuing public goods: the purchase of moral satisfaction. *Journal of Environmental Economics and Management* 22, 57–70.

Kahneman, D. and Tversky, A. (1979) Prospect theory: an analysis of decision under risk. *Econometrica* 47, 263–291.

Kemp, M.A. and Maxwell, C. (1992) *Exploring a Budget Context for Contingent Valuation Estimates*. Cambridge Economics Inc., Cambridge, Massachusetts.

Kirwan, J.R., Chaput de Saintonge, D.M., Joyce, C.R.B. and Curry, H.L.F. (1984) Clinical judgement in rheumatoid arthritis III: British rheumatologists' judgements of change in response to therapy. *Annals of the Rheumatic Disease* 43, 686–694.

Lancaster, K. (1966) A new approach to consumer theory. *Journal of Political Economy* 74, 132–157.

Loomes, G. and Sugden, R. (1982) Regret theory: an alternative theory of rational choice under uncertainty. *The Economic Journal* 92, 805–824.

Loomis, J. (1996) A sampler of uses of contingent valuation methodology in the United States. In: Bateman, I. and Willis, K.G. (eds) *Valuing Environmental Preferences*. Oxford University Press, Oxford.

Loomis, J.B. and duVair, P.H. (1993) Evaluating the effect of alternative risk communication devices on willingness to pay: results from a dichotomous choice contingent valuation experiment. *Land Economics* 69(3), 287–298.

Loomis, J., Lockwood, M. and DeLacy, T. (1993) Some empirical evidence on embedding effects in contingent valuation of forest protection. *Journal of Environmental Economics and Management* 24, 45–55.

Macmillan, D., Hanley, N. and Buckland, S. (1994) Valuing biodiversity losses due to acid deposition: a contingent valuation survey of uncertain environmental gains. Paper presented to the European Association of Environmental and Resource Economists' annual conference, Dublin. Macaulay Land Research Institute, Aberdeen.

Mitchell, R.C. and Carson, R.T. (1989) *Using Surveys to Value Public Goods: The Contingent Valuation Method.* Resources for the Future, Washington DC.

Parkman, A.M. (1985) The multiplier in English fatal accident cases: what happens when judges teach judges economics. *International Review of Law and Economics* 5, 187–197.

Randall, A. (1991) Self-reported values and observable transactions: is there a trump in the deck? *Invited Paper, W-133.* Western Regional Science Association Meeting, Monterey, CA. 27/2/91. Department of Agricultural Economics and Rural Sociology, Ohio State University, Columbus, Ohio.

Seller, C., Stoll, J.R. and Chavas, J.P. (1985) Validation of empirical measures of welfare change: a comparison of non-market techniques. *Land Economics* 61, 156–175.

Smith, V.K. and Kaoru, Y. (1990) Signals or noise? explaining the variation in recreation benefit estimates. *American Journal of Agricultural Economics* 72, 419–433.

Tolley, G.S., Randall, A., Blomquist, G., Fabian, R., Fishelson, R., Frankel, J.P., Krumm, R. and Mensah, E. (1986) *Establishing and Valuing the Effects of Improved Visibility in the Eastern United States.* Report for USEPA. US Environmental Protection Agency, Washington DC.

Tunstall, S. M. and Coker, A. (1992) Survey based valuation methods. In: Coker, A. and Richards, C. (eds) *Valuing the Environment: Economic Approaches to Environmental Evaluation.* Belhaven, London.

Tversky, A. and Kahneman, D. (1982) The framing of decisions and the pyschology of choice. *New Directions for Methodology of Social and Behavioural Science: Question Framing and Consistency Response* 11, 3–20.

Walsh, R.G., Johnson, D.M. and McKean, J.R. (1989) Issues in non-market valuation and policy application: a retrospective glance. *Western Journal of Agricultural Economics* 14, 178–188.

Willig, R.G. (1976) Consumer's surplus without apology. *American Economic Review* 66, 589–597.

Willis, K.G. and Whitby, M.C. (1985) The value of green belt land. *Journal of Rural Studies* 1, 147–162.

Willis, K.G. (1994) Paying for heritage: what price for Durham Cathedral? *Journal of Environmental Planning and Management* 37, 267–278.

Willis, K.G. and Garrod, G.D. (1991) Landscape values: a contingent valuation approach and case study of the Yorkshire Dales National Park. *Countryside Change Working Paper Series, WP 21.* Countryside Change Unit, Department of Agricultural Economics and Food Marketing, University of Newcastle upon Tyne.

Willis, K.G. and Garrod, G.D. (1993a) Landscape values: a contingent valuation approach. *Journal of Environmental Management* 37, 1–22.

Willis, K.G. and Garrod, G.D (1993b) Valuation of the South Downs and Somerset Levels and Moors Environmentally Sensitive Area Landscapes by the General Public. *Appendices Report of the Ministry of Agriculture, Fisheries and Food.* Centre for Rural Economy, Department of Agricultural Economics and Food Marketing, University of Newcastle upon Tyne.

Willis, K.G. and Garrod, G.D. (1993c) The benefits of low flow alleviation in the River Darent. *Report to the National Rivers Authority.* Centre for Rural Economy, Department of Agricultural Economics and Food Marketing, University of Newcastle upon Tyne.

Willis, K.G. and Garrod, G.D. (1993d) The benefits of a Northumberland Wildlife Trust Programmes. *Countryside Change Working Paper Series, WP 47.* Countryside Change Unit, Department of Agricultural Economics and Food Marketing, University of Newcastle upon Tyne.

Willis, K.G., Garrod, G.D, and Saunders, C.M. (1993a) Valuation of the South Downs and Somerset Levels and Moors Environmentally Sensitive Area Landscapes by the General Public. *Report of the Ministry of Agriculture, Fisheries and Food.* Centre for Rural Economy, Department of Agricultural Economics and Food Marketing, University of Newcastle upon Tyne.

Willis, K.G., Nelson, G.B., Bye, A.B. and Peacock, G. (1993b) An application of the Krutilla–Fisher model for evaluating the benefits of green belt preservation versus site development. *Journal of Environmental Management* 36, 73–90.

_____ **9** _____

Alternative Valuation Techniques: A Comparison and Movement to a Synthesis[1]

Vic Adamowicz

University of Alberta

Introduction

Measuring the value of environmental goods and services has become an integral part of environmental economics over the past 30 years. As an area of research, this subject has grown rapidly. This increase in research activity has resulted in an increased understanding of the scope and limitations of non-market valuation methods. This chapter outlines the advantages and disadvantages of each of the major methods of valuing environmental goods and services. It does not concentrate on the advantages and disadvantages of valuation *per se* but simply assumes that valuation measures provide information that is useful to decision makers.

In order to assess alternative valuation techniques, it is first necessary to define the various types of value that economists are interested in, and to describe the major approaches to measuring these values. Some of the advantages and disadvantages of the various techniques will arise directly from these descriptions and definitions. Describing the techniques in more detail reveals some further pros and cons associated with each technique. Finally, attention is turned to a more detailed analysis of a new form of valuation method, the stated preference method, that arises from market research techniques common in the marketing literature. This new technique offers some advantages relative to current methods. Also, the stated preference technique shares a common theoretical base with current non-market valuation techniques and can be used in conjunction with them.

[1] Thanks to Ken Willis, Guy Garrod, and Colin Price for helpful comments on a draft of this paper.

144

Types of Values and Valuation Techniques

There are two broad classes of value, use values and passive use values. Use values are values related to some form of activity or expenditure (of money or time). Values associated with outdoor recreation are the most frequently cited examples of use values. Passive use values (or non-use values) are values that are not associated with any 'economic' behaviour.[2] Existence values are passive use values as there is no change in behaviour (expenditures, etc.) associated with this value. Similarly, there are two broad classes of valuation techniques, direct and indirect. Direct techniques (or conversational techniques) involve descriptions of situations to individuals and assessment of their valuations through direct questions. Contingent valuation and stated preference are examples of direct techniques. Indirect techniques use information on actual behaviour to build economic models of choice. These models are then used to determine the value of environmental change. Typical examples of indirect methods are the travel cost model of recreation demand and the hedonic price method.

As illustrated in Table 9.1, use values are measurable using either direct or indirect techniques. However, passive use values are only measurable using direct techniques.[3] Therefore, a large class of economic values are not measurable using indirect techniques. This is clearly a limitation of the approach. Nevertheless, there still exist a large number of cases in which use values are important (property value changes, recreation) thus indirect methods will continue to be required.

A second distinction in types of value is the measurement of total values associated with environmental goods (e.g. parks) or activities

Table 9.1. Values and valuation techniques.

Types of value	Valuation technique	
	Direct	Indirect
Use values	X	X
Passive use values	X	?

---

[2] The concept of passive use value is not an uncontroversial one. There are still several economists who suggest that values cannot exist without some form of behavioural trail. However, recent court judgements in the US have included passive use values as legitimate forms of value.

[3] There are some efforts to uncover passive use values from observed behaviour. See Larson (1992) for an example of such research.

(e.g. hiking) versus measurement of values associated with quality changes. The latter have become more important since most major environmental issues typically involve a change in quality rather than total losses. Thus, techniques that cannot measure quality changes are limited in scope.

Finally, use values and passive use values can be measured as willingness to pay values or willingness to accept compensation. The former have dominated the literature as they appear to be easier to elicit. However, the differences between willingness to pay and willingness to accept compensation may be significant in a policy context. This topic is explored further later in the chapter.

Given this introduction to valuation, the following sections will examine the two major approaches to valuation, direct and indirect, with primary focus on the ability of these techniques to value changes in environmental quality.

Revealed Preference Techniques

Revealed preference techniques (RP) are based on models of actual market behaviour. Examples of RP techniques include travel cost models and hedonic price models. Reviews of the technical aspects of these methods can be found in Braden and Kolstad (1991). In general, these techniques use observations of actual choice and observations of factors affecting choice (price, environmental quality attributes, individual specific attributes, etc.) to develop models of demand for goods or services.

An advantage of RP techniques is the fact that they are testable (can be validated using 'holdout data' or data from subsequent periods). In most cases direct techniques, especially contingent valuation, cannot be easily validated. Indirect techniques are based on traditional economic theory which provides several decades of experience in empirical modelling. Therefore, economists have preferred to use these approaches and have defended them strenuously.

However, revealed preference methods have a number of drawbacks. First, they can only be used to measure use values. This immediately removes them from consideration for a large class of environmental effects. Second, the behavioural implications of the models used are often somewhat unusual. The traditional travel cost model, for example, assumes that individuals reach a decision on the number of trips they will take at the beginning of a 'season' and are not affected by occurrences throughout the season. Travel cost models also make specific assumptions on the value of time. These problems arise, as they do in any form of demand analysis, because a relatively simple model is being used to describe choice behaviour. The behavioural model becomes a maintained hypothesis in the modelling process.

Since revealed preference models rely on statistical estimation of parameters, they suffer from a host of statistical problems. Revealed preference models often suffer from measurement error. In analysing environmental impacts, for example, it is the individual's perception of the environmental change that should affect their behaviour, and not, in general, the parts per million change measured by the scientist. Revealed preference models also rely on information that is currently available. If the environmental change involves a state that is not within the current realm of experience, it will be difficult to estimate the impact of such a change. Finally, revealed preference models suffer from collinearity. Physical variables (or even prices) are often correlated in reality, and models have difficulty in separating the effects of individual variables. This problem has been recognized in the hedonic price literature and is currently being recognized in the discrete choice travel cost literature.

While revealed preference models are easily criticized on the grounds above, they still have the advantage of being based on actual behaviour. Furthermore, it seems that the best way to model learning, dynamic effects and habit forming behaviour is through the use of revealed preference models, or perhaps models combining revealed and stated preference information.[4]

An interesting development in the revealed preference literature is the movement towards random utility models for the analysis of choice. Random utility models originated in the transportation field where they were used to study travel mode choice. This approach was adapted by recreation demand modellers because it offered a useful method for analysing choices as a function of quality attributes as well as price (or travel cost). Recent results in the hedonic price literature suggest that random utility specifications may offer substantial gains in the measurement of the value of environmental improvements reflected in real estate values (Cropper *et al.*, 1993). Finally, random utility theory forms the basis for referendum contingent valuation and for stated preference methods of choice analysis. Both of these topics are discussed below. The fact that these three major forms of valuation employ the same underlying theoretical model provides a framework to compare and combine the various methods.

---

[4] Hensher (1994) discusses how stated preference techniques may be used to help identify learning and other forms of dynamic behaviour.

Contingent Valuation

Contingent valuation (CV) has been increasing in use and popularity over the past ten years. Rather than relying on specific models of behaviour, contingent valuation practitioners avoid the entire issue by directly eliciting value. Contingent valuation appears in open-ended forms, directly eliciting payments, and in closed-ended (referendum) forms, eliciting a yes–no response to a particular payment amount. A variety of extensions and modifications of these two methods are discussed in Carson (1991). Contingent valuation has the advantage of being able to measure passive use values and use values. Therefore, it has become the method of choice for many applied environmental economists.

Contingent valuation exercises typically involve informing the individual about current conditions (prices, income, environmental conditions, property rights, etc.), and then informing them about a change. The individual is asked to value an 'event,' or a particular change in environmental conditions. This format leads to a number of difficulties. First, there is always the possibility of strategic behaviour. Individuals may understate their willingness to pay if they feel that they can free-ride or they may overstate their willingness to pay if they feel provision of the improved situation is not conditional on their actual payment. Second, and somewhat conversely to the item discussed above, individuals may become 'yea-sayers.' The phenomenon of supporting environmental 'good causes' regardless of the amount it will cost the individual, seems to be quite pervasive in the literature. Third, the hypothetical nature of the process requires careful structuring of information to inform respondents about the salient points while not overloading them with unnecessary description. Accurate assessments of the environmental change require appropriate information provision. A variety of other problems that can arise with contingent valuation, including responses bias, starting point bias, etc., are discussed in Mitchell and Carson (1989) and Carson (1991).

One of the most controversial findings about contingent valuation is the possibility of embedding effects. Embedding is best explained by an example. If there is one environmental good (A) and a subset of this good (S), one would expect the subset to be worth less than the overall good. However, several researchers are finding that A is valued more than S if the same individuals are asked these questions but if one group is asked to value A and another S, their values do not differ. This implies that the value of good S depends on the question order (first or second) and that individuals place the same value on goods A and S if they are both in the first position. This unusual result led Kahneman and Knetsch (1992) to suggest that individuals were paying for moral satisfaction rather than for goods as they would be priced in a market. While there have been a number of heated debates on this issue, the issue remains controversial and worthy of concern.

The recent experience in the US with the Exxon Valdez case has raised the issue of valuation to new heights within the academic community. The result has been the publication of the National Oceanic and Atmospheric Administration (NOAA) report on contingent valuation (Arrow *et al.*, 1993). This report highlights some of the issues that must be considered when conducting CV experiments. These include, survey administration, information provision, use of referendum questions, choice of conservative values, etc. The NOAA proceedings suggest that contingent valuation can be used to produce credible estimates of passive use values. However, there are a number of traps that the researcher can fall into and care must be taken in the design and administration of such processes. Contingent valuation, however, is only one type of 'conversational' approach to eliciting preferences. In the marketing and decision research literature other methods have been devised, and these methods are now discussed.

Stated Preference Methods

Stated preference (SP) analysis, or the experimental analysis of choice, has its roots in conjoint analysis. Conjoint analysis is a form of analysis used to represent individual judgements of multiattribute stimuli (Batsell and Louviere, 1991). Conjoint analysis is a well-known technique and has been applied in marketing for over 20 years. However, conjoint techniques have more recently been applied in geography, transportation, and economics (Louviere, 1991). The particular type of conjoint analysis discussed here is the experimental analysis of choice. This method involves the analysis of the choice situation in terms of attributes and the design of experiments that allow for the estimation of discrete choice models reflecting the tradeoffs an individual makes between attributes. This particular approach is worthy of note because it parallels the Random Utility Model structure (McFadden, 1974; Ben-Akiva and Lerman, 1985) that is common in referendum CV (Mitchell and Carson, 1989) models and in discrete choice travel cost models (Bockstael *et al.*, 1991).

Contingent valuation involves describing to the respondent, through the use of various information provision instruments, the precise changes that will occur in the good or service (the environment). The individual is then typically asked to respond to a tradeoff question regarding paying for the improved good or service. The problem with this approach is that it relies heavily on the accuracy of the 'information', and any errors in the description discovered after the fact cannot be changed. The SP approach, on the other hand, relies on the representation of the choice situation (rather than the specific change in the good or service) using an array of attributes.[5] The SP approach relies less on the accuracy and completeness of any particular description of the good or service, but more on the accuracy and completeness of the characteristics and features used to describe the situation. Rather than being questioned about a single event in detail, therefore, consumers are questioned about a sample of events drawn from the universe of possible events of that type (Louviere, 1994).

Using these attributes and levels, experimental design procedures are then used to make 'packages' of attributes and levels that reflect different states of the world. Individuals are then asked to choose their preferred alternative from a 'choice set' made up of two or three different 'packages.' This choice process reflects the tradeoffs that each individual makes between the attributes of the situation.

The choice process is examined using random utility theory. Each alternative (i) in the choice set has an associated utility level for each individual represented by:

$$U_i = V_i + \varepsilon_i$$

This utility contains an objective component (V_i) and an error component (ε_i). In the economics literature this function is also known as a conditional indirect utility function since it is conditional on the choice of the object (i). Selection of one object (package of attributes) over another implies that the utility (U_i) of that object is greater than the utility of the other (U_j). Since overall utility is a random one it can only analyse the probability of choice of one package over another, or:

$$Pr\{i \text{ chosen}\} = Pr\{V_i + \varepsilon_i > V_j + \varepsilon_j; \forall j \text{ in } C\}$$

Specific choices of error distributions lead to methods for the estimation of the parameters of this utility function, and quantitative representations of tradeoffs between attributes. If the errors are Type I extreme value distributed,[6] the probability of choice can be represented by the multinomial logit distribution. The probability of choice is expressed as a function of the attributes.

The random utility model described above provides the basis for the experimental choice process. In typical stated preference experi-

---

[5] Price (1978) discussed methods that considered the attributes of landscapes in valuation methods. While researchers in marketing, transportation and psychology have adopted these types of techniques, economists have been hesitant to use stated preference, attribute based, techniques.

[6] A Type I extreme value distribution is a particular statistical distribution. An alternative assumption would be normally distributed errors, leading to the use of multinomial probit model.

ments, the levels of various attributes of the choice situation (including the 'price') are varied in a systematic fashion. Therefore, SP can provide values associated with the attributes of the change, as well as the overall change.[7] Also, SP typically entails repeated measure responses from the individual while CV and RP (revealed preference) methods do not.[8] Nevertheless, both techniques arise from the same theoretical background.

Stated preference methods, since they are structured as choices, have the same survey design advantages as referendum CV methods. That is, there are likely to be fewer refusals and the choice approach is more familiar to the respondent. Issues of information provision (attribute definition), and other survey implementation problems arise just as in any CV experiment. However, the repeated sampling method employed in SP can alleviate some of the concerns regarding lower informational efficiency that affects the referendum CV model (Carson, 1991). Furthermore, SP methods, appropriately designed, should alleviate the problem of 'yea saying' since there is no clear environmental good cause to support. Whether SP suffers from embedding or not is a topic for further research. In one sense, SP can avoid embedding by structuring subsets of the overall environmental good within the attribute set. However, this may not be the best solution to the embedding problem (Arrow *et al.*, 1993).

Revealed preference (RP) models also employ random utility theory. Typically these are models of recreational site choice or some other form of qualitative choice (Bockstael *et al.*, 1991). In this case the objective component of the utility function is composed of measures of attributes of the 'real' alternatives. SP techniques directly parallel these qualitative choice models, however, SP approaches avoid measurement error and collinearity effects common in RP methods.

Stated preference methods can be used as complements to CV and RP methods or as substitutes. They can be complements in that the information from these approaches can be combined to yield a richer overall result (Swait and Louviere, 1993; Adamowicz *et al.*, 1994). They can be substitutes since SP methods on their own are representations of individual choice consistent with random utility theory. Furthermore, SP can examine situations (attributes, levels) that do not exist in currently available options. In such cases, RP is limited in scope since it relies on currently available attributes in generating behavioural representations of choice. Furthermore, SP methods may be very useful

[7] Being able to value attributes may be important if the actual physical effect being valued is uncertain. A CV experiment would have to be performed for each level of the environmental change. The SP approach would provide values for each level.

[8] There has been some movement toward a type of repeated measures response in CV via the double bounded or triple bounded referendum CV models (e.g. Hanemann *et al.*, 1991).

in benefits transfer exercises.[9] If the attribute space in the model includes the characteristics under study in the region one wishes to transfer benefits to, and the model is segmented to take into account differences in socioeconomic factors, the benefit transfer process is feasible.[10] To illustrate the application of the SP approach, an example is now provided of recreational site choice. This application also includes a RP analysis and a combined SP–RP analysis.

Example: The Impact of Water Resource Development on Recreational Values

In this example the stated preference approach is used to characterize recreationist choice of sites (Adamowicz *et al.*, 1994). Some of these sites will be affected by a water resource development project that will affect fishing quality and other attributes of the sites. The attributes used to describe the sites in the stated preference model were chosen based on the actual ranges of attributes of the sites in the study region. These ranges of actual values were used to develop categories or levels of the attributes. For example, distances travelled by recreationists living in this region range from about 25 km to about 150 km. A set of four levels of distance (25 km, 50 km, 100 km and 150 km) were used in the stated preference experiment to describe the attribute distance. Information on actual choice was also elicited from these recreationists. This information was used to develop a discrete choice model of actual site choice, based on the same type of factors as the stated preference model. Thus, the two techniques use similar factors to explain choice; revealed choice and stated choice.

In order to design the choice sets, a set of attributes affecting the choice of recreational sites was developed to reflect actual character- istics of water-based recreational resources in the study area. These 13 attributes and the levels chosen for the analysis are listed in Table 9.2. The set of attributes and levels displayed in Table 9.2 can be viewed as setting the space to be spanned in the choice experiment. If each attribute is treated as discrete, as in Table 9.2, there are $2^6 \times 4^5$ possible standing water alternatives, and an additional $2^5 \times 4^5$ possible running water alternatives. The problem of choice set construction, therefore, can be viewed as sampling from the universe of possible pairs of standing and running water alternatives. The survey was designed such that respondents had to choose among: (i) a standing water option,

---

[9] Benefits transfer is the process of using a valuation study in one region to value changes in a similar environmental situation in a different region.

[10] Also, the fact that SP models alleviate collinearity problems in RP models suggests that SP (or combined SP and RP) models may perform better in benefits transfer exercises.

Table 9.2. List of attributes used in the stated preference experiment of water recreation site choice.

1. Terrain
    Flat prairie
    Rolling prairie
    Foothills
    Mountain
2. Fish size
    Large
    Small
3. Fish catch rate
    1 fish per 4 hours
    1 fish per 80 minutes
    1 fish per 45 minutes
    1 fish per 35 minutes
4. Water quality
    Good
    Bad
5. Facilities
    None
    Day-use only
    Limited facility campsite
    Fully serviced campsite
6. Swimming
    Yes
    No
7. Beach
    Yes
    No
8. Distance
    25 km
    50 km
    100 km
    150 km

Standing water	*Running water*
9. Water feature	9. Water feature
Natural lake	River
Reservoir	Stream
10. Fish species	10. Fish species
Pike and perch	Mountain whitefish
Pickerel, pike and perch	Rainbow trout and mountain whitefish
	Rainbow trout, mountain whitefish and brown trout
	Cutthroat trout, mountain whitefish and bull trout

11. Boating
    None
    Small crafts
    Power boats (limited)
    No restrictions

Table 9.3. Example of stated preference question.

Recreational opportunities:
Suppose last August that you could have chosen only from the recreational opportunities described below.

	A. Standing water	B. Running water	C. Non-water
Water feature	Reservoir	River	
Terrain	Rolling prairie	Foothills	
Driving distance	25 km	150 km	
Fishing:			Any other
Types of fish	Pike and perch	Mountain whitefish	non-water related
Fish size	Small	Large	recreational
Typical fishing			activity or
success	1 fish every 35 minutes	1 fish every 35 minutes	stay at home
Camping facilities	Day-use only	None	
Water quality	Good	Good	
Boating	No restrictions	None	
Swimming	Yes	No	
Beach	Yes	No	

Had the above opportunities been available last August, which one would you have most likely chosen? (Check one and only one box.)

❑	❑	❑
A	B	C

(ii) a running water option, or (iii) staying at home and not participating in water-based recreational activity.

The final design, therefore, consisted of 64 choice sets chosen from the $2^{11} \times 4^{10}$ full factorial of possible attribute level combinations using a main effects design strategy. In essence, the design tells us exactly how to define the 64 pairs of standing and running water alternatives such that the model parameters of interest can be estimated. Table 9.3 illustrates an example of the resulting design. It is unrealistic to assume that individuals can or will respond to all 64 choice sets in an interview setting. Consequently, the experiment was blocked into four sets of 16 choice sets by using an additional four-level column as a factor in the design.

Data

The data for both the revealed preference analysis and the stated preference analysis were obtained from a multiphase survey sponsored by Alberta Environment. Random digit dialling techniques were used to contact individuals within the study region (an area in and around the city of Calgary, Alberta). In the telephone portion, individuals were asked if they participated in water-based recreation, where they participated in such activities, what type of recreation they engaged in, and a variety of socioeconomic characteristics. Each person who responded that they participated in water-based recreation was asked if they would be willing to complete a mailed-out questionnaire which contained the stated preference experiment. After a period of 3 weeks, 413 accurately completed mail-out portions were returned (45%).

Individuals were also asked to discuss specific details of the trips they took in August of 1991 (the survey was administered in the fall of 1991). These 730 trips are the basis for the revealed preference analysis, described below.

Results

The stated preference parameter signs were consistent with expectations. Larger fish, increased catch rates, good water quality, and the availability of swimming and beaches positively affected utility. Mountains and foothills were preferred to flat prairie and rolling prairie. More fish species were preferred to fewer, with the package of rainbow trout, mountain whitefish and brown trout providing the highest utility. Fully serviced campsites were preferred on both standing and running water sites. Distance was a negative factor as expected (for details see Adamowicz *et al.,* 1994).

Formulated in such a manner, the stated preference model is described exactly like a revealed preference travel cost model. Welfare measures from that model can be developed using the theory applied to revealed preference discrete choice models (Hanemann, 1984). Per trip welfare measures were calculated for the set of water quality changes proposed in the project. The per-trip welfare measures vary by residence zone from a maximum of $8.06 to a minimum of $4.33.[11]

Revealed preference analysis

Information on the actual choices of recreation sites was collected from the same sample of individuals who provided responses to the stated preference survey. A multinomial-logit discrete-choice model of site

---

[11] Some other examples of welfare results are: a 10% change in travel costs results in an average (across sites) loss of $3.48 per trip (revealed preference), $4.68 per trip (stated preference) and $3.60 (joint model). A 10% increase in the fishing catch rate results in an average benefit of $1.74 per trip (revealed preference), $0.11 per trip (stated preference) and $0.43 (joint model).

choice was specified and estimated. Travel cost (distance) and other site attributes were used to explain site choices. The quality factors could not all be entered into the statistical analysis due to collinearity. The final model contained a subset of the parameters estimated in the stated preference model.

The resulting welfare measures, for each residence zone, ranged from $0.46 per trip to $3.99 per trip. Note that while the stated preference welfare measures were higher than the revealed preference measures for each residence zone, the differences were not constant. The revealed preference measure for one zone was eight times smaller than the corresponding stated preference measure. On the other hand, the stated preference measure for a different zone was only twice the revealed preference measure. The models represent a different quantification of the tradeoffs between site attributes, or scaling differences due to different magnitudes of the respective random components.

Joint revealed-stated preference analysis

A likelihood-ratio test of the difference between parameters, incorporating the relative scale effect (the possibility of difference variances between the models) implied that one cannot reject the hypothesis of equal parameters (see Swait and Louviere (1993) for a discussion of these hypothesis tests). Therefore, a joint model was also used for welfare analysis. All parameters in the joint model had the same sign as the parameters in the stated preference model. Many more factors were found to be significant in the joint model relative to the revealed preference model (see Adamowicz *et al.*, 1994). This is probably because the collinearity in the revealed preference model was reduced (or perfect collinearity no longer existed). The welfare measures were recalculated using the parameters estimated from the joint model. These new measures were closer to the revealed preference model than the stated preference model.

In summary, this examination of SP and RP illustrates the use of the SP method in measuring environmental values and the benefits of joint SP–RP analysis. Interestingly, in this case the RP and SP data were found to be generated by similar preference structures, once the scale effect was taken into account. This shows that the direct technique and the indirect technique produced representations of choice that did not differ.

Discussion

Environmental valuation has come a long way since the days of simple travel cost models and simple contingent valuation questions.

Complex nested choice models of recreation demand are used to reflect the complexity of spatial choice decisions. Sophisticated contingent valuation surveys employ 'verbal protocol analysis', optimal statistical bid designs and a host of elicitation devices designed to reveal accurate willingness to pay measures. Stated preference research has moved to the point of using computer-generated graphics to present attributes on self-administered video based surveys. The state of the art continues to improve our understanding of the processes and problems of environmental valuation. However, some basic issues constantly arise. Revealed preference techniques are appealing because they have a market base, but their applicability to measuring passive use values appears to be limited. Contingent valuation, the most common method of measuring passive use value, is being carefully scrutinized because of embedding and other difficulties that arise from its use.

Stated preference is relatively new in the economics realm. Perhaps some of the problems associated with CV can be alleviated using SP. Also, the fact that SP, RP and CV techniques can all be represented using random utility theory suggests that combinations of, and comparisons between, the techniques may be used to further refine the measurements. SP research has been used successfully in marketing and transportation economics. Valuation economists may be able to learn from that literature. SP type techniques have been successfully applied to transportation planning, and hazardous waste siting problems, as well as to recreational site choice problems (Mackenzie, 1993; Opaluch *et al.*, 1993; Hensher, 1994).

Even though valuation research has come a long way there are a few items that have not been adequately addressed. First, the temporal dimension remains largely unexplored. There are two aspects to temporal analysis. The first deals with environmental values over time. Valuation work performed today is typically static and the values are placed into benefit–cost analyses and subjected to discounting. Is this the appropriate way to treat environmental values? Research by Cropper *et al.* (1992) found that values associated with health risks do not appear to follow traditional discounting patterns. Price (1993) argues that environmental goods should not be subject to discounting. Suffice it to say that relatively little has been done in the area of intertemporal environmental valuation even though this aspect of valuation is very important. A second, and not entirely unrelated, aspect of temporal analysis that has not been explored is the possibility for learning, habit formation, variety seeking and other dynamic effects within valuation models. There is no doubt that recreation demands are affected by such dynamic effects. It is probably true that passive use values also involve learning and dynamic elements.

Finally, almost all of our current valuation efforts measure willingness to pay, either because they are structured to measure willingness to pay or because the values arise from models that assume that willingness to pay and willingness to accept are similar. Whether one takes the Knetsch (1989) stance that indifference curves are non-reversible (different preferences for gains and losses) or one takes the Hanemann (1991) stance that the difference between willingness to pay and willingness to accept can be large depending on the availability of substitutes, it is clear that we should not rule out significant differences for some goods. Environmental valuation often examines losses, thus willingness to accept will often be the correct measure of impact. Furthermore, environmental goods may not have good substitutes. Therefore, using willingness to pay will understate the loss. This argument has been raised elsewhere (Knetsch, 1990) yet there appears to be little movement towards appropriate methods for measuring compensation amounts.

In conclusion, there are advantages and disadvantages associated with each environmental valuation technique, but there are many more techniques to choose from than there were 20 years ago. Current research into using market methods for passive use value measurement (Larson, 1992) may yield some interesting approaches. Stated preference techniques may soon be used more widely and may add to the pool of information on choices and values. Environmental valuation research is also attracting some of the most capable economists and there is more collaboration between economists and other social scientists. This will undoubtedly add to the quality of research produced.

References

Adamowicz, W.L., Louviere, J. and Williams, M. (1994) Combining stated and revealed preference methods for valuing environmental amenities. *Journal of Environmental Economics and Management* 26, 271–292.

Arrow, K., Solow, R., Portnoy, P., Leamer, E., Radner, R. and Schuman, H. (1993) Report of the NOAA Panel on Contingent Valuation. *Federal Register* 58(10), 4601–4614.

Batsell, R.R. and Louviere, J.J. (1991) Experimental choice analysis, *Marketing Letters* 2, 199–214.

Ben-Akiva, M. and Lerman, S. (1985) *Discrete Choice Analysis: Theory and Application to Travel Demand.* MIT Press, Cambridge, Massachusetts.

Bockstael, N.E., McConnell, K.E. and Strand, I.E. (1991) Recreation. In: Braden, J.B. and Kolstad, C.D. (eds) *Measuring the Demand for Environmental Quality.* North-Holland, Amsterdam.

Braden, J.B. and Kolstad, C.D. (1991) *Measuring the Demand for Environmental Quality.* North-Holland, Amsterdam.

Carson, R.T. (1991) Constructed markets. In: Braden, J.B. and Kolstad, C.D. (eds)

Measuring the Demand for Environmental Quality. North-Holland, Amsterdam.

Cropper, M., Aydede, S. and Portney, P. (1992) Rates of time preference for saving lives. *American Economic Review* 82, 469–472.

Cropper, M., Deck, L., Kishor, N. and McConnell, K.E. (1993) Valuing product market attributes using single market data: a comparison of hedonic and discrete choice approaches. *Review of Economics and Statistics* 75, 225–232.

Hanemann, W.M. (1984) *Applied Welfare Analysis with Qualitative Response Models,* Working Paper No. 241. University of California, Berkeley, pp.26.

Hanemann, W.M. (1991) Willingness to pay and willingness to accept: how much can they differ? *American Economic Review* 81, 635–647.

Hanemann, W.M., Loomis, J. and Kanninen, B. (1991) Statistical efficiency of double-bounded dichotomous choice contingent valuation. *American Journal of Agricultural Economics* 73, 1255–1263.

Hensher, D.A. (1994) Stated preference analysis of travel choices: the state of practice. *Transportation* 21, 107–134.

Kahneman, D. and Knetsch, J.L. (1992) Valuing public goods: the purchase of moral satisfaction. *Journal of Environmental Economics and Management* 22, 57–70.

Knetsch, J.L. (1989) The endowment effect and evidence of nonreversible indifference curves. *American Economic Review* 79, 1277–1284.

Knetsch, J.L. (1990) Environmental policy implications of disparities between willingness to pay and compensation demanded measures of value. *Journal of Environmental Economics and Management* 19, 227–237.

Larson, D.M. (1992) Can non-use values be measured from market behavior. *American Journal of Agricultural Economics* 75, 1114–1120.

Louviere, J.J. (1991) Experimental choice analysis: introduction and overview. *Journal of Business Research* 23, 291–297.

Louviere, J.J. (1994) *Relating Stated Preference Measures and Models to Choices in Real Markets.* Paper presented at the DOE/EPA Workshop on Using Contingent Valuation to Measure Non-Market Values, Herndon, Virginia, May 1994.

Mackenzie, J.A. (1993) Comparison of contingent preference models. *American Journal of Agricultural Economics* 75, 593–603.

McFadden, D. (1974) Conditional logit analysis of qualitative choice behavior. In: Zarembka, P. (ed.) *Frontiers in Econometrics.* Academic Press, New York, pp.105–142.

Mitchell, R.C. and Carson, R.T. (1989) *Using Surveys to Value Public Goods: The Contingent Valuation Method.* Johns Hopkins University Press for Resources for the Future, Baltimore.

Opaluch, J.J., Swallow, S., Weaver, T., Wessels, C. and Wichlens, D. (1993) Evaluating impacts from noxious waste facilities: including public preferences in current siting mechanisms. *Journal of Environmental Economics and Management* 24, 41–59.

Price, C. (1978) *Landscape Economics.* Macmillan, London.

Price, C. (1993) *Time, Discounting and Value.* Blackwell, Oxford.

Swait, J. and Louviere, J.J. (1993) The role of the scale parameter in the estimation and comparison of multinomial logit models. *Journal of Marketing Research* 30, 305–314.

10

The Pros and Cons of Alternative Valuation Methods

Colin Price

University College of North Wales, Bangor

Introduction

Let me begin by quoting the first verse of a modern carol by John Rutter (1985):

> How do you capture the wind on the water?
> How do you count all the stars in the sky?
> How can you measure the love of a mother,
> Or how can you write down a baby's first cry?

The sentiments may evince a certain adolescent mawkishness – and perhaps I value them for just that reason. But, taken literally, the words set the agenda for environmental valuation in context: in a sense I feel that I have spent half my life trying to capture the wind on the water, and performing parallel feats of environmental appraisal. Thus nowadays, when people ask me, 'How do you put a cash value on a beautiful sunset?', I tend to answer ,'Which of the eight major ways do you want me to start with?' Or else enquire what the size of the budget is: if they have £25 to spend, I can value a beautiful sunset; if they have £25,000 I can't, but I know a man who can ...

Of course all these 'how do you ... ?' questions are asked rhetorically. They are in reality *statements* of a belief that such valuation is impossible. In his book *Ecology into Economics Won't Go*, McBurney (1990) develops this theme with a magnificent lack of clarity, adumbrated by the picture on the front cover. It shows a hand emerging from a pin-striped sleeve (symbolic, presumably, of a faceless, heartless, soulless bureaucrat), attempting to crush a cabbage (a rather ill-chosen symbol of unmodified ecosystems) into a tin (a symbol of the industrial economy). Clearly we are meant to be overwhelmed by this cogent visual argument. And yet, to the environmental economist at any rate, the moral is clear: if ecosystems will not fit into the present conception of economics, we need to design a bigger tin – to enlarge that conception of economics.

On the other hand, the mawkish sentimentality and the intuitive rejection of monetization closely represent my own emotional position. When people (e.g. Bowers, 1990) reproduce cartoons in which pin-striped bureaucrats murmur such profundities as, 'My heart leaps up when I cost out a rainbow in the sky' I feel affronted precisely because I, too, care about nature. I too would prefer to walk through a world of beauty forever unthreatened, forever intuitively appealing. I too recognize that the value of the natural world is derived partly from a sense that the natural world is beyond value.

Therefore, if I set out to value the natural world in cash terms, I must not do so for trivial purposes. I must cause minimum disturbance of my fellow-citizens' equanimity. I must be prepared to make myself a guinea pig in my own valuation experiments – a notice on my door in Bangor reads: 'The world is a wonderful place as you experience it: it's only depressing when you start to evaluate it', and that indicates the kind of emotional martyrdom one must steel oneself to suffer if necessary.

Finally, I must accept that judgement will often be required: the purpose of valuation techniques is to *inform* one's judgement, not to replace it. Hence the pros and cons of alternative valuation methods are a function of how well they perform that role. This approach to economics is not concerned, in the first instance, with the issues of public cost–benefit analysis, but with questions like: should I give money to supporting Durham Cathedral's fabric fund, or to saving endangered wildlife, or to keeping children in the Sudan from starvation? It does not have to be smart, or trendy, or in receipt of massive research council funding; it has to help me to make decisions in my life.

Judging the Scope of Judgement

My remit is to review a number of alternative techniques, and I can start with two to cross off your list.

Many studies, dating from Gregory (1955), have imputed what environmental benefits must have been, from the costs that land managers in the past were prepared to incur in order to promote those benefits. The suppressed premises are that such managers made rational decisions; that their view of cost (including discounting calculations) matched our own; and that they had some independent means of knowing how big the benefits were – means which, mysteriously, are inaccessible to the present generation of land managers.

Voluntary contributions to maintain publicly accessible amenities are rightly regarded with suspicion by economists. Marwell and Ames (1981) have raised the question of whether only economists are free-riders – that is, consumers who enjoy the benefits of public amenities without voluntarily contributing to their support. But the evidence for widespread free- (or at least cheap-) riding is impressive. For example, until recently, Britain's cathedrals collected only voluntary contributions from the visiting public, including a derisory 3–4p per visitor at Lincoln, widely regarded as Britain's finest medieval building. Financial stringency is forcing several to introduce entry charges upwards of £2, but visitor numbers seem little affected (Price, 1994). Clearly what people voluntarily pay gives no reliable indication of what they are, if pressed, *willing* to pay.

The next judgement to be made is: is judgement appropriate to a particular valuation problem? Typical of the seat-of-pants judgements which characterize debates on upland land use is this: 'Forestry profits come nowhere near balancing the financial value of the water losses where the [hydroelectric generation] catchment is afforested' (Reynolds, 1979).

The best thing I can do is to *avoid* such judgements, and get out there to measure the effect of forests on items with real market prices: for example, hydroelectricity. Our study of 41 sample points in Scotland (Barrow *et al.*, 1986) showed that, at 35 sites, forestry would in any case have been unprofitable, so hydroelectricity losses were irrelevant. At three further sites the losses were trivial; at the remaining three they were significant.

This point is worth stressing, for lurking half-concealed behind statements about information bias in contingent valuation studies, there is sometimes a suggestion that citizens need to be informed about ecosystem functions before they can deliver appropriate valuations (Minter, 1994). In fact there should be a clear distinction between the *functional* properties of ecosystems which experts should *measure*, and their *aesthetic properties*, which it is proper that citizens should *judge*.

On the other hand, not all production functions are accurately quantified, even by experts. There is wide disagreement on the physical concomitants of CO_2 emissions, in consequence of which suggested shadow prices for emissions range from 20p to £240 per tonne carbon equivalent (figures mostly derived from Cline, 1992).

And when economists go into the scientific aspects of a problem, they often get it wrong. The most widely quoted source of a carbon price is Nordhaus (1991, 1992, 1993). But the whole canon of Nordhaus-inspired work is based on a bogus regression of changing atmospheric concentrations on emissions (Price, 1995). As a result, most concerned economists appear to believe that one third to one half of annual CO_2 emissions 'disappear somewhere' (Schelling, 1992) – by which they do not mean 'are taken up by oceans or terrestrial ecosystems', but, apparently, 'totally dematerialise'. Moreover, according to the Nordhaus model, the oceans are an infinite sink: those CO_2 emissions which do not immediately 'disappear somewhere' are all eligible for eventual uptake. This supposition yields a *convenient* negative exponential for the future costs of present emissions, but is not scientifically *accurate*. According to the Intergovernmental Panel on Climate Change (IPCC) (1990) about 15% of all CO_2 emissions remain in the atmosphere indefinitely, and the associated costs so continue too.

Judgement and Representativeness

On the other hand, valuation of landscape, and of wildlife as an aesthetic resource, can hardly escape the need for judgement. Traditionally, judgements of landscape value have been made by landscape experts. Four questions arise in relating such judgements to environmental valuation.

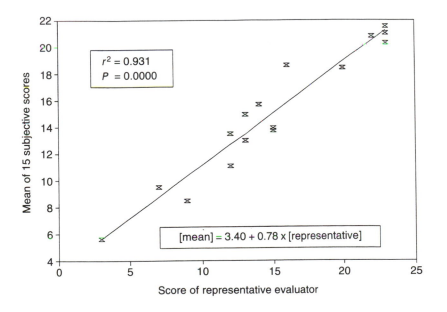

Fig. 10.1. Representative judgement of overall landscape value.

1. How representative are expert judgements of judgements made by the general public?
2. Do judgements show any relationship with objectively measurable factors?
3. On what kind of scale are judgements made?
4. How is judgement to be given a cash equivalent?

Some disagreement has been recorded between expert and public perceptions of the detail of aesthetic value (Lee, 1990). None the less, a statistically impressive group consensus can be found on the overall merit of several landscapes, judged on a quantitative scale. In particular, one individual can calibrate himself or herself to represent the judgements of the group. The correlation shown in Fig. 10.1 has an r^2 value for which many financial analysts would give their right arm.

Do Judgements Show any Relationship with Objectively Measurable Factors?

Holistically judged landscape values can be well predicted by models based on numerous measurable landscape attributes (Coventry–Solihull–Warwickshire, 1971). A strong correlation is shown even in a highly simplified model, as illustrated by Fig. 10.2, which aggregates scores only for land form, diversity of land use, and presence of water features.

Such an impressive prediction from objective factors raises the question of whether judgement could, after all, be dispensed with; whether a cash value of landscape attributes can be derived from regressions of house price (for example) on those attributes. My own belief is that it cannot. Let me illustrate the problem from Willis and Garrod's (1992) hedonic pricing model.

This found, among other results, that lower house price was associated with the presence in the same kilometre grid square of Sitka spruce plantations older than 50 years. On the other hand, presence of younger Sitka spruce plantations had no adverse effect. But I don't need this result to tell me about the aesthetic quality of Sitka spruce. I *know* that young Sitka spruce is aesthetically offensive, but that the offence becomes less in later life – about the age of 50 – when the canopy becomes more broken and interesting. When such a clear conflict of information and judgement arises, only three honourable courses of action are available:

1. I should accept that my aesthetic judgement is no good at all, and give up lecturing on forest landscape design – this I reject utterly.
2. Willis and Garrod should accept that hedonic pricing is no good at

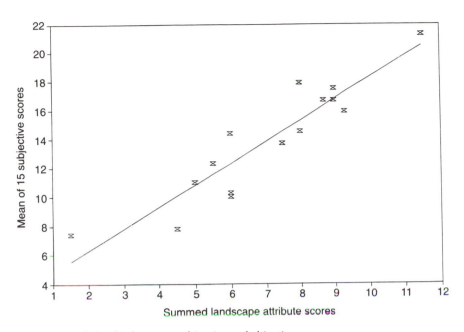

Fig. 10.2. Relationship between subjective and objective scores.

all, and should give up building models – this I reject with equal confidence.

3. We should jointly seek an explanation of the anomaly, and consider what its implications may be – this I think we should do.

Figure 10.3 illustrates two of the many possible explanations. That on the left-hand side suggests that height (concomitant of the trees' physiological age) is the problem, raising the plantation's unwanted serrated profile above intervening skylines. More extensive visibility with age is appropriately curtailed by shortening spruce rotations. By contrast, the right-hand explanation is that more recent spruce plantations have received greater design attention: better shaping of boundaries, more judicious blending with broadleaved species. This is a concomitant of unfolding human history, not of increasing tree age, and it would be wholly inappropriate to respond by shortening rotations.

There are many other ways of making the results of the statistical model compatible with aesthetic judgement. The important point is that the *right explanation* has to be known, before the hedonic model can give guidance in decision making.

However, my wariness about hedonic pricing goes deeper than interpretation of particular puzzling results: rather it is based on a

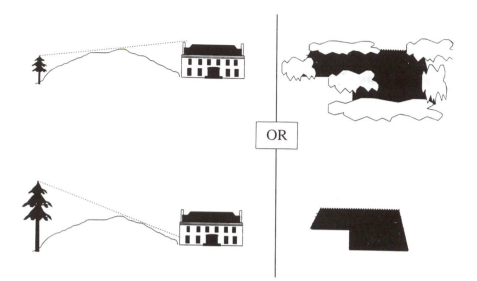

Fig. 10.3. Explanations of the Garrod–Willis effect.

theoretical expectation of problems (Price, 1978, 1991), which are illustrated in Fig. 10.4. Aesthetic value is complex: it is based on a vast number of visible features and qualities, as well as on invisible atmospheric variables. And, while the major factors – such as topography and diversity of land uses – may be quite evident, the significance of others is in itself a matter of judgement (Fig. 10.4a), as is the most appropriate way to measure them (10.4b). If we add the difficulty of establishing the functional relationship between attributes and value (10.4c), the likelihood that the attributes affect the dependent variable interactively (10.4d) and the fact that they are often inter-related as independent variables (10.4e), then it would actually be surprising if hedonic pricing models were able to distinguish accurate values for the separated attributes of a landscape. At best, it may assign a value to different levels of aesthetic quality judged – I emphasize that word – holistically.

On What Kind of Scale Are Judgements Made?

Even in pure landscape terms, it is rarely sufficient to judge 'what landscape is better'. When the complex comparisons of the real world

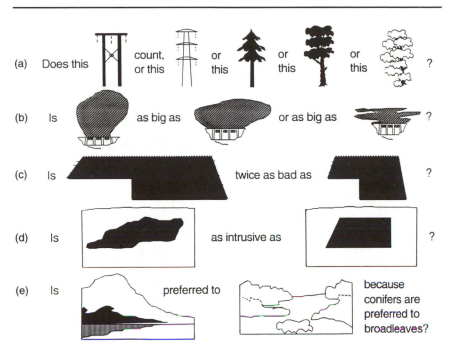

Fig. 10.4. Problems of the hedonic pricing method illustrated.

are involved it is also imperative to decide *'how much better'*. It is here that the stated preference method (Hoinville, 1971; Adamowicz, Chapter 9, this volume) may offer useful, and perhaps surprising insights.

Consider Fig. 10.5, which depicts four urban landscapes graded on an ordinal scale, whose full range is −II to +X. The choice offered is a walk embracing either the views on the left-hand side, or those on the right. (Here I gloss over the problem that the value of the walk may depend on the sequence in which the views are seen (Ross and Simonson, 1991).) If the grade −I landscape plus the grade VIII landscape are preferred to grade II plus grade V, the conclusion would be that the (cardinal) value interval between grade −I and grade II is less than the interval between grade V and grade VIII. Approximate equality of intervals can be arrived at, throughout the scale, by adjusting the elements of the choice. My own feeling − one which is consonant with the original scale of landscape value proposed by Fines (1968) − is that value intervals become greater, higher up the scale of grades.

This choice is posed in the context of a sequence of landscapes traversed incidentally, or visited deliberately, by the viewer. A conclusion that took my judgement by surprise is that relative values may be very different for landscapes that are inhabited by the viewer. Here we

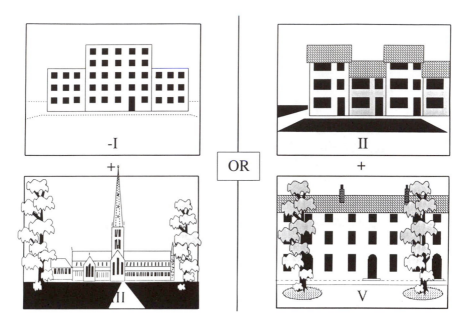

Fig. 10.5. Cardinalizing scales from preferences.

are involved not with sequences of experience, but with a single outlook. Let the choice in Fig. 10.5 be restructured as follows:

> *50% probability of grade −I outlook*
> *plus*
> *50% probability of the grade VIII outlook*

OR

> *50% probability of the grade II outlook*
> *plus*
> *50% probability of the grade V outlook*

The dire possibility of 25 years looking at −I may now suffice to offset the potential great delights of outlook VIII: value intervals may be more nearly equal between adjacent grades on the scale.

On the other hand, in conjectured landscapes (the landscapes of existence value), it is likely that the highest quality views (VIII to X) will be given an extremely high weighting, relative to the ordinarily attractive ones (V to VII), while lower grades will have hardly any significance.

How Is Judgement to Be Given a Cash Equivalent? – Contingent Valuation

Willingness to pay is normally not an absolute, but a 'separational' value between two alternative states – that indeed is the heart of marginal analysis. Researchers are good at describing the changed state of an environment for which willingness to pay is apparently sought: the datum from which the change is made is often more vague. Moreover, we are, avowedly, concerned with 'environmental valuation in context', and the significance of separation of states may depend on changes that are going on in the background.

Consider these problems in relation to contingent valuation. I was quite happy with the technique when, back in 1970, I asked visitors to a peri-urban woodland how far they would be prepared to drive for recreation in a similar wood, if housing development destroyed this one. The scenario was probable, the two separated states clear, and the outcome predictable. It all becomes more complex when we seek willingness to pay to save the greenshank or the snail-darter from extinction, because the mechanisms whereby people might be able to do that are quite obscure.

In these unfamiliar circumstances, Hanley (Chapter 4, this volume) shows that willingness to pay for existence values is a function of information given to the respondent, presumably because information heightens awareness of the separation of the with/without states. But information given to 1 in 100,000 of the population does not give a *better valuation* for a given product: rather it gives an equally appropriate valuation for a *different perceived product*. It does not represent the willingness to pay for existence values among the 99,999 out of 100,000 of the population who were *not* sampled, *not* informed, and who therefore have *no changed perception*.

Valuation must, moreover, take place within an overall context of environmental valuation. The problem can be represented schematically as in Fig. 10.6a, in which there are only six species of importance each shown in a different shading style. Before a particular conservation issue arises, the greenshank ranks sixth in this hierarchy. Then a threat (say, blanket afforestation of the Flow Country) arises. Information becomes more general, the greenshank 'goes to the top of the league', and contingent valuation studies, which inform respondents of what they are about to lose, will record a high separation value. But other species are not unaffected. There is a certain 'mental account' of *concern* about

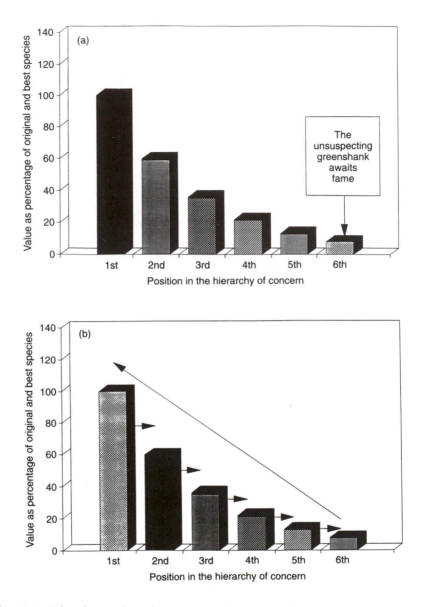

Fig. 10.6. Value changes through contingent valuation and extinction. (a) Values in the initial position; (b) after information on the greenshank; (c) after 'celebrity' extinction; (d) after 'non-entity' extinction.

species preservation, just as there is a *cash* mental account which restricts how much people are willing to pay for environment. Preoccupation with the greenshank is likely to mean other species become, for the time

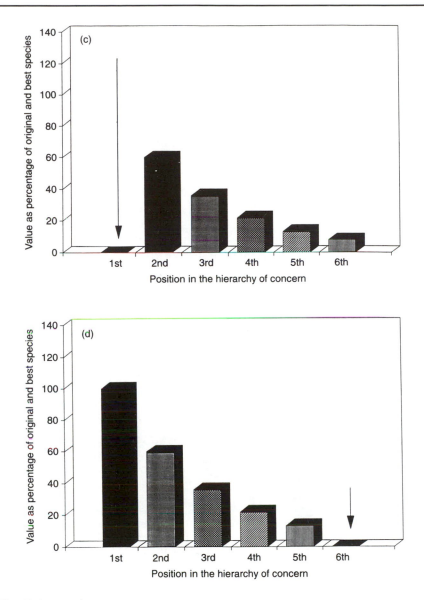

Fig. 10.6. *contd*

being, of less perceived importance, as shown in Fig. 10.6b.

Suppose that the greenshank does in fact become extinct: what value is to be ascribed to this loss? Initially, the last-recorded separational value is relevant (to the population which knows about it): the difference of the two states is the difference between Figs 10.6b and

10.6c. However, as time passes and other conservation issues draw upon the 'mental account of concern', the remembered greenshank may lapse to its former position in the hierarchy. The difference of the two states is the (much smaller) difference between Figs 10.6a and 10.6d.

As well as loss of positive utility with an extinction, there is an actual disutility due to a *sense of loss* (or outrage or injustice), which in the case of celebrated extinctions like that of the dodo may prove extraordinarily durable (Price, 1985): *knowing that a species has been made extinct* is a different value from *no longer enjoying the fact of its existence*. Seen from this perspective, information not only rearranges positive utilities, but actually may create additional disutilities, by promoting interest in species generally, and, in particular, in a species which subsequently becomes extinct. The differences shown in Fig. 10.7 represent this sense of loss: they result not from extinction *per se*, but from rearranging and enhancing potential disutilities through contingent valuation studies. The disutility exists, irrespective of whether concern for other species is affected. But the difference between Figs 10.6c and 10.6d is a further negative, though transient consequence of the act of valuation. Increasing a particular separational value by officiously imparting information increases the potential for unhappiness.

The conclusion is clear: we should confine our informative contingent valuations to species that are unlikely to become extinct, like starlings. This seems to be quite the opposite of current practice.

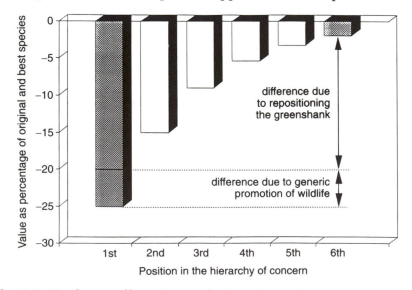

Fig. 10.7. Disutility caused by contingent valuation and extinction.

Whatever the effect of information, these environmental changes are implicitly assumed to take place within a constant context. An individual flower species is evaluated on the basis that survival of all other flower species is assured. The modern children's hymn which begins 'Think of a world without any flowers...' (Newport, 1983) suggests a whole sequence of alternative reference levels. Compared with each of these, separational values would be far more significant than are current valuations, which habitually refer to marginal reduction in number of species.

Giving a Cash Value – Travel Cost Method

The value given by the currently unfashionable travel cost method is also commonly interpreted as an absolute. Again, however, in reality it should be regarded as a separational value. In this case the implicit datum is the net value of the next-best alternative destination. As specified by Clawson (1959), the travel cost method derives data of the form:

For V visits per 1000 population,

[Willingness to pay (WTP) for travel to the destination]

$$\geqslant$$

[Cost incurred in travel to it]

If, however, alternative destinations exist, rational choice is more properly represented as:

[WTP for the destination] – [Cost incurred in travel to it]

$$\geqslant$$

[Net value of the best alternative destination]

This can be rearranged as:

[WTP for the destination] – [Net value of alternative]

$$\geqslant$$

[Cost incurred in travel to it]

– again for V visits per 1000 population. The demand curve compiled from such data thus represents the value-surplus over the best alternative. This of course is the value that is actually lost if the original destination becomes unavailable, and the next best alternative is substituted for it. The conditions under which this argument is valid are discussed and demonstrated by Connolly and Price (unpublished).

But the standard travel cost method gives an approximation to value only within the current context, not in the normal dynamic context, where environmental attrition affects alternative destinations as well as the destination being valued. With successive removal or degradation of sites, the separational value increases between with-and-without-destination states. The possibility that the datum provided by high-quality alternatives might decline without limit over time provides a strong rationale for maintaining 'critical natural capital' in the form of inviolable designated areas (Price, 1975, 1977).

Giving a Cash Value – House Prices

The hedonic pricing model is also capable of rendering a plausible separational value, not for individual landscape attributes, but for holistically judged qualities of view. For example, the view of Durham Cathedral from South Street is considered, anecdotally, to be worth an extra £30,000 on the price of a house (for those who can afford to live in this prime location).

However, even this valuation requires rephrasing. What is worth £30,000 is the *high quality* view, as valued by the *marginal* inmover, probably *rich*, in relation to the package available at alternative locations. The premium over alternatives includes elements for the view itself; for being rich; and for a banner to which the well-to-do may rally, safe in the knowledge that people of lower income group and different political orientation will not be able to afford to become neighbours. This separational value may be interpreted as *depression* of prices in low-quality and low-income environments, as much as premium for the obverse conditions. To the extent that this is true, the view does not create value, but simply redistributes socioeconomic groups, with no guarantee that the result is an overall improvement. I have used this £30,000 premium myself in illustrative valuations of cityscapes (Cobham Resource Consultants and Price, 1991): but I have a haunting fear that it will be quoted in prescriptive studies, by those who have not thought through the caveats outlined above.

Discounting

At the end of the valuation process, no matter how much care has been expended in deriving a unit benefit in cash terms, it is probable that some wrecker will spoil everything by discounting the future stream of values at a 6% rate, and thus cause much that is important to become of no account whatever. To illustrate this point consider Fig. 10.8. Of this the salient features are:

1. the time scale of around 500 years on the horizontal axis, that is, the

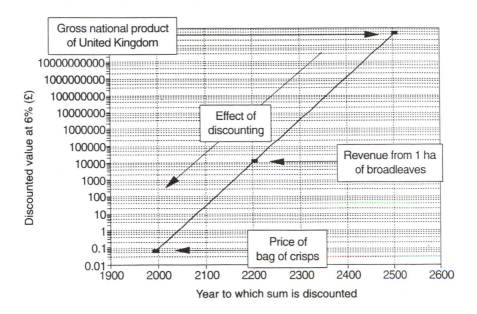

Fig. 10.8. Effect of discounting on a very large sum of money.

kind of period over which monumental environmental problems like the possible melting of the Antarctic ice sheet might develop;
2. the 6% discount rate as recommended not only by the Treasury (1991), but also the Department of the Environment (1991);
3. the logarithmic present value scale;
4. the reduction, under these conditions, of the entire current gross national product of the United Kingdom to a present equivalent value of one small packet of potato crisps.

This result does not *inform* our judgement, but *defies* it. We might well prefer to ask ourselves more explicitly: what kind of processes we could envisage as changing values over this time period; and whether the standard discounting procedure is at all likely to reflect them. Prolonged deliberation suggests that it is not (Price, 1993).

Conclusion

The approach to valuation which I have described as a process of informing judgement is, I judge, unlikely to become the standard form of cost–benefit analysis. But in an academic sense, I don't care two buttons for that. No economist ever asked me whether I approved of the standard approach of cost–benefit analysis, and obversely I do not need their approval to proceed with my own.

The approach offers three useful functions:

1. it helps me to make up my mind about what I think is right and proper;

2. it gives scope for those with some political influence to indulge in Machiavellian paternalism – using the process to suggest what the best outcome is, then manipulating political processes to improve the chances of that outcome being reached;

3. it lays out a relatively transparent route to an environmental valuation, in which decision makers are able to check expert judgements, to replace these judgements with their own where they disagree, and to present the effects of their dissenting judgements for wider scrutiny.

In the last sense, the approach is more democratic and accountable, as well as being more reliable, than the arcane techniques which are so widely promoted for environmental valuation.

References

Barrow, P., Hinsley, A.P. and Price, C. (1986) The effect of afforestation on hydroelectricity generation: a quantitative assessment. *Land Use Policy* 3, 141–151.

Bowers, J.K. (1990) *Economics of the Environment.* British Association of Nature Conservationists, Telford.

Clawson, M. (1959) *Methods of Measuring the Demand for and Value of Outdoor Recreation.* Resources for the Future, Washington DC.

Cline, W.R. (1992) *The Economics of Global Warming.* Institute for International Economics, Washington DC.

Cobham Resource Consultants and Price, C. (1991) *The Benefits of Amenity Trees.* Report to Department of the Environment, London.

Coventry–Solihull–Warwickshire (1971) *A Strategy for the Sub-region, Supplementary Report 5: Countryside.* Coventry–Solihull–Warwickshire Sub-regional Study Group.

Department of the Environment (1991) *Policy Appraisal and the Environment.* HMSO, London.

Fines, K.D. (1968) Landscape evaluation: a research project in East Sussex. *Regional Studies* 2, 41–55.

Gregory, G.R. (1955) An economic approach to multiple use. *Forest Science* 1, 6–13.

Hoinville, G. (1971) Evaluating community preferences. *Environment and Planning A* 3, 33–50.

IPCC (1990) *Climate Change.* Cambridge University Press, Cambridge.

Lee, T. (1990) *Attitudes Towards and Preferences for Forestry Landscapes*. Report to Forestry Commission, Edinburgh.

Marwell, G. and Ames, R.E. (1981) Economists free ride, does anyone else? experiments in the provision of public goods 4. *Journal of Political Economy* 15, 295–301.

McBurney, S. (1990) *Ecology into Economics Won't Go*. Green Books, Bideford.

Minter, R. (1994) Sharing common values? *Landscape Research* **19**(1), 2–4.

Newport, D. (1983) In *Hymns and Psalms*. Methodist Publishing House, Peterborough.

Nordhaus, W.D. (1991) To slow or not to slow: the economics of the greenhouse effect. *Economic Journal* 101, 920–937.

Nordhaus, W.D. (1992) An optimal transition path for controlling greenhouse gases. *Science* 258, 1315–1319.

Nordhaus, W.D. (1993) Rolling the 'DICE': An optimal transition path for controlling greenhouse gases. *Resource and Energy Economics* 15, 27–50.

Price, C. (1975) *Right Use of Land in National Parks*. University College of North Wales, Bangor.

Price, C. (1977) Cost–benefit analysis, national parks and the pursuit of geographically segregated objectives. *Journal of Environmental Management* 5, 87–97.

Price, C. (1978) *Landscape Economics*. Macmillan, London.

Price, C. (1985) Economics, natural justice and the conservation of marine mammals. *Proceedings of the Symposium on Endangered Marine Mammals and Marine Parks, Cochin* 1, 5–12. Cochin, India.

Price, C. (1991) *Landscape Valuation and Public Decision Making*. Report to the Countryside Commission, Cheltenham, and Countryside Commission for Scotland, Perth.

Price, C. (1993) *Time, Discounting and Value*. Blackwell, Oxford.

Price, C. (1994) Donations, charges and willingness to pay. *Landscape Research* 19(1), 9–11.

Price, C. (1995) Emissions, concentrations and disappearing CO_2. *Resource and Energy Economics* (in press).

Reynolds, G. (1979) Discussion: the effect of afforestation on water resources in Scotland. In: Thomas, M.F. and Coppock, J.T. (eds) *Land Assessment in Scotland*. Aberdeen University Press, Aberdeen.

Ross, W.T. Jr and Simonson, I. (1991) Evaluation of pairs of experiences: a preference for happy endings. *Journal of Behavioral Decision Making* 4, 273–282.

Rutter, J. (1985) *Candlelight Carol*. Oxford University Press, Oxford.

Schelling, T.C. (1992) Some economics of global warming. *American Economic Review* 82, 1–14.

Treasury (1991) *Economic Appraisal in Central Government: A Technical Guide for Government Departments*. HMSO, London.

Willis, K.G. and Garrod, G.D. (1992) Amenity value of forests in Great Britain and its impact on the internal rate of return from forestry. *Forestry* 65, 331–346.

11

Uncertain Values in Environmental Policy Analysis

Chris Hope

University of Cambridge

Introduction

How much is a view worth? What is the value to society of an endangered species? Economists seek to answer questions of this kind with contingent valuation methods. Some critics of economics (Kelman, 1981; Sagoff, 1988) are sceptical about the expression of such values in money terms. Others seek reassurance that the questions are adequately framed (worth to whom? in what context?) (Ekins, 1992, p.37).

The discussions in this chapter assume that it is sensible to express these values in money terms, and that the questions have been adequately framed. However, it is recognized that people may still be uncertain about what the answer to the questions should be. Perhaps the view is worth $10 to them, or perhaps it is worth $20.

This chapter sets out the rules of thumb that people often use to make judgements about uncertain quantities like these, the biases that these rules of thumb can introduce, and why these biases might matter. It concludes that the biases mean that we don't know the answers to contingent valuation questions as well as we think we do, and this could affect the quality of our decision making. There are, however, steps available to combat this.

The Existence of Uncertainty

It should not be difficult to persuade people that uncertainty is all-pervasive in environmental valuation. In designing and running several models for environmental policy analysis (EPA), in areas such as acid rain and the greenhouse effect (Dixon, 1989; Hope *et al.*, 1993), and obtaining the inputs for the valuation sections of these models, experts have always been at pains to stress just how uncertain the valuations are.

Contingent valuation methods, however refined they become, can never deliver answers that have anything like the precision of real prices observed in real markets. Partly, this is because the methods will always involve only a sample of the people likely to be affected, and so the results will always be subject to sampling error. The main difficulty, however, is the artificiality of the valuation process. People are asked to say what they would pay to avoid some environmental harm that is described, briefly or at length. But, at least in the valuation phase, the payment is not actually made, nor does the environmental harm actually occur.

Now of course researchers in many areas have to ask artificial questions all the time. Staying with the environmental field, people have been asked for their estimate of a scientific parameter, such as the rise in equilibrium temperature caused by a doubling of carbon dioxide concentration, or the frequency with which a component of a nuclear power station will fail. The values of these parameters are uncertain. So researchers have explicitly encouraged people to give probabilistic answers, perhaps initially in a crude form such as low – medium – high, but ultimately as complete subjective probability distributions.

Researchers now have several decades of experience of asking this type of question. They discovered fairly early on that in giving their answers, people used certain rules of thumb, and that these rules of thumb could introduce systematic biases into the answers obtained. So, quite elaborate protocols were developed to ensure that these biases were minimized (Watson and Buede, 1987, chapter 7.4; Morgan and Henrion, 1990, chapter 7). These protocols are used today by essentially all reputable decision scientists who are engaged in asking questions of this type.

However, these protocols are not routinely used by economists in contingent valuation studies. In fact, in many studies, the researchers have made no attempt to elicit a range, or probability distribution, but have concentrated on single point estimates, which are then sometimes expressed to three or four significant figures. So it may be that many economists are unaware of the rules of thumb that their respondents are likely to be using, and the biases that they can introduce, as they grope for an answer to contingent valuation questions.

Rules of Thumb and the Biases Uncertainty Can Introduce

The three main rules of thumb are called *representativeness, availability,* and *anchoring and adjustment.* They were identified by Tversky and Kahneman as long ago as 1974, and the following description of them draws heavily on their seminal paper (Tversky and Kahneman, 1974), to which interested readers should turn for more details.

Representativeness

For an illustration of judgement by representativeness, consider the occupation of an individual who has been described as follows: 'Steve is very shy and withdrawn, invariably helpful, but with little interest in people, or in the world of reality. A meek and tidy soul, he has a need for order and structure, and a passion for detail.' Using the representativeness heuristic, the probability that Steve is a librarian, for example, is assessed by the degree to which this description is representative of, or similar to, the stereotype of a librarian. Thus many respondents say that it is quite likely that Steve is a librarian.

The fact that there are far more shop workers than librarians in the population should enter into any reasonable estimate of the probability that Steve is a librarian rather than a shop worker. The main bias that representativeness can introduce is a neglect of this kind of base rate frequency information, since it does not affect the similarity of the description of Steve to the stereotypes of librarian and shop worker.

In the environmental policy area, one bias that can be blamed upon representativeness is that people can be too willing to be convinced that detailed scenarios are likely actually to occur. As more and more detail is added to the scenarios, they become more and more representative in people's minds of the kind of future that they expect to see, and so they are rated as more likely to occur than other less detailed descriptions. In fact it is logically certain that adding more detail to a scenario makes it less likely to be exactly fulfilled, not more.

Availability

To illustrate judgement by availability, consider a group of ten people who form committees. How many different two-person committees can be formed? How many different eight-person committees? When people were asked these questions, the median estimate of the number of two-person committees was 70, while the median estimate for eight-person committees was 20. The correct answer is 45 in both cases, as any two-person committee automatically forms an eight-person committee out of the remaining members of the group. The reason for the bias is that instances of two-person committees are much more available, by which is meant they come to mind much more readily, than instances of eight-person committees.

In the environmental field, the well-documented concern of people with rare but catastrophic events can be explained by a reliance upon availability. Catastrophic events that do occur, such as Flixborough or Chernobyl, are extensively reported in the media, and so are highly available to people when they are considering what their concerns should be. Smaller scale, routine hazards escape this type of scrutiny, and hence are not so available.

Experts are not immune to availability bias. Forecasts that are made of even the distant future tend to bear an uncanny resemblance to a continuation of trends from the recent past. Fig. 11.1 shows projections made in 1981 of the world oil price through to year 2000 from ten well-respected models (EMF, 1982). As the report from which this figure is taken states, 'The unmistakable long-run projected trend of world oil prices, adjusted for inflation, is upward.'

It is easy to be critical of these projections in 1994, with hindsight, at the end of a decade of falling oil prices (the mid-1994 price of about

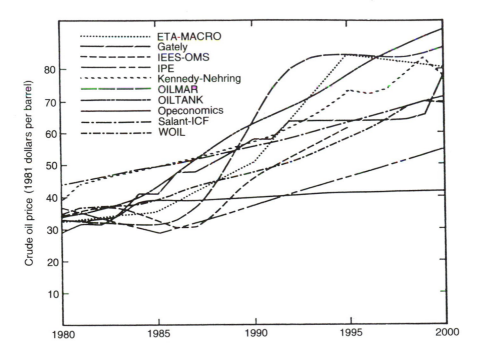

Fig. 11.1. World oil price projections to the year 2000 by ten models. Source: EMF (1982).

$15 per barrel, equates to about $9 per barrel in the 1981 dollars of the figure). But recall that these projections were made in 1981, at the end of a decade that had seen a marked upward movement of oil prices. This experience was more readily available to the forecasters than the long period of declining oil prices before 1971. Today's generation of forecasters who are tempted to project continuing stable or falling oil prices should reflect that they might be in the grip of the 1990s version of availability bias (Caddy *et al.*, 1992; Adelman, 1993 makes a similar point).

Anchoring and adjustment

To illustrate this rule of thumb, try estimating the product $8 \times 7 \times 6 \times 5 \times 4 \times 3 \times 2 \times 1$ in five seconds. Alternatively, try estimating $1 \times 2 \times 3 \times 4 \times 5 \times 6 \times 7 \times 8$ in the same time. The correct answer in both cases is 40,320, but the five second time does not allow enough time to calculate this. In an experiment, the median answers produced for the two sums were 2250 for the first, descending sequence, and 512 for the latter, ascending one. What is happening is that people perform the first few steps of the required calculation, which provides an anchor, and then make an adjustment. Because adjustments are typically too small, this leads to an underestimate. The underestimate is more pronounced for the ascending sequence because the anchor produced by a few steps of calculation is smaller.

In many situations people make estimates like this, by starting from an initial anchor value and then adjusting it to give the final estimate. The fact that adjustments are typically too small is well documented. One of the main aims of elicitation protocols in the decision sciences is to avoid the use of anchoring and adjustment, as far as is possible.

If these protocols are not used, and people are asked to give their answer in the form of a range within which they expect the answer to lie with, let us say, 98% confidence, they will give ranges that are too narrow. Typically, 30% of true values fall outside ranges that people have expressed a 98% confidence in (Lichtenstein *et al.*, 1982, Table 1).

In contingent valuation, people are typically asked for point estimates and not ranges, but a similar bias can occur if the researchers, aware of the rather fragile nature of the estimates, make an attempt to provide a range themselves. An extract from Nordhaus (1991) shows this process:

> We estimate that the net economic damage from a 3 degree warming … is likely to be around 0.25 percent of national income for the United States in terms of those variables we have been able to quantify. This figure is

clearly incomplete, for it neglects a number of areas that are either inadequately studied or inherently unquantifiable. We might raise the number to around 1 percent of total global income to allow for these unmeasured and unquantifiable factors, although such an adjustment is purely ad hoc. It is not possible to give precise error bounds around this figure, but my hunch is that the overall impact upon human activity is unlikely to be larger than 2 percent of total output.

This is classic anchoring and adjustment. First an incomplete calculation is made, which is then adjusted to give a best estimate for the desired quantity. It is then adjusted again to give an upper limit. As adjustments are typically too small, it would be prudent to be cautious about the status, particularly of the 2% upper limit, for all its subsequent prominence in the literature.

Why the Biases Matter

Most researchers accept the seriousness of biases which affect people's best estimates of uncertain quantities, as all of the three rules of thumb described above can do. However, there is much less agreement about the importance of biases that lead to too small a range, which is the main effect of anchoring and adjustment.

Two arguments against worrying too much about this type of bias are first, that if no better information can be obtained, the best estimate of the value is the one on which decisions should be based; and second, that if many uncertain quantities are combined together, in a model say, any uncertainties and biases will tend to cancel each other out.

A simple moderately realistic environmental example that provides a counter-argument against the first point goes as follows:

Suppose you are considering whether to take action to cut emissions of the gases that cause global warming. You believe that there is a threshold in the damage function for global warming. Any rise in temperature that is less than 3°C will cause essentially no damage, but above this the damage could be substantial. You decide to look ahead to 2050. With business as usual emissions, your modellers tell you that, global temperature is expected to rise by 2°C by 2050, with a range of from 1–3°C. If you act upon their best estimate, you will clearly not want to cut emissions, as a 2°C rise is less than the threshold. If you believe their range you will also take no action, as even the top of the range is not above the threshold.

But what if your modellers have been affected by anchoring and adjustment and their range is too narrow. Suppose it is in fact from 0°C to 4°C, with an unchanged best estimate of 2°C. Now there is a chance that the rise in temperature will exceed the threshold. The chance could

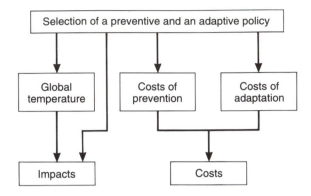

Fig. 11.2. Overall structure of the PAGE model. Source: Hope *et al.* (1993).

perhaps be as high as about 20% if the range follows a normal distribution with 0°C and 4°C as the 5% and 95% points. If you believe the damage will be substantial if the threshold is exceeded, and the costs of cutting emissions somewhat are not large, you might decide not to run the 20% risk that the threshold will be exceeded. Cutting emissions might be the right thing to do. Further calculations are needed to show if it is the right thing to do, but already it is clear that using the best estimate alone for decision making is not sensible, and that using a range that is too small can also lead to error.

The PAGE model (for Policy Analysis of the Greenhouse Effect) was developed to make just this sort of further calculation under uncertainty. Figure 11.2 shows its overall structure. Hope *et al.* (1993) provide a full description of the PAGE model; but to understand the results in this chapter it is necessary to know that the PAGE model works with triangular probability distributions for many inputs, such as the equilibrium rise in temperature for a doubling of CO_2 concentrations, and the unit valuation of impacts, and produces probabilistic results.

An Experiment with the PAGE Model

Using some illustrative but realistic inputs to the PAGE model, the second argument against worrying too much about biased ranges can also be addressed. Recall that this argument says that if many values are combined together in a model, the uncertainties will be reduced enormously and any biases will tend to cancel each other out.

Table 11.1 shows some illustrative inputs used in a PAGE calcula-

Table 11.1. Inputs for an experiment with PAGE.

	Minimum	Mode	Maximum	s.d. as percentage of mean
Climate:				
°C rise for $2 \times CO_2$	1.5	2.5	4.0	20
Warming halflife (y)	25	45	70	20
Tolerance:				
Tolerable °C in EU	0	0.5	1.0	30
Multiplier for rest of OECD	0.5	1.0	1.5	20
Valuation:				
Transport in EU (billion ECU)	1	5	17	40
Multiplier for rest of OECD	0.8	1.6	2.4	20

s.d., Standard deviation

tion of the global temperature rise by 2050, and consequent global economic damage, of business as usual emissions. The inputs are triangular probability distributions, and the first three columns show the minimum, modal and maximum values that completely define the distribution. The final column shows the standard deviation of each input as a percentage of its mean value, which is one useful summary measure of the uncertainty in each input.

The rows show the inputs. The first two relate to the climate model that is part of PAGE. The first row shows the range of values for the equilibrium warming caused by a doubling of CO_2 concentration – a minimum of 1.5°C, a most likely value of 2.5°C and a maximum value of 4.0°C. These values correspond closely to the IPCC findings (IPCC, 1990, p.xxv). The final column shows this input to have a standard deviation that is 20% of its mean value. For a normal distribution, 95% of the values lie within two standard deviations of the mean value. For this asymmetric distribution the minimum value is 40% below, and the highest value 60% above the most likely value.

The second row shows the thermal response rate of the Earth to a warming stimulus, ranging from 25 years to 70 years for just over half (actually $1-e^{-1}$) of the response to occur. These values come from calibrating PAGE against IPCC scenarios A and D (Hope, 1992). Again, the standard deviation of this input is 20% of its mean value.

The next two rows relate to the rise in global mean temperature that can occur before any impacts are felt. The first row shows that in the European Union (EU), this experiment assumes that somewhere between 0°C and 1°C rise can take place before impacts occur. The next row shows that in the rest of the OECD, the global temperature rise that can take place before impacts occur is somewhere between 0.5 and 1.5 times the rise that can occur in the EU.

The last two rows show an example of the valuation inputs in PAGE. The first shows that the impacts of global warming on the transport sector in the EU are assumed to be between 1 billion and 17 billion ECU (European Currency Units; 1 ECU is about $1) for every year that the temperature is 1°C above the tolerable level. These values come from a large study carried out for the European Commission (CRU/ERL, 1992), and are mainly caused by the sea level rise and subsequent inundation of ports and roads that will accompany global warming. These are the impacts in the base year of the model, 1990, they grow in line with GDP as time goes on.

The last row shows that the impacts in the rest of the OECD will be somewhere between 0.8 and 2.4 times the impacts in the EU, per year and per degree Celsius, with a most likely value of 1.6 times, because the rest of the OECD has an activity level in vulnerable areas that is about 1.6 times the activity in vulnerable areas of the EU (CRU/ERL, 1992).

The point of describing the inputs has been to show that they are reasonable, and not special pathological values designed to give a particular result. What of the claim that uncertainty in input values will be reduced greatly when they are combined together to give model outputs?

The claim has its origins in the mathematics of the sums of random variables. If you add together n identical independent normal variables, each with a standard deviation that is $x\%$ of its mean value, then the resulting sum will be a normal distribution with a standard deviation that is $x/\sqrt{n}\%$ of its mean value. The Central Limit Theorem tells us that, remarkably, this result also holds true, for reasonably large n, for any independent random variables (Meyer, 1969), not just normally distributed ones.

So, for instance, if a 'model' simply adds together 25 identical inputs, each of which has a standard deviation that is 20% of its mean value, like many of the inputs shown in Table 11.1, the output will be a normal distribution whose standard deviation is only $20/5 = 4\%$ of its mean value. In other words, the output of the model will have a 95% confidence interval that is only plus or minus 8% on either side of its mean value. This indeed is a great reduction in uncertainty compared with the uncertainty in the inputs.

Table 11.2 shows what the results of the PAGE experiment are in practice. The first three columns show the 5% point, mean value and 95% point on the output distribution. The fourth column interprets this, as in Table 11.1, in terms of the summary statistic of standard deviation

Table 11.2. Results of an experiment with PAGE. BAU policies in the year 2050.

	5 % point	Mean	95% point	s.d. as % of mean	No. of inputs
Temperature:					
Global (°C > 1990)	1.0	1.7	2.6	20	5
Above tolerable (°C)	0.4	1.3	2.4	40	7
Damage (billion ECU):					
EU transport sector	10	60	140	60	8
EU all sectors	300	800	1600	40	26
All regions, all sectors	1200	3000	6000	40	32

s.d., Standard deviation.

as a percentage of the mean value. The final column shows how many uncertain inputs the PAGE model uses to produce this particular output.

The first two rows show the temperature results. PAGE calculates the global mean temperature will be between 1.0°C and 2.6°C higher in 2050 than in 1990, with a mean value of 1.7°C higher. This range has a standard deviation that is 20% of its mean value, which is comparable to the uncertainty in the inputs shown in Table 11.1. The last column shows that PAGE has only used five uncertain inputs to produce this result, so perhaps it is not too surprising that the uncertainty has not greatly reduced. The second row shows how much the global mean temperature exceeds what is tolerable in 2050. The mean value is very close to the 1.7°C mean temperature rise minus the 0.5°C most likely tolerable rise from Table 11.1. Because the mean value is smaller, the uncertainty is greater, with a standard deviation that is 40% of its mean value.

The next three rows show the economic impacts calculated by the model. The damage to the EU transport sector is calculated to be somewhere between 10 and 140 billion ECU in 2050, with a mean value of 60 billion ECU. Some readers may be puzzled that this mean value is much higher than the 1.3°C by which the temperature rise exceeds the tolerable multiplied by the most likely valuation of 5 billion ECU per degree Celsius. It is higher for two reasons. The first is that the valuation input is highly asymmetrical, as can be seen from Table 11.1, and has a mean value that is about 8 billion ECU. The second is that the valuation increases with GDP, which is assumed to grow at about 2.5% per year in the EU from 1990 to 2050. For comparison, the impact of 60 billion ECU is about 0.2% of EU Gross Regional Product in 2050. The uncertainty here is even higher, with a standard deviation that is 60%

of its mean value, even though the model has used eight uncertain inputs to obtain this result.

The final two rows show the impacts including all other economic sectors as well as transport and other regions than the EU. The economic damage in all sectors for the EU of between 300 and 1600 billion ECU is between about 1% and 5% of EU Gross Regional Product in 2050. The actual values do not have great policy significance; remember that the inputs are only plausible illustrative ones. What is important is that the uncertainty in the output remains high, with a standard deviation at 40% of its mean value, both for total EU economic damage, and for whole world economic damage, despite the use of 26 uncertain inputs to calculate the former result and 32 uncertain inputs to calculate the latter. Thus the expectation that combining the uncertain inputs in a model would greatly decrease the uncertainty has not been borne out in practice.

It is worth asking why the uncertainty does not decrease. The first reason is that some inputs are simply more important than others. Their variation has a bigger effect on the output. PAGE itself calculates the importance of each input in each output calculation (see Hope *et al.*, 1993). For this experiment, the most important input turns out to be the equilibrium temperature rise for a doubling of CO_2 concentration, followed by the valuation on the services sector (because of inundation of cities), followed by the warming halflife and so on. The valuation of the transport sector comes 23rd in this list. So although the model may use 32 inputs to produce the result, it may well be that only the variation in the first five or so have any significant effect. Thus an n of 5 rather than an n of 32 would appear in the $1/\sqrt{n}$ reduction in uncertainty. The second reason is that the PAGE model is performing calculations that are more complex than simply adding the inputs together. For instance, the climate part of PAGE uses the warming halflife as a constant in a negative exponential expression, and the valuation input is used as a multiplier of the temperature rise above the tolerable level. A third reason that is not allowed in the PAGE model, but is often the case in reality is that some of the inputs are not independent. For instance, if the valuation of damage is high in one economic sector, it may be more likely that the damage will be high in others as well. With positive correlation like this among inputs, the reduction in uncertainty will again be less than expected.

Conclusions

The two main conclusions of this chapter are that the judgements people use to answer contingent valuation questions are likely to include rules of thumb that will lead to systematic biases in their answers, and that we cannot assume that these biases will be rendered harmless by the combination of values that goes on in policy analysis. In particular, any ranges of values elicited or inferred are likely to be too narrow. The combination of these ranges with others inside policy models will lead to broad ranges for the outputs of the models, not the much more precise outputs that a naive view of uncertainty might lead us to expect.

As stated in the introduction to this chapter, these conclusions do not include any consideration of the difficulties of protest votes, inadequate framing of questions, category mistakes or other philosophical objections that some commentators have raised.

Two pieces of practical guidance can be offered to minimize the difficulties identified. First, use an appropriate elicitation protocol whenever uncertain values are sought (such as those in Morgan and Henrion, 1990). These protocols encapsulate many years' experience of trying to minimize the biases that would otherwise occur. Second, do not assume that mean values are sufficient for policy analysis. Any models built to use uncertain values should have a complete probabilistic treatment of uncertainty. Prototypes of such models already exist, in the environmental policy field, as well as others (Dowlatabadi and Morgan, 1993; Hope *et al.*, 1993).

Acknowledgement

The PAGE model was developed by a team at Cambridge Decision Analysts and Environmental Resources Management, with funding from DG XI of the Commission of the European Communities.

References

Adelman, M.A. (1993) Modelling world oil supply. *The Energy Journal* 14(1), 1–32.

Caddy, P., Hawdon, D., Jordan, R.M., Stevens, P. and Toalster, J. (1992) *Prospects for Oil Prices in 1992 and Beyond.* SEEDS Discussion Paper No. 63, Surrey Energy Economics Centre, Guildford.

CRU/ERL (1992) *Economic Evaluation of Impacts and Adaptive Measures in the European Community,* Phase 3, final report. Commission of the European Communities, DG XI, Brussels.

Dixon, E. (1989) Modelling under uncertainty: comparing three acid-rain models. *Journal of the Operational Research Society (Oxford)* 40(1), 29–40.

Dowlatabadi, H. and Morgan, M.G. (1993) A model framework for integrated studies of the climate problem. *Energy Policy* 21(3), 209–221.

Ekins, P. (1992) *Wealth Beyond Measure*. Gaia, London.

EMF (1982) *World Oil*. Energy Modeling Forum Summary Report 6. Stanford University, Stanford.

Hope, C. (1992) *A Fast and Simple Model of Global Warming from Greenhouse Gas Emissions*. Research paper 1992/1993 No. 2. Judge Institute of Management Studies, University of Cambridge.

Hope, C., Anderson, J. and Wenman, P. (1993) Policy analysis of the greenhouse effect. *Energy Policy* 21(3), 327–338.

IPCC (1990) *Climate Change: The IPCC Scientific Assessment*. Cambridge University Press, Cambridge.

Kelman, S. (1981) Cost–benefit analysis: an ethical critique. *Regulation* 5(1), 33–40. Reprinted in: Glickman, T.S. and Gough, M. (eds) (1990) *Readings in Risk*. Resources for the Future, Washington DC.

Lichtenstein, S., Fischhoff, B. and Phillips, L.D. (1982) Calibration of probabilities: the state of the art to 1980. In: Kahneman, D., Slovic, P. and Tversky, A. (eds) *Judgement under Uncertainty: Heuristics and Biases*. Cambridge University Press, Cambridge.

Meyer, P.L. (1969) *Introductory Probability and Statistical Applications*, 2nd edn. Addison-Wesley, Reading, Massachusetts.

Morgan, M.G. and Henrion, M. (1990) *Uncertainty: A Guide to Dealing with Uncertainty in Quantitative Risk and Policy Analysis*. Cambridge University Press, Cambridge.

Nordhaus, W.D. (1991) To slow or not to slow: the economics of the greenhouse effect. *Economic Journal* 101, 920–937.

Sagoff, M. (1988) *The Economy of the Earth*. Cambridge University Press, Cambridge.

Tversky, A. and Kahneman, D. (1974) Judgement under uncertainty: heuristics and biases. *Science* 185, 1124–1131.

Watson, S.R. and Buede, D.M. (1987) *Decision Synthesis*. Cambridge University Press, Cambridge.

12

Transferability of Benefit Estimates

Ken Willis and Guy Garrod

University of Newcastle upon Tyne

Introduction

The transferability of benefits refers to the extent to which the process, demand function, and values, estimated for one particular site or policy can be applied to estimate the benefits attributable to another site elsewhere or to an alternative policy proposal.

In considering the environmental benefits and costs associated with another development proposal, or the extension of environmental protection to other areas, decision makers must decide whether the benefits and costs estimated for one site or policy can be extrapolated to another; or whether instead to commission a new benefit assessment study for the new site or policy. It is simply not feasible on the grounds of time and resource constraints to conduct new research projects to analyse the benefits of every policy, regulatory change, or the addition of new protected areas to an existing programme. Thus interest has arisen, especially in government, in investigating the extent to which the benefits estimated, by travel cost methods (TCMs), hedonic price methods (HPMs), contingent valuation methods (CVMs) or other benefit estimation techniques, in one specific policy context or location, can be transferred to other sites and policies.

The Treasury 'Green Book' explicitly recognizes that:

> Approaches to valuation can sometimes be borrowed from other contexts or from similar programmes, but that the values derived are often quite specific to a particular area of application. For example,
> (i) the characteristics of the consumers or client group may differ,
> (ii) the demand for units of output will depend in part on relative prices of other goods and services. These may vary.

191

Such factors limit the extent to which values can be generalised

(HM Treasury, 1991)

In some contexts, such as the appraisal of transport, health, safety regulations, and industrial schemes, values of life appear in practice to be readily transferred between activities, areas and policies.[1] A standard value of life is often applied in valuing improvements in safety across many policies and across individuals affected. In this way the transfer of a statistical average benefit estimate is routinely undertaken. However, this benefit transfer procedure is crude and, where fatality numbers are small, rarely accounts for differences between age, income, and other characteristics of individuals. These results are in contrast to those found in economic research which has shown that different individuals attach different values to safety, and have different attitudes towards risk.[2] Furthermore, psychologists have revealed that individuals do not view dying from different causes with equal equanimity, and have different values for avoiding death according to the particular context.[3]

Where relatively large numbers of individuals die across a number of areas for which government has regulatory responsibility towards safety and protection, the value of life will tend towards the average. However, the average value argument may not be appropriate in environmental cases especially if individual cases are few in number; and hence, the transferability of values may be less applicable and acceptable in the environmental area.

[1] However, variations in the value of life abound as revealed in the implicit decisions of environmental and safety regulators. Recently van Houtven and Cropper (1994) have pointed out for the EPA in the USA, which administers the Clean Air Act; Clean Water Act; Federal Insecticide, Fungicide, and Rodenticide Act; and the Toxic Substances Control Act; that: (i) regulations under different Acts imply different values of life for cancer cases avoided, from $52 million for cancer cases avoided amongst pesticide applicators; $49 million per case for asbestos regulations; (ii) for air pollution regulations to reduce carcinogens risks from vinyl chloride, benzene, inorganic arsenic, and radio-nuclides, $15 million per cancer case avoided if the risk was less than 1 in 10,000, both before and after the vinyl chloride decision of the US Court of Appeals for the District of Columbia in 1987, but for risks greater than 1 in 10,000 and infinite value of life; (iii) these values were much higher than the value of life implicit in workers' occupational choices of about $5 million.

[2] Indeed Jones-Lee and Loomes (1994) have pointed out that because of preferences and attitudes to risk, there is no reason to suppose that willingness to pay (WTP) to prevent a fatality on the London Underground need be the same as on roads. They suggest that WTP is 1.75 times greater for the Underground than for roads.

[3] Similar arguments about individual values and average values occur in other professions. British medicine operates on reasonable doctor and patient standards which precludes strict liability for damages to remote chances (1% to 2%) of serious unintended consequences of operations (Brahams, 1985), although allowing negligence. American clinical–legal practice is patient orientated, based on the patient's need to know. The American rule would have found in favour of the plaintiff in the Sidaway case; whereas under British law Mrs Sidaway lost her case for compensation when the court ruled that although the surgeon had not told her about the 1% to 2% chance of becoming paralysed as result of a laminectomy to relieve back pain, negligence had not occurred, and a reasonable patient might well have accepted such a risk (Schwartz and Grubb, 1985).

Nevertheless, in environmental regulation, physical standards apply in air and water pollution, which are also assumed to be readily transferable between different locations. Moreover, many environmentalists in evaluating policy make comparisons between countries and policies. So to some extent the concept of transferability has already been implicitly accepted. Brookshire and Neil (1992) have argued that 'benefit transfers are valid under well defined conditions, and that no one appears to argue that they are impossible. Thus, the debate becomes one of limits and the protocol associated with transfers as against whether benefit transfers should be accomplished.'

In trying to estimate the benefits of a policy proposal, decision makers have a choice of the following:

1. commissioning new research;
2. explicitly predicting environmental benefits by extrapolating benefits estimated from previous studies using TCM, HPM, CVM, or other techniques;
3. implicitly using their own intuitive judgement, which invariably involves the transferability of benefits based upon their 'professional experience'.

If neither of the first two options are undertaken, decision makers invariably extrapolate, on the basis of cognitive knowledge, in an intuitive and ill-structured way with little analysis. Given the problems of biases that affect judgement at this basic level on the cognitive continuum (see Hamm, 1984), a more structured approach to the transferability of benefits is surely better. Thus the debate becomes one about the protocol associated with the transferability of benefits in particular situations, and the limits to transferability.

Travel cost methods and hedonic price models have been used in the past to predict the benefits associated with future developments and proposed policies, from existing demand functions and benefit estimates. However, for a number of reasons greater controversy surrounds the transferability of benefits estimated by CVMs. First, concerns about the inaccuracy of CVMs with respect to non-market goods, and to the passive use value of goods, may mean that the transferability of the process, and benefit estimates to other goods and policies simply compounds the existing problems and inaccuracies. Second, CVM studies reporting empirical estimates, have tended to value goods with unique characteristics, and have not incorporated sufficient variables in a conventional demand model $[q = f(p, s, c, y, a)$, where q = quantity, p = price, s = substitutes, c = complements, y = income; a = attitudes or preferences] to permit the transferability of benefit estimates. Third, in the environmental field, CVM has frequently been applied to valuing the risk of a change or the risk of an irreversible change such as the extinction of a particular species. Respondents typically experience great difficulty in articulating small probability changes in terms of utility to themselves (see Jones-Lee *et al.*, 1985). Moreover, unlike studies into the value of life and safety, in environmental economics individuals are requested to respond and to value changes without knowledge of the probability of the loss. They also experience difficulty in valuing an irreversible change, given their demand uncertainty for the good. Fourth, for a variety of reasons they often fail to adhere to an expected utility solution (see Kahneman and Tversky, 1979). Fifth, CVM studies have typically valued environmental goods in a partial equilibrium framework; and have usually also valued the first site in the programme, and ignored other sites such as the last marginal site. The partial equilibrium framework suggests that people would simultaneously be willing to pay to save almost every environmental programme suggested. Moreover, valuing only the first item or area in an environmental programme renders it impossible to value the whole programme, since nothing is known about the value of marginal increments to the programme.

This chapter first explores transferability of environmental values from experts' opinions through intuition; before moving on to review transferability through travel cost models; and finally considering transferability in contingent valuation methods.

Transferability of Benefits and Costs from Expert Opinion

The opinions of experts, whether professionals or administrators, is perhaps the most ubiquitous form by which the transferability of benefits is imputed and accomplished.

One of the most famous studies in which the opinions of experts was employed, in the transferability of benefits and costs, was that of the Third London Airport (Commission on the Third London Airport, 1970: the Roskill Commission). The opinions of estate agents were employed by the Roskill Commission to estimate the utility loss (cost) of environmental externalities associated with noise at the site of the proposed Third London Airport, from knowledge of the effect of noise on house prices around Heathrow and Gatwick airports. The Roskill Commission valued environmental externalities (bads) at the minimum households would be willing to accept (WTA) as just compensation for their loss. This was evaluated in terms of:

1. depreciation in house prices as a result of the increase in noise [from estimates by estate agents using their intuitive judgements];

2. transactions costs to households of moving house to avoid the increase in noise [which could have been estimated from the market prices of legal, removal, and other associated costs];
3. loss of consumer surplus over and above the market price of the house [from a CVM survey of households].

The consumer surplus and removal expenses were elicited by a sample survey, from the following CVM question:

> Suppose your house was wanted to form part of a large development scheme and the developer offered to buy it from you, what price would be just enough to compensate you for leaving this house (flat) and moving to another area?
>
> (Commission on the Third London Airport, 1970)

The market price of houses, and estimates of depreciation in price because of noise, were obtained from estate agents in comparable situations around Gatwick and Heathrow, on the argument that:

> The professional valuer is constantly in touch with the prices at which houses change hands and with the valuations made for other purposes (e.g. estate duty). His professional skill lies largely in making suitable allowance for the multitude of factors entering into the valuation of any particular house i.e. that part of the problem which causes difficulty for the statistician
>
> (Commission on the Third London Airport, 1970)

While some research has suggested a close correlation between estate agents' estimates of total house price and estimates derived from an HPM (Dodgson and Topham, 1990); other research has revealed discrepancies between estate agents in their total valuation of the same property, greater discrepancies (up to 100%) in their valuation of the effect of an environmental attribute even when all other variables were held constant, and extremely high estimates of value for the attribute compared with those derived from an hedonic price model (Willis and Garrod, 1993).

Owing to the problem of quantifying in monetary terms the value of benefits to patients' and their families, resource allocation decisions in health care operate on the basis of expert opinions and professional judgements. Even in cost–utility analysis, the enumeration of quality-adjusted life years (QALYs) for various health-care operations is often based upon experts' opinions[4] rather than on utility assessments of recipients (patients and relatives), although occasionally the latter are

---

[4] See for example the study by Stason and Weinstein (1977), where it was assumed on the basis of expert consensus, not independently verified, that a year with side effects from hypertension therapy to avoid a stroke was equivalent to 0.99 of a healthy year. Other examples of this approach include Weinstein (1980), Willems *et al.* (1980), Churchill *et al.* (1984), Williams (1985).

incorporated.[5] While some investigators have found little difference between the utility estimates of patients and those of doctors (Sackett and Torrence, 1978; Kaplan and Bush, 1982; Wolfson *et al.*, 1982); others have detected differences (see Williams, 1985). Moreover, a large number of empirical studies in the clinical field have revealed that intuitive judgements are subject to considerable biases and errors. For example, McGoogan (1984) revealed that 39% of main clinical diagnoses were not confirmed at autopsy, and even in cases where physicians were reasonably confident of their diagnosis, their main diagnosis was not confirmed in 25% of cases. de Dombal (1984) found that the accuracy of diagnosis of cases in an accident and emergency department of a hospital varied from 42% for admitting doctors; to 71% for house surgeons; 79% for registrars; 82% for senior clinicians; and 91% for a computer aided system. Renwick *et al.* (1991) found that radiographers disagreed with radiologists in 9.4% of examinations: there were 7% false positives and 14% false negatives.[6]

In the environment field, intuitive, rule of thumb, measures employed in assessing water supply projects frequently turn out to be inaccurate. Pearce and Warford (1993), for example, report a study by Whittington *et al.* (1990) in Haiti which estimated an average willingness to pay (WTP) of 1.7% of household income for stand-pipes and 2.1% for private connections, both significantly lower than the assumed WTP of 3% to 5% of household income by The World Bank in appraising the feasibility of water supply projects.

People, including experts, have limited information processing abilities, and this (bounded rationality) affects how people interpret values and make choices.[7] Tversky and Kahneman (1974) point to representativeness, availability, and anchoring as heuristics employed for making judgements under uncertainty and numerical predictions. These heuristics, while highly economical, lead to systematic and predictable errors. Given these findings it is surely preferable to rely on more objectively validated techniques.[8]

---

[5] In the study by Boyle *et al.* (1983) the QALYs added by a neonatal intensive care programme were calculated using paediatricians' forecasts of lifetime outcomes, and utility assessments of health states made by a random sample of parents.

[6] A false positive occurs where a patient is diagnosed as having a disease, but doesn't actually have it. A false negative occurs where a patient is diagnosed as not having a disease, whilst he or she actually has the disease.

[7] Indeed, a linear model of the decision maker's own judgements invariably outperforms the intuitive predictions of the expert himself (see Dawes and Corrigan, 1974; Dawes *et al.*, 1989). By estimating the implicit weights used by the human judge, and eliminating any noise or inconsistencies, such bootstrapping models (so called because an individual can improve his judgement or pull himself up by his own mental bootstraps) typically outperform the human judge.

[8] And if you still don't believe in the ability of experts to value goods incorrectly by several orders of magnitude, then recall the auction at Christie's on 19th May 1993 when auctioneers expected an early 19th century German mechanical calculator to fetch £15,000, and eventually sold it for £7.7 million!

Transferability of Benefits from Travel Cost Models

Some of the earliest examples of the more systematic transfer of benefits occur in recreational demand studies employing travel cost models. The early travel cost models developed by Clawson and Knetsch (1966) were zonal travel cost models (ZTCMs); in which the quantity of participation (demand), expressed as visits per unit of population per zone of origin, was related to the price of access, and the characteristics (income, and so on) of residents in each zone:

$$V_{ij}/N_i = f(TC_{ij}, T_{ij}, Y_i, S_i, A_k)$$

where:

V_{ij} = trips from zone i to site j
N_i = population of zone i
TC_{ij} = travel costs from zone i to j sites,
T_{ij} = travel time from zone i to j
Y_i = average income in zone i
S_i = socioeconomic characteristics of zone i
Q_j = recreation quality at site j
A_k = measure of the cost and quality of substitute site k to origin i.

ZTCMs estimate the demand for existing recreational activities. The benefits to consumers from proposed facilities are estimated by transferring the demand functions from existing facilities, where the prospective facility closely resembles the existing facility in the type of recreation it provides. If the catchment areas of the two sites are mutually exclusive, then multiplying the existing site coefficients by the values of the independent variables for the new site would give a reasonable estimate of both the use and benefits attributable to the new site. Thus only by chance would the same social valuation be placed on the new facility as the old, despite the fact that the same basic relationship is assumed. Loomis (1992) argued that this approach is likely to yield a more accurate estimate of the benefits of a new site than simply applying an average value of benefit per visitor day to the new site, since benefits are a complex function of site characteristics, user characteristics, and spatial characteristics of the site relative to visitors' residences (i.e. each site has a unique matrix of own price and substitute prices).

Where a new facility is situated within the catchment area of an existing facility, a demand curve is estimated for each site as if it were the only one. If consumer surplus from the proposed facility exceeds the existing one, then the net gain from having the proposed facility is taken as the difference between the two consumer surplus values, summed over all zones.

Often the proposed site does not exactly resemble any existing site, due to differences between the mix of recreation facilities offered, or differences in the scenic backdrop between the two sites. The lack of homogeneity in product mix may be remedied by valuing the different recreational activities separately and aggregating, rather than developing a demand curve for the site as a whole (see for example, Lewis and Whitby, 1972). With the development of multi-site or regional TCMs incorporating variations in site quality (e.g. reservoir size, water quality, fish catches, etc.) it is no longer necessary to find a similar site: a new site could be represented by any linear combination of site characteristics from existing sites (see Dwyer *et al.*, 1977). The problem of scenic backdrop was, and remains, more difficult. Mansfield (1971) attempted to estimate the recreation benefits from the proposed Morecambe Bay Barrage. The new site was closer to the Liverpool–Manchester conurbation than the Lake District, resulting in a diversion of trips. If sites are perfectly homogeneous, of course, then, in theory, as soon as the price for one becomes cheaper everyone should divert. However, the qualities associated with the Lake District suggested this was unlikely to happen. Hence Mansfield assumed that the degree of diversion depended upon the price reduction, according to the following formula

$$(PL - PB) / 0.5(PL + PB)$$

where PL = price of visiting the Lake District, and PB = price of visiting the Barrage. The formula indicates an increasing willingness to substitute one site for the other as the price differentials grow. Thus when PB falls to $0.333(PL)$, complete diversion occurs.

The problems of transferability of benefit estimates from both ZTCMs and individual travel cost models (ITCMs) stem from the many potential errors in estimating recreational demand functions and the calculation of implied benefits. McConnell (1992) lists errors in the demand function as:

1. Choosing the wrong functional form $f(\cdot)$. Different functions produce very different estimates of consumer surplus.[9]
2. Selecting an incomplete or inappropriate set of arguments, e.g. ignoring some of the q values. Thus, truncated maximum likelihood estimates are significantly lower than the usually reported ordinary least squares estimates.
3. Measuring arguments incorrectly, as frequently occurs with income,

---

[9] Smith (1988) calculated consumer surplus increased by 50% with a semi-log function rather than a linear model; while in the Kling (1988) study it doubled. Larger variations were observed by Willis and Garrod (1991): the double log being unbounded, the semi-log (dependent) being 20 times larger than the linear model, but with the semi-log (independent) and the linear model being reasonably close.

the value of time, cost of access (price per mile for car usage).[10]
4. Measuring the dependent variable with error: the frequency of visits is especially important for the ITCM.[11]

The presence of substitute sites in TCMs is also important, deflating the expected consumer surplus. However, Donnelly and Price (1984) have shown, through a simulation model, that if sites are randomly distributed substitution effects cancel out and a ZTCM correctly estimates the contribution of the site to the value of a recreation system. In theory clustered sites should be over-valued by a simple ZTCM which ignores substitutes, and systematically spaced sites under-valued.

The calculation of benefits also provides opportunities for error, for example in estimating the number of participants and the extent of the market.[12]

Loomis (1992) assessed the validity of the transferability of TCM benefit estimates by comparing site-specific benefit estimates with those derived from transferring TCM equations: a multi-site TCM demand equation for steelhead fishing in Oregon was estimated for $n - 1$ of the Oregon steelhead rivers and then the equation used to predict the nth or missing river. The percentage difference between total recreation benefits estimated from the full multi-site TCM and from the transferred model (omitting the specified river) ranged from a few percentage points to 17.5%. Transferring the equation to the unstudied site rather than simply using average benefits per trip from the full model, provided a better indicator of benefit for the unstudied site: the 10-year average benefit per trip frequently had percentage differences of 25% or greater, while the transferred equation benefit per trip only once differed from the actual site-specific estimate by more than 10%. Loomis (1992) did note, however, that cross-state benefit transfers, even for identically defined activities between Idaho, Oregon and Washington, were more inaccurate, and suggested further investigation of factors affecting transferability between states and

[10] Estimates of consumer surplus vary depending upon whether access costs are based on petrol costs only, or include depreciation and services costs associated with car usage. Adding in time costs of travel similarly increases consumer surplus associated with recreational facilities (Willis and Garrod, 1991).

[11] McConnell (1992) reported a study which found estimated annual fishing trips were 27% higher with an annual recall period than a 6-month period, with the annual mean from an annual recall of an in-person interview being almost twice the annual mean from a 2-month recall in a telephone interview.

[12] Gibson (1974) demonstrated that the semi-log and double log model produced substantial differences in the estimated numbers of participants from changes in admission prices; while Willis and Garrod (1991) showed that linear, semi-log and double log models varied significantly in their prediction of visits compared with actual visits to sites, and in the correlation between predicted and actual visit numbers across distance zones.

how to incorporate systematic differences between states to make models more transferable.

Contingent Valuation and Environmental Assets

Whether CVM estimates are transferable depends upon their accuracy, and whether the new good to be valued is sufficiently similar to the existing good for which CVM estimates are available.

CVM estimates have been shown to roughly match market values where the methodology has been applied experimentally to situations in which market values exist (see Bishop and Heberlein, 1979; Dickie *et al.*, 1987). This criterion validity of CVM estimates suggests they are transferable in these circumstances.

For specific goods, different assessment methods have been shown to produce convergent results in certain circumstances (see Smith *et al.*, 1986). Cummings *et al.* (1986) report reasonably strong convergent validity for CVM, with studies they reviewed producing estimates within a ± 50% range: an error which may not affect a cost–benefit analysis outcome, but which might appall a polluter faced with a bill for damages under CERCLA! (Comprehensive Environmental Response, Compensation and Liability Act, 1980).

In terms of theoretical validity (the degree to which the findings of a study, and especially the coefficients of the independent variables, are consistent with theoretical expectations), explained variation in individuals' WTP has varied between 1% and 48% in different studies, with more consistency in the size and even greater robustness in the sign of the coefficients explaining WTP.

CVM is the most widely employed technique for valuing environmental assets, especially where passive (non-use) values also need to be derived. However, CVM is commonly applied to environmental, natural and wildlife, resources:

1. with unique sets or combinations of attributes;
2. to a good less than perfectly described;
3. measured in relation to an incomplete substitute set;
4. measured in a single focus CV question rather than as part of a more inclusive set;
5. valued as an intramarginal unit rather than a marginal unit of the resource;
6. assessed from a partial rather than a general equilibrium perspective.

These issues need to be addressed if greater transferability of values is to be achieved. There are two basic methods by which they can be tackled:

1. assessing the *product* and improving *CVM methodology* more thoroughly: the economists' solution;
2. investigating the *process* of economic thought: the psychologists' and sceptical economists' solution.

Both should be advanced simultaneously to ensure confidence in the transferability of values.

The product

CVM estimates for private goods are generally readily transferable to other private goods, where homogeneity prevails, with the same protocols as those applying to travel cost estimates. In public good situations recommendations for improving the *product* and *methodology* have been advocated by the Arrow–Solow (1993) Panel, and by Gregory *et al.* (1993). These revolve around greater concentration on valuing the attributes of the good; and tighter definitions of the description of the good, substitute set, the focus of WTP questions, embedding and scoping effects.

For use values, stated preference methods can further unpack the contribution of attributes to the value of a specific good or site, thus aiding the transferability of values as in TCMs by addressing the issue of different combinations of attributes associated with a resource. Stated preference methods such as tradeoff and conjoint analysis 'are decompositional methods that estimate the structure of a consumer's preference ... given his/her overall evaluation of a set of alternatives that are pre-specified in terms of levels of different attributes' (Green and Srinivasan, 1978; quoted in Kroes and Sheldon, 1988).

Moreover, as Adamowicz *et al.* (1994) have shown, stated preference (SP) and revealed preference (RP) methods yield similar results for water based recreation use values, while SP can improve the quality of estimates of a RP model by avoiding colinearity which is so often a feature of RP models.

The transferability of non-use values remains more problematical, since for example in nature conservation it involves attribute concepts such as size, diversity, naturalness, rarity, typicalness, fragility, recorded history, position in an ecological and geographical unit, potential value, and intrinsic appeal. But evaluating these is not necessarily intractable. Gregory *et al.* (1993) argue that this requires a Multi-Attribute Utility Theory (MAUT) approach since open-ended holistic responses are poor in terms of construct validity for goods with several value relevant attributes.[13] MAUT also tackles the embedding problem

---

[13] Studies have found that when people are asked to make holistic judgements about multidimensional stimuli, they typically make use of fewer cues than they say they (*continued over*)

because it focuses responses to the specific problem rather than to general 'moral satisfaction'; and because responses are more sensitive to specifications.

Hanemann (1994) also points out that demand is context specific, i.e. people will perceive broadleaved trees differently in different landscapes. The more that is known about these contexts, the greater the confidence that can be placed in benefit transfers.

Transferability may be improved with respect to these concerns by following more closely the Arrow–Solow (1993) recommendations to the National Oceanic and Atmospheric Administration, namely:

1. accurate description of the good being evaluated;
2. reminder of undamaged or alternative substitute commodities;
3. alternative expenditure possibilities: a mental accounting approach to avoid a single focus WTP response;
4. the accumulation of standard damage assessment values, so that new benefit (opportunity costs forgone) estimates can be judged in context.

Hanemann (1994) argued that more empirical information is required on scope effects: by how much should people value preventing 200,000 bird deaths more than 2000 in the central flyway? If q_0 is the number of birds in the population; q_r the number of birds at risk from dying; and q_s the number of those saved: are q_0, q_r, and q_s perfect substitutes? Economic theory is silent on this issue: empirical tests are required to trace out these relationships. Neoclassical economics provides no theoretical basis for specifying the shape and content of the utility function.

The process

Psychologists use 'verbal protocol' to gain insight into how respondents arrive at particular answers. Verbal protocols can provide an indication of respondents' thought processes while answering a CVM question. This is important since research suggests that CVM responses can be sensitive to some irrelevant factors[14] and insensitive to some relevant ones.[15]

---

[13](*contd*) do (see Willis and Powe 1995). Faced with complexity people resort to simplifying strategies. The more complex the decision problem the more likely that expressions of value will be constructed based only on a subset of the available information. Thus accurate and transferable values are more likely to be obtained from decompositional procedures than from holistic ones.

[14] For example the payment vehicle, sequence of commodities, WTP versus WTA, gain/loss framing, sunk costs, etc.

[15] Embedding, the question of capital versus annual payments, dichotomous choice versus open-ended question formats.

Verbal protocols should be able to establish under what conditions CVM estimates for one good, or site, can be applied to others. Conditions under which values can be transferred, because they derive from common processes in formulating values, are where:

1. Respondents have well-formed and articulated values which can be retrieved through an appropriate CVM elicitation question. If on the other hand WTP responses are constructed during an elicitation question, then such responses might be highly sensitive to the task and context of a particular CVM survey, and hence less readily transferable.

2. Respondents adopt the same rational economic model. Even though values may differ across individuals, because they have different utility functions, or across situations because some things are worth more than others, the process by which values are calculated should be the same in all cases (whether the maximization of expected utility, minimization of regret, or whatever). If different people use different strategies, or the same person uses different strategies in similar situations, then transferability of values will be invalid. Similarly, transferability will be enhanced where people adopt the same strategy with regard to the ambient tendencies in the environment (base rate information) and features of the current situation (case-specific information).[16]

3. Expressed values are not highly labile. However, in practice many expressed values do appear to be highly labile: subtle aspects of how problems are posed, questions are phrased, and responses are elicited can have substantial impacts on judgements that supposedly express people's 'true values'. If values for particular goods are labile, then the transferability of such values poses problems. Fischhoff *et al.* (1980) argued that in tackling this problem there may be no substitute for an interactive, dialectical elicitation procedure, one that acknowledges the elicitor's role in helping the respondent to create and enunciate values. Such help might include a conceptual analysis of the problem, and of the personal, social and ethical issues to which the respondent might wish to relate, and the provision of tools including education in economics, etc., and training in decision making.

4. Procedural invariance does not exist. Equivalent procedures should result in the same order of preference for a set of objects. Preference reversals, where A is preferred to B under one method of measurement

---

[16] People typically ignore base rates and over-emphasize case-specific information in decisions. For an accurate estimate of WTP for a good this is important; but it is not important for the transferability of values, since all values will be equally biased.

while B is preferred to A under a different but equivalent measurement procedure,[17] violates procedural invariance. Procedure invariance is likely to hold if people have well established preferences; or have an algorithm for computing the answer.[18]

Meta Analysis

CVM estimates of annual WTP by individuals or households per year for landscape and nature conservation in Britain vary enormously (see Table 12.1). However, many of the differences between estimates from various studies can often be accounted for, or explained, by differences in populations of reference; different values held by users compared with non-users; the different number of benefit issues estimated by the study; whether a marginal change in quantity is being valued or the value of the good in total is being assessed; whether the change is irreversible or not; the elicitation format employed by the CVM study; the extent to which embedding is a problem in the valuation of the good; the framing of the study and the questions; the uniqueness of the good; and whether substitutes are available and considered in the valuation of the specific good. This list is not exhaustive, but provides some flavour of the factors which can give rise to different CVM benefit estimates for nature conservation objectives, objectives which conserve many distinct and different goods.

In a similar comparison, but across a wider range of goods, Bateman *et al.* (1994) have argued by intuitive inspection that:

1. where many substitutes exist in a local area then low WTP valuations are elicited;
2. as the number of substitutes falls, then WTP valuations rise significantly;
3. where there are no local substitutes, and where the landscape would

---

[17] For example, most subjects choose an H bet (8:9 chance to win $4) over an L bet (1:9 chance to win $40). When asked to state the minimum price they would sell each gamble if they owned it, most subjects put a higher price on the L bet. Preference reversals have been observed in a range of situations (see Slovic and Lichtenstein, 1983, Tversky *et al.*, 1990).

[18] Consider two traffic safety improvement proposals. Programme A saves 30 lives each year at an annual cost of $12 million. Programme B saves 100 lives each year at an annual cost of $55 million. When a sample of people are asked which programme they prefer, a substantial majority indicate a preference for Programme B. A second sample are asked to state the cost that would make the programmes equally attractive, and an even greater majority gave figures smaller than $55 million. Tversky and Thaler (1990) quote this as an example of preference reversal. Jones-Lee (personal communication, 1990) argues that two meanings can be placed on 'equally attractive': (i) equal value for money, i.e. equal B/C ratios, (ii) such that one would be indifferent between the two programmes. Respondents who adopt (i) as a decision criterion for computing an answer, requiring *equality in cost per life saved,* would logically quote a value less than $55 million., i.e. $40 million to be exact.

Table 12.1. Comparison of some CVM estimates of WTP for landscape and nature conservation in Britain.

Author	WTP	Aggregate WTP	Good being valued
Willis (1990)	£0.82 Skipwith Common £0.61 Derwent Ings £1.29 Upper Teesdale (per year) (non-use plus option values)		Three SSSIs
Hanley and Craig (1991)	£16.79 (capital payment/household)	£68,419,000 (for Scottish population)	Preservation value of the Flow Country in Scotland
Hanley and Spash (1993)	£0.74 per visit £9.73 per visit £25.57 capitalized payment		Heathland conservation in Dorset
Willis and Garrod (1992)	£26.03 per visitor £22.12 per resident (household per year)	£41,760,000 (visitors) £120,000 (residents)	Preservation of today's landscape in the Yorkshire Dales
Bateman et al. (1992)	£76.04 (OE) visitors £224.01 (DC) visitors £4.08 (OE) non-user (household per year)	£5,989,000 to £7,773,000 (user values) £109,852,000 (non-use benefits)	Preservation of the landscape of the Norfolk Broads from increased risk of flooding
Willis et al. (1993)	£27.52 (OE) resident £19.47 (OE) visitor £1.98 (OE) non-user } South Downs £17.53 (OE) resident £11.84 (OE) visitor £2.45 (per household per year) } Somerset Levels and Moors	£48,682,000 (user values) £31,153,000 (non-use benefits) £10,758,000 (user values) £41,879,000 (non-use benefits)	South Downs ESA Somerset Levels and Moors ESA

change in a significant way, then WTP valuations rise further again by a significant amount (e.g. for the Yorkshire Dales);

4. where the good is a truly unique resource, for which there is no substitute, and for which the change would be irreversible (e.g. flooding of the Norfolk Broads), then WTP rises even higher;

5. household WTP values for large areas such as Environmentally Sensitive Areas (ESAs) are much greater than WTP estimates for smaller Sites of Special Scientific Interest (SSSIs), and for less well-known sites.

Meta analysis improves upon intuitive judgement by using data based aids in terms of regression analysis to explain variations in WTP estimated in different studies. Meta analysis attempts to take stock of current benefit estimates by investigating the relationship between WTP, the features of the goods, and the assumptions of the models; with the explicit aim of applying past results to future resource policy decisions.

The study by Walsh *et al.* (1989) of 287 benefit estimates (156 TCMs, 129 CVMs, and 2 HPMs) sought to explain variations in net economic benefits per activity day in terms of site, location, and methodological variables. Three models of recreational benefits were reported: one of all observations; and one each for TCM and CVM studies. Around two thirds of the explanatory variables were significant at the 0.01 level, with the models explaining between 36% and 44% of the total variation in reported values. Their principle findings were that:

1. omitting travel time in TCM studies reduced benefit estimates by 34%;

2. ITCM estimates were about 46% greater than ZTCM estimates, using the same functional form;

3. omitting an effective cross price term for substitution raised TCM values by about 30%;

4. if TCM were accepted as the standard for benefit estimation, then CVM estimates needed to be adjusted upwards by 20% to 30%, but that dichotomous choice CVM estimates were closer to TCM values;

5. significant spatial variations in recreation values existed; along with significantly different values for different activities, e.g. various kinds of fishing and hunting (the value of the product varied).

Smith and Kaoru (1990) found both the type of recreation site involved, and the assumptions implicit in the TCMs, to be instrumental in explaining TCM results, specifically that:

1. site usage measurement in terms of days produced smaller values than for trips;

2. truncated maximum likelihood estimators reduced consumer surplus estimates substantially;

3. trips to national parks were worth $20 more than trips of comparable length to coastal areas;
4. inclusion of substitute sites and exclusion of the value of time decreased consumer surplus estimates.

Walsh *et al.* (1989) suggested that controlling for the effects of payment vehicle, functional form, dichotomous choice, information, uncertainty, and substitute possibilities might permit the transferability of benefit estimates; while Smith and Kaoru (1990) believed meta analysis could best serve as a consistency check to the processes used in benefit transfer analysis for policy. Apart from these two studies, meta analysis has not been further developed to assist the transferability of benefit estimates. However, meta analysis should not be seen just as modifying existing estimates to produce a value for a new policy situation, but also as a means of investigating the factors and issues involved in the transferability of values.

Conclusion

While broad trends in environmental values are discernible, past applications of environmental valuation techniques do not bode well for benefit transfer studies. Valuation exercises tend not to be designed with future benefit transfers in mind, but rather to explore new methodologies, survey design, data modelling, or to test specific hypotheses. So whither benefit transferability? Progress could be made by:

1. Constructing a database of all UK environmental benefit estimates, plus details of the modelling procedures used, and all relevant assumptions. An elementary form of this has already been initiated by the Department of the Environment, and is held by CSERGE at University College, London (see Georgiou, 1994).
2. Requiring researchers to bear transferability in mind when undertaking valuation studies. A broad code of practice for the conduct of benefit studies should be drawn up to ensure that the outputs from valuation studies would be usable in future benefit transfers. To ensure the success of such a code of practice, government departments and other agencies funding research should make adherence to it a condition for commissioning work. Desvouges *et al.* (1992) recommended that as well as a site-specific model, valuation studies should include a transfer model which would concentrate only on those explanatory variables that are available at the majority of sites of that type.
3. Investigating the theoretical conditions under which benefit transfers would be possible. For example, the value of statistical life, and

values for morbidity avoided, are readily transferable between geographical areas. What other values fall into this category? What types of environmental value are more difficult to transfer?

4. Undertaking a series of empirical studies specifically designed to test the feasibility of benefit transfer. Boyle and Bergstrom (1992) suggested concurrently determining non-market values at both study and policy sites. Values would then be transferred from the study site to the policy site based on the study site valuation models, and compared with the values estimated directly at the policy site from primary data. The research would determine whether the values were biased, the size and direction of the bias, and adjustments required to mitigate bias in benefit transfers.

While research documenting the value of environmental outcomes and goods needs to continue in order to build a more comprehensive picture of values in different contexts; the process whereby outcomes are generated should also be explicity incorporated into the analysis, since people patently care about how outcomes are generated.[19] Simultaneously assessing the extent to which benefits can be transferred also requires the factual assumptions implicit in CVM studies to be tested,[20] and psychological techniques applied to understand the contexts in which individuals express rational choices and values and those in which expressed preferences are subject to biases.

Until a research agenda is developed and undertaken to establish the credibility of benefit transfers, only pragmatism remains: decision makers are left arguing whether a benefit transfer value is 'tenable', whether they 'feel comfortable' with that value, and whether the value is 'close enough'.

References

Adamowicz, W., Louviere, J. and Williams, M. (1994) Combining revealed and stated preference methods for valuing environmental amenities. *Journal of Environmental Economics and Management* 26, 271–292.

Arrow, K., Solow, R., Portney, P.R., Leamer, E.E., Radner, R. and Schuman, H. (1993) Report of the NOAA Panel on Contingent Valuation. *Federal Register* 58(10), 4601–4614.

Bateman, I.J., Willis, K.G., Garrod, G.D., Doktor, P., Langford, I. and Turner, R.K. (1992) *Recreation and Environment Preservation Value of the Norfolk Broads: A*

---

[19] The death of an estimated 70,000 sea birds, washed up on shores around the North Sea in the winter of 1994, from starvation through severe weather, was newsworthy. But imagine the outcry which would have occurred if they had been killed through industrial pollution.

[20] e.g. the extent to which individuals care only about the size of a wildlife population, rather than how many were in the original population, at risk, or saved.

Contingent Valuation Study. Report to the National Rivers Authority. CSERGE, University of East Anglia, Norwich.

Bateman, I.J., Willis, K.G. and Garrod, G.D. (1994) Consistency between contingent valuation estimates: a comparison of two studies of UK National Parks. *Regional Studies* 28, 457–474.

Bishop, R.C. and Heberlein, T.A. (1979) Measuring values of extra market goods: are indirect measures biased? *American Journal of Agricultural Economics* 61(5), 926–930.

Boyle, K.J. and Bergstrom, J.C. (1992) Benefit transfer studies: myths pragmatism and idealism. *Water Resources Research* 28, 657–663.

Boyle, M.H., Torrance, G.W., Sinclair, J.C. and Horwood, S.P. (1983) Economic evaluation of neonatal intensive care of very-low-birth-weight infants. *New England Journal of Medicine* 308, 1330–1337.

Brahams, D. (1985) Doctor's duty to inform patient of substantial or special risks when offering treatment. *Lancet* 528–530.

Brookshire, D.S. and Neil, H.R. (1992) Benefit transfers: conceptual and empirical issues. *Water Resources Research* 28, 651–655.

Churchill, D.N., Lemon, B.C. and Torrance, G.W. (1984) A cost-effectiveness analysis of continuous ambulatory peritoneal dialysis and hospital hemodialysis. *Medical Decision Making* 4, 489–500.

Clawson, M. and Knetsch, J. (1966) *Economics of Outdoor Recreation.* Johns Hopkins University Press for Resources for the Future, Baltimore.

Commission on the Third London Airport (1970) *Papers and Proceedings Vol. 111 (Parts 1 and 2) – Stage 111 Research and Investigation – Assessment of Short-Listed Sites.* HMSO, London.

Cummings R.G., Brookshire D.S. and Schulze W.D. (1986) *Valuing Environmental Goods: An Assessment of the Contingent Valuation Method.* Rowman and Allanheld, Totowa, New Jersey.

Dawes, R.M. and Corrigan, B. (1974) Linear models in decision making. *Psychological Bulletin* 81, 95–106.

Dawes, R.M., Faust, D. and Meehl, P. (1989) Clinical vs. actuarial judgement. *Science* 243, 1668–1673.

Desvouges, W.H., Naughton, M.C. and Parsons, G.R. (1992) Benefit transfer: conceptual problems in estimating water quality benefits using existing studies. *Water Resources Research* 28, 675–683.

de Dombal, F.T. (1984) Computer-aided diagnosis of acute abdominal pain: the British experience. *Revue d'Epidemiologie et de Sante Publique* 32, 50–56.

Dickie, M., Fisher, A. and Gerking, D. (1987) Market transactions and hypothetical demand data: a comparative study. *Journal of the American Statistical Association* 82, 69–75.

Dodgson, J.S. and Topham, N. (1990) Valuing residential properties with a hedonic price method: a comparison with results of professional valuations. *Housing Studies* 5, 209–213.

Donnelly, D.S. and Price, C. (1984) *The Clawson Method and Site Substitution: Hypothesis and Model.* Department of Forestry, University College of North Wales, Bangor.

Dwyer, J., Kelly, J. and Bowes, M. (1977) Improved procedures for valuation of the contribution of recreation to national economic development. *Report*

128, Water Resources Centre, University of Illinois at Urbana-Champaign.

Fischhoff, B., Slovic, P. and Lichtenstein, S. (1980) Knowing what you want: measuring labile values. In: Bell, D.E., Raiffa, H. and Tversky, A. (eds) *Decision Making: Descriptive, Normative and Prescriptive Interactions.* Cambridge University Press, Cambridge.

Georgiou, S. (1994) *UK Studies of the Economic Valuation of Environmental Impacts: Central Directory.* CSERGE, University College London, London.

Gibson, J.G. (1974) Recreation cost–benefit analysis: a review of English case studies. *Planning Outlook (Special Issue Panning for Recreation).*

Green, P.E. and Srinivasan, V. (1978) Conjoint analysis in consumer research: issues and outlook. *Journal of Consumer Research* 5, 103–212.

Gregory, R., Lichtenstein, S. and Slovic, P. (1993) Valuing environmental resources: a constructive approach. *Journal of Risk and Uncertainty* 7, 177–197.

Hamm, R.M. (1984) Clinical intuition and clinical analysis: expertise and the cognitive continuum. *Medical Decision Making* 4, 427–447.

Hanemann, W.M. (1994) *Contingent Valuation in Economics.* Draft paper, Department of Agricultural and Resource Economics, University of California, Berkeley.

Hanley, N. (1991) Wilderness development decisions and the Krutilla–Fisher model: the case of Scotland's 'flow country'. *Ecological Economics* 4, 145–164.

Hanley, N. and Spash, C.L. (1993) *Cost–Benefit Analysis and the Environment.* Edward Elgar, Aldershot.

HM Treasury (1991) *Economic Appraisal in Central Government: A Technical Guide for Government Departments.* HMSO, London. (See Annex B, p.48.)

Jones-Lee, M.W. and Loomes, G. (1994) Towards a willingness-to-pay based value of Underground safety. *Journal of Transport Economics and Policy* 28, 83–98.

Jones-Lee, M.W., Hammerton, M. and Philips, P.R. (1985) The value of safety: results of a national sample survey. *The Economic Journal* 95, 49–72.

Kahneman, D. and Tversky, A. (1979) Prospect theory: an analysis of decision under risk. *Econometrica* 47, 263–291.

Kaplan, R.M. and Bush, J.W. (1982) Health related quality of life measurement for evaluation research and policy analysis. *Health Psychology* 1, 61–80.

Kling, C.L. (1988) The reliability of estimates of environmental benefits from recreation demand models. *American Journal of Agricultural Economics* 70, 892–901.

Kroes, E.P. and Sheldon, R.J. (1988) Stated preference methods. *Journal of Transport Economics* 22, 11–25.

Lewis, R.C. and Whitby, M.C. (1972) Recreation benefits from a reservoir. *Research Monograph No. 2.* Agricultural Adjustment Unit, Department of Agricultural Economics, University of Newcastle upon Tyne.

Loomis, J.B. (1992) The evaluation of a more rigourous approach to benefit transfer: benefit function transfer. *Water Resources Research* 28, 701–705.

McConnell, K.E. (1992) Model building and judgement: implications for benefit transfers with travel cost models. *Water Resources Research* 28, 695–700.

McGoogan, E. (1984) The autopsy and clinical diagnosis. *Journal of the Royal College of Physicians of London* 18, 240–243.

Mansfield, N.W. (1971) The estimation of benefits from recreation sites and the provision of a new recreation facility. *Regional Studies* 5, 55–69.

Pearce, D.W. and Warford, J.J. (1993) *World Without End.* Oxford University Press, Oxford, p.114.

Renwick, I.G.H., Butt, W.P. and Steele, B. (1991) How well can radiographers triage X-ray films in accident and emergency departments. *The Radiographer* 38, 112–114.

Sackett, D.L. and Torrance, G.W. (1978) The utility of different health states as perceived by the general public. *Journal of Chronic Diseases* 31, 697–704.

Schwartz, R. and Grubb, A. (1985) Why Britain can't afford informed consent. *Hasting Centre Report* 15, 19–25.

Slovic, P. and Lichtenstein, S. (1983) Preference reversals: a broader perspective. *American Economic Review* 73, 596–605.

Smith, V.K. (1988) Selection and recreation demand. *American Journal of Agricultural Economics* 70, 29–36.

Smith, V.K. and Kaoru, Y. (1990) Signals or noise? Explaining the variation in recreation benefit estimates. *American Journal of Agricultural Economics* 72, 419–441.

Smith, V.K., Desvouges, W.H. and Fisher, A. (1986) A comparison of direct and indirect methods for estimating environmental benefits. *American Journal of Agricultural Economics* 68, 280–290.

Stason, W.B. and Weinstein, M.C. (1977) Allocation of resources to manage hypertension. *New England Journal of Medicine* 296, 732–739.

Tversky, A. and Kahneman, D. (1974) Judgement under uncertainty: heuristics and biases. *Science* 185, 1124–1131.

Tversky, A. and Thaler, R.H. (1990) Anomalies: preference reversals. *Journal of Economic Perspectives* 4, 201–211.

Tversky, A., Slovic, P. and Kahneman, D. (1990) The causes of preference reversal. *American Economic Review* 80, 204–217.

Van Houtven, G.L. and Cropper, M.L. (1994) When is a life too costly to save? The evidence from environmental regulations. *Resources*, No. 114. Resources for the Future, Washington DC.

Walsh, R.G., Johnson, D.M. and McKean, J.R. (1989) Issues in nonmarket valuation and policy application: a retrospective glance. *Western Journal of Agricultural Economics* 14, 178–188.

Weinstein, M.C. (1980) Estrogen used in postmenopausal women – costs, risks, and benefits. *New England Journal of Medicine* 303, 308–316.

Whittington, D., Briscoe, J., Mu, X. and Barron, W. (1990) Estimating the willingness to pay for water services in developing countries: a case study of the use of contingent valuation surveys in Southern Haiti. *Economic Development and Cultural Change* 38, 293–312.

Willems, J.S., Sanders, C.R., Riddiough, M.A. and Bell, J.C. (1980) Cost-effectiveness of vaccination against pneumococcal pneumonia. *New England Journal of Medicine* 303, 553–559.

Williams, A. (1985) Economics of coronary artery by-pass grafting. *British Medical Journal* 291, 326–329.

Willis, K.G. (1990) Valuing non-market wildlife commodities: an evaluation and comparison of benefits and costs. *Applied Economics* 22, 13–30.

Willis, K.G. and Garrod, G.D. (1991) An individual travel-cost method of evaluating forest recreation. *Journal of Agricultural Economics* 42, 33–42.

Willis, K.G. and Garrod, G.D. (1992) Assessing the value of future landscapes. *Landscape and Urban Planning* 23, 17–32.

Willis, K.G. and Garrod, G.D. (1993) Not from experience: a comparison of experts' opinions and hedonic price estimates of the incremental value of property attributable to an environmental feature. *Journal of Property Research* 10, 193–216.

Willis, K.G. and Powe, N. (1995) Planning decisions on waste disposal sites. *Environment and Planning B: Planning and Design* 22, 93–107.

Willis, K.G., Garrod, G.D. and Saunders, C.M. (1993) *Valuation of the South Downs and Somerset Levels and Moors Environmentally Sensitive Area Landscapes by the General Public*. Report to the Ministry of Agriculture, Fisheries and Food. Centre for Rural Economy, University of Newcastle upon Tyne.

Wolfson, A.D., Sinclair, A.J., Bombardier, C. and McGeer, A. (1982) Preference measurement for functional status in stroke patients: inter-rater and inter-technique comparisons. In: Kane, R. and Kane, R. (eds) *Values and Long-term Health Care*. D.C. Heath, Lexington, Massachusetts.

13

Towards a Willingness-to-pay Based Value of Underground Safety[1]

Michael Jones-Lee[*], and Graham Loomes[†]

[*]*University of Newcastle upon Tyne and* [†]*University of York*

Introduction

It is self-evident that London Underground Limited (LUL)[2] does not have access to unconstrained funding to finance safety improvement. This means that LUL faces hard choices in its appraisal of proposed safety projects. These choices will be virtually impossible to make in a systematic and consistent manner unless LUL has a monetary measure of the *value* of safety improvement so that value can be weighed against cost in reaching an informed decision as to whether or not any particular Underground safety project should be undertaken.

This then raises the question of *how* monetary values of safety should be defined and estimated for use in the Underground context. The clue to an answer lies in LUL's business objective which calls for it to *'maximise net social benefit within available funds and subject to a defined gross margin target'* (London Underground Limited, 1991). Clearly, any satisfactory definition of 'social benefit' (or 'social value') must take account of the interests and well-being of members of the public, and for present purposes this plainly means the travelling public (including, ideally, those who will benefit from the lower casualty rates, as well as the reduced road congestion and pollution, that will result from a substitution of Underground travel for road use). If one also allows that the interests and well-being of members of the

[1] The research reported in this chapter was carried out under contract to London Underground Limited. However, the opinions expressed in the chapter are solely the responsibility of the authors and do not necessarily reflect the views of London Underground.

[2] London Underground Limited is the state-owned operator of London's underground railway system.

213

travelling public are in large part determined by the nature of their *preferences,* then it follows that in LUL's case 'social benefit' should be defined in such a way as to reflect those preferences.

Given all of this, it is evident that LUL will require a measure of its customers' preferences – and more particularly their *strength* of preference for safety. Such a measure is naturally provided by customers' *willingness to pay* for safety, in that the maximum amount that a person is willing to pay for a good or service is a direct indication of what that good or service is worth to the person, relative to his or her other potential objectives of expenditure. Furthermore, willingness to pay, being conditioned by ability to pay (that is, income), is an indication of strength of preferences, taking due account of resource constraints.

In summary, if LUL's safety expenditure decisions are to be systematic, consistent and pursuant of LUL's business objective, then:

1. These decisions must involve a balancing of social benefit and cost, where the measure of social benefit reflects customers' strength of preference for safety.

2. Since strength of preference is naturally measured by willingness to pay, LUL should ideally work with appropriately estimated *willingness-to-pay* (WTP) based values of safety.

Lest it be thought that this proposal is unduly radical, it should be appreciated that the UK Department of Transport and the Health and Safety Executive *both* inform their decisions by reference to WTP based values of safety (see Department of Transport, 1988, and Health and Safety Executive, 1992, Appendix 3), as do corresponding agencies in the USA, Canada, Sweden and New Zealand, with other countries showing clear signs of moving in the same direction. *More significantly, the Treasury has given unequivocal and emphatic advice that bodies such as LUL should adopt the WTP approach to the valuation of safety* (see HM Treasury, 1991, Annex B).

In the light of considerations such as these and because, hitherto, no estimates of WTP based values of Underground safety have been available, LUL instituted a programme of research, to be undertaken by the authors of this paper, aimed at obtaining such estimates. Following a desk study (designated 'Phase 0') intended to identify the key issues and questions to be addressed, the first substantial phase of the research programme ('Phase 1') involved a pilot study, conducted during November 1992, designed to assess the feasibility of our proposed estimation procedures and provide some first indications of the possible order of magnitude of WTP based values of Underground safety. It is hoped that the main phase of the research programme ('Phase 2'), involving a large-scale sample survey, will be conducted in the near future. The purpose of this chapter is to report the findings of the Phase 1 pilot study.

The Department of Transport's WTP Based Value of Preventing a Road Fatality

In principle, under the WTP approach one seeks in the first instance to establish the amounts that affected individuals would be willing to pay for typically very small improvements in their own or others' safety. These (usually quite modest) amounts are then aggregated across all affected individuals to arrive at an overall monetary value for the safety improvement concerned. If the improvements in individual safety are standardized so that – taken over the affected group – they can be expected, on average, to prevent one fatality, then the resultant aggregate willingness to pay is naturally referred to as the 'value of preventing a *statistical* fatality' or more succinctly as the 'value of a statistical life'. Because it is cumbersome and somewhat forbidding, the term 'statistical' is often dropped and one refers simply (but not entirely accurately) to the 'value of preventing a fatality' or the 'value of life'.

Of course, in the process of aggregating WTP across different individuals – in order to arrive at an overall value of safety – it is necessary to make a judgement about the *relative* social value of a £1 gain to different income groups. In conventional social cost–benefit analysis the aggregation is typically carried out on an unweighted basis, so that a £1 gain is effectively treated as having a constant social value, irrespective of the income level of the individual to whom it accrues. By contrast, in weighted cost–benefit analysis distributional weights are employed to reflect judgements about the way in which the social value of a £1 gain should vary with the income level of the recipient of the gain. All aggregate values referred to in this paper are unweighted.

To get a feel for the composition and magnitude of a WTP based value of statistical life it will be instructive to consider the figure currently used by the Department of Transport (DoT) in its analysis of proposed road projects.[3] This is shown in Table 13.1 in 1991 prices.

As can be seen, apart from the pure WTP component (which is the DoT's estimate of aggregate WTP for small safety improvements that, taken together, can be expected to prevent one road fatality) there are two further components. These components are included because there

---

[3] The DoT decided to adopt the WTP approach in place of its former gross-output based procedure in 1988 following a comprehensive review of the literature and careful consideration of the various issues involved. See Dalvi (1988) and Department of Transport (1988).

Table 13.1. Breakdown of DoT WTP based value of preventing a road fatality.

Pure WTP component	£634,600
Component reflecting medical and ambulance costs	£450
Component reflecting avoided output loss, net of consumption	£48,100
Total	£683,150

is strong evidence that individuals tend not to take account of them in determining their own individual WTP for safety (see, for example, Jones-Lee, 1989, pp. 169–174). While the rationale for inclusion of the first of these additional components is self-evident, the reason for including the component reflecting avoided output loss, net of consumption, is somewhat less obvious. Essentially, this component is included because when an individual dies prematurely the rest of society (in the first instance, the individual's dependants, the Inland Revenue and Department of Social Security) loses the excess of what the individual would have produced during the remainder of his or her working life *over and above* what he or she would have consumed. The output loss is in fact an estimated *average* for this loss, net of consumption.

Towards a WTP Based Value for Preventing an Underground Fatality[4]

How might a corresponding WTP based value for the prevention of an Underground fatality be expected to break down? We would suggest that the following constitute the key components:

1. pure WTP component;
2. component reflecting the avoided medical and ambulance costs;
3. component reflecting the avoided cost of legal compensation (or, equivalently, the cost of insuring against claims for compensation).

As can be seen, the only component that has no obvious counterpart in the DoT breakdown for the road value is that for avoided costs of legal compensation. However, English courts award damages to the surviving dependants of the deceased victim of tortious negligence in an amount that is principally intended to compensate for their financial loss. In particular, the compensation awarded is intended to reflect the victim's 'net income' – that is, the excess of his/her income

---

[4] For a brief discussion of the value of preventing non-fatal Underground injuries, see Appendix A.

over and above his/her consumption, had he/she survived. As such, one might therefore expect that the average compensation award for a fatality would be broadly similar to the net output loss component in the DoT road breakdown, though the former will of course be net of direct tax while the latter will be gross.

As far as the other components in the LUL breakdown are concerned, we would make the following observations:

1. As argued in Annex B of the Treasury 'Green Book', there is no a priori reason why the pure WTP component for a mode such as the Underground should have the same numerical magnitude as its DoT road counterpart (see HM Treasury, 1991, Annex B). In particular, it will be recalled that these components are intended to reflect the preferences and attitudes to risk of Underground passengers and road users respectively, and there are not grounds for supposing that these preferences and attitudes need necessarily be the same on the two modes.[5]

2. By contrast, averaged over all Underground fatalities, medical and ambulance costs might not be expected to differ greatly from the corresponding costs averaged over all road fatalities.

Material Damage, Police and Administrative Costs and Lost Revenue

So far, we have said nothing about the damage to vehicles and property or the police and administrative costs that might be expected to accompany the typical road fatality; nor have we alluded to the system damage and lost revenue that may result from an Underground accident. The reason for this is that while allowances for avoided material damage, police and administrative costs *are* included in the DoT's value for the prevention of a fatal road *accident*, no such allowances are included in the corresponding figure for a fatal casualty. The DoT's reason for proceeding in this way is that material damage and other things are '... part of the cost of an injury accident but ... are not specific to casualties' (Department of Transport, 1991).

While we are not entirely comfortable with the DoT's distinction on this point, we are prepared to concede that averaging damage, police and administrative costs over fatal injury accidents is slightly less arbitrary than doing so over fatal casualties. In any case, as far as road fatalities are concerned, the avoided material damage, police

---

[5] It is also possible that differences in the perceived levels of the risks concerned may cause people's willingness to pay for risk reduction on the Underground to differ from that on the roads, though the direction of this effect is not unambiguous (see Jones-Lee, 1989, p.38).

and administrative cost component of the value of preventing a fatal injury accident is only in the region of £3500, so that excluding this component from the corresponding casualty figure has a relatively minor effect. However, in the case of Underground fatalities matters are rather different. In particular, whereas even a large-scale road accident involving many vehicles will rarely, if ever, result in material damage costs in excess of £1m, LUL has estimated that the system-damage costs and lost revenue caused by the King's Cross fire amounted to some £30m. Furthermore, there are grounds for supposing that over an extended period, the total number of fatalities in large-scale Underground accidents (such as occurred at King's Cross in 1987 or Moorgate in 1975) might reasonably be expected to be similar to the overall number resulting from 'small-scale' accidents, each involving only one or two fatalities (see Appendix B). It is therefore clear that averaged over *all* Underground fatalities, system-damage costs on the scale of King's Cross could be very substantial indeed.

Admittedly, given the very rare and quite unique nature of large-scale Underground accidents, it is impossible to predict with any measure of accuracy precisely what system-damage costs and lost revenue might be expected to be. However, in the light of the remarks in the previous paragraph it would not surprise us if, averaged over all Underground fatalities occurring during the next 50 or 100 years, such costs were to amount to several hundred thousand pounds. Indeed, as a 'back-of-the-envelope' calculation, suppose:

1. that over a protracted period the total number of fatalities in large-scale and small-scale Underground accidents *are* approximately equal;
2. that large-scale accidents will, on average, involve about 30 fatalities;[6] and
3. that the system-damage and lost-revenue costs associated with the King's Cross fire can be taken as indicative of what might be expected in a large-scale accident.

On these assumptions, an estimated £30m of system-damage costs and lost revenue will be 'spread' over 60 fatalities, giving an average figure of about £500,000 per fatality. Indeed, even if one assumes that large-scale accidents account for only about 20% of all Underground fatalities, the average system-damage and lost-revenue costs would amount to some £200,000 per fatality, though admittedly this figure would fall somewhat if one also averaged the cost over those non-fatal injuries that might be expected to occur in a large-scale accident.

[6] This approximation is obtained from LUL's estimated *F–N* curve (see Appendix B) treating large-scale accidents as those involving between 10 and 100 fatalities.

This having been said, we are not necessarily advocating that LUL should break with the DoT convention of averaging damage costs and lost revenue over accidents rather than casualties. What does concern us, however, is that given the possible magnitude of system-damage costs and lost revenue, these costs should not be overlooked in LUL's safety project appraisal. In short, while on a per accident (or per casualty) basis such costs are arguably small beer on the roads, they are almost certainly *not* in the Underground context.

Estimating the Pure WTP Component of the Underground Value

Regardless of how one elects to deal with the costs of system damage and lost revenue, the key question in determining a WTP-based value of preventing an Underground fatality concerns the appropriate means by which to set about estimating the pure WTP component *per se*. Broadly speaking, two types of approach have been adopted in obtaining empirical estimates of pure WTP values in other contexts. Under the first of these approaches one seeks to observe situations in which people actually do trade off wealth or income for risk as in, for example, labour markets where riskier jobs can be expected to command identifiable wage premiums. Under the other approach one asks members of a representative sample of the affected population more or less directly about their individual willingness to pay for small improvements in their own and possibly others' safety.

It is our considered judgement that neither of these approaches is likely to be workable in the case of Underground risks.

As far as the first approach is concerned, its application would require that passengers should face a choice from a spectrum of *different* safety levels and a corresponding inversely-related fare structure on any particular Underground journey (for example, 'very safe and expensive' versus 'less safe but cheap'), and this is patently not the case, in that on any given journey on the Underground there is just one level of safety and one fare for each type of passenger (such as a one-day visitor to London or a season-ticket holder).

The difficulties with the second approach are more subtle but, we believe, none the less real. The first problem is that Underground risks are very small in relation to, say, road risks. This means that respondents in a sample survey would have to be asked about their willingness to pay for minuscule reductions in risk. While one might well get answers to these questions, the process by which such answers are then converted into an estimated value of statistical life would produce results with error bands so large as to render these results virtually worthless.[7]

The second difficulty with a process of direct questioning is that Underground passengers are *fare-paying*. Asked about their willingness to pay for safety improvement, passengers are therefore likely to believe that their responses could have a significant influence on future fare levels, so that one might reasonably expect that their answers would be subject to a substantial downward 'strategic' bias.[8]

All of this suggests that if one is to form an empirical estimate of the pure WTP component of a value of statistical life for Underground risks it will be necessary to proceed *indirectly*, by trying to measure how members of the travelling public value reductions in the risk of death on the Underground *relative* to reductions in comparable risks on the roads. If such a measure can be obtained then it can be combined with the DoT figure for the roads to estimate the appropriate value to be used by LUL. Thus the main objective of Phase 1 of the study was to explore the feasibility of obtaining such a measure, and give some indication of its possible magnitude.

Summary of Phase 1 Fieldwork

Given the nature and complexity of the issues involved, and the importance of eliciting considered responses rather than instant, and therefore probably unreliable reactions, it was decided to organize 12 'focus' groups, each comprising six or seven members of the public who would initially discuss the issues in an open-ended way (which was nevertheless guided by the group moderators) and who would then be presented with more formal quantitative questions at a later stage in the proceedings.

These quantitative questions addressed the two key characteristics of accidents with respect to which the Phase 0 desk study suggested that people's attitudes to safety on the Underground might differ from their attitudes to safety on the roads, namely: the *scale* of possible accidents; and the *context* in which death or injury might be sustained (see Jones-Lee and Loomes, 1992).

The scale issue arises from the fact that whereas only a very small proportion of all deaths on the roads are likely to occur in accidents in

---

[7] Thus, suppose that an individual indicates that she would be willing to pay £v for a reduction dp in the probability of being killed in an Underground accident during the coming year. Calculation of a value of statistical life then involves approximating the individual's 'marginal rate of substitution' of wealth for risk of death by £v / dp. Suppose further that the person concerned is able to report her 'true' WTP only to an accuracy of ± £e. The error band for the relevant marginal rate of substitution will then be ± £e / dp which will clearly increase very rapidly as dp gets smaller.

[8] For a discussion of strategic bias, see, for example (Cummings *et al.*, 1986).

which 10 or more people are killed at the same time, such multiple-fatality accidents, although rare, are likely to account for a much higher proportion of all fatalities on the Underground over, say, a 20–30 year period. Some of the literature reviewed in the Phase 0 desk study suggested that reducing the risks of such multiple-fatality accidents might be given a disproportionately heavy weight in people's preferences relative to reductions in the risks of single-fatality accidents. Whether this is true, and if so, whether it is because of the sheer numbers involved, or because of the greater unpredictability associated with such events – or indeed, simply because of the greater media attention that such accidents typically receive – were questions we sought to explore during the discussion phase of each group meeting. Following the discussion phase, focus group members were asked to complete mini-questionnaires which contained at least one question intended to elicit some measure of the relative weights attached to reducing the risks of accidents according to their scale.

When asking about scale, the question held the context constant; that is to say, the 'scale' question referred to different scales of accident *on the Underground*. The other main question, concerning contextual factors, held the scale of the accident constant and tried to focus purely on how people felt about a particular reduction in risk on the Underground *vis-à-vis* a comparable reduction in risk on the roads. The open-ended discussion on the context issue typically covered topics such as people's preferences for (a sense of) greater control over their safety, the degree of voluntariness involved in their decisions about the mode of transport used and the risks incurred, and their feelings about the extent to which responsibility for safety was (or ought to be) distributed differently when comparing public transport with private transport. In addition, it seems likely that many people will be particularly averse to the prospect of being involved in an accident in a remote and confined space deep below the surface of the earth. After the open-ended discussion, the corresponding more formal 'context' question in the mini-questionnaire tried to elicit some measure of the relative weights involved.

During November 1992, 12 focus groups were convened. While the participants in these groups could not be regarded as a genuinely random sample of the London travelling public, care was taken to ensure a reasonable spread of ages, gender and social class. In addition, the locations used for these meetings were scattered around the area served by the Underground so as to obtain reasonable coverage of most of the lines.

The first four group meetings, held on 2–3 November 1992, each lasted approximately one and a half hours and were largely exploratory, with each group being presented with a somewhat different mini-questionnaire, so that different types of formats of questions could be tried out. The emphasis in these groups was less upon obtaining quantitative data and more upon allowing participants to express their feelings and concerns about safety (to ensure that there were no important elements or considerations that we had overlooked) and to make comments and suggestions about the question formats used and the likelihood that particular forms of questions would elicit quantitative responses which were usable for our purposes, and in which we could have some confidence. More detailed discussion on these questionnaires and the responses to them is provided in the Phase 1 report (see Jones-Lee and Loomes, 1993), but particular points which surfaced repeatedly in the discussion in the first four group meetings – and were confirmed or expanded upon in the subsequent eight groups – were the following:

1. When asked about the factors that influenced their decisions concerning choice of transport mode, safety was usually not one of the first two or three items to be volunteered by group participants; more frequently it was time, convenience and cost. Furthermore, in almost every group, the first thing that came to participants' minds when asked to think about safety on the Underground was the risk of *assault* and often the second thing was the risk of *bombs*.

2. Initially, many participants expressed the view that 'there is no limit' to the amount that should be spent to reduce risks and that putting a money value on safety is 'callous'. However, when encouraged to explore the matter further, many people saw that they themselves place some limits on what they will do to reduce risk, that resources are not unconstrained, and that hard choices have to be made, though these are found to be more palatable when expressed in 'opportunity costs' (for example, time) rather than 'money cost' terms.

3. The main reason given for using the Underground rather than the roads was the congestion on the latter and/or the difficulty or expense of finding a parking space. Indeed, for these reasons many participants believed that they had no real option but to use the Underground.

4. Most of those who would have chosen to travel by car if travel time and cost were the same for both modes readily acknowledged that travelling by car was statistically more dangerous. To some extent this was offset against the greater sense of *control* that people felt when driving, together with the greater convenience and comfort. By contrast, people felt that the responsibility for safety on the Underground rested to a much greater extent with the management of LUL.

5. Notions of responsibility and control also appear to have influenced a number of participants in their attitudes to large-scale as opposed to small-scale Underground accidents, though such considerations could work in one of two *opposite* directions. Thus, some people expressed the view that a number of single-fatality Underground accidents might have been avoidable if the victims themselves had taken greater care, whereas multiple-fatality Underground accidents merited extra weight because there was nothing that the victims could do to prevent this kind of accident. On the other hand, a feeling that there was relatively little that *anyone* could do to prevent the unpredictable coincidence of human and mechanical failure that often lay behind catastrophic accidents caused some people to prefer to target safety expenditure on the more 'regular' – and in their view, preventable – small-scale types of accident. A related point concerned doubts about getting 'value for money' from expenditure aimed at reducing the risk of large-scale accidents. Thus, suppose that large sums were to be spent in the hope of attenuating such risks and that, in the event, no large-scale Underground accidents were to occur. How would one know whether such an accident *would not have occurred anyway* and that the safety expenditure had therefore been effectively 'wasted'?

In the final eight group sessions, each of which also lasted about one and a half hours, the preliminary discussion was also open-ended, but more structured than in the first four sessions, making greater use of certain standard (verbal) questions raised by the moderator, as well as exposing participants to tape-recorded 'clips' of various (sometimes conflicting) expert opinions about road and rail safety policy. On the basis of the first four groups, the questionnaires had been refined and consisted of one 'scale' question, one 'context' question, and one 'overview' question, as described below. The format used with the four groups held on 11–12 November was modified slightly for the remaining four groups held on 24–25 November, but the modifications were small – the basic structure did not change, and in what follows, the responses from all eight groups are pooled.

The 'scale' question asked participants to consider two alternative ways of spending extra money on safety on the Underground. The first option was to reduce the risk of multiple-fatality accidents to an extent expected to prevent one such accident occurring during the next 25 years, where such an accident, if it were to occur, would on *average* be likely to involve 25–30 fatalities. The alternative option was to spend the money on reducing the risks of single-fatality Underground accidents. Participants were asked to consider different possible levels of effectiveness of this alternative option, in terms of the total number of fatalities expected to be prevented over the same 25-year period and to indicate at what levels they would definitely prefer the first option to the second, at what other levels they would definitely prefer the second option to the first, and at what (intermediate) levels – if any –

they would be unable to state a clear preference for one or the other. This way of eliciting responses was intended to allow for the possibility that people might not have well-honed, precise preferences 'immediately to hand' and might need to be allowed to feel their way towards a sort of 'grey indifference' region in a more gradual manner.

For example, someone who placed a premium on reducing the risk of a multiple-fatality accident might continue to prefer the first (multiple-fatality accident prevention) option even if the second option were expected to prevent as many as 35–40 single-fatality accidents during the same period; might be undecided over the range 40–60, but might express a definite preference for switching the money to prevent single-fatality accidents if this were expected to prevent more than 60 fatalities. This sort of pattern of responses is probably most fruitfully thought of as reflecting a kind of 'personal confidence interval' for the premium to be accorded to the value of preventing a fatality in a large-scale Underground accident. Accordingly, in summarizing the results we have treated such a pattern of responses as entailing a 'minimum' scale premium of $[(37.5 / 27.5) - 1] \times 100 = 36\%$; a 'maximum' scale premium of $[(60 / 27.5) - 1] \times 100 = 118\%$; and a 'best estimate' scale premium of $[(50 / 27.5) - 1] \times 100 = 82\%$.[9]

Alternatively, someone else might prefer the first, multiple-fatality accident prevention option if the second would prevent only 10–15 single-fatality accidents, but might switch to the second option if it were expected to prevent more than 15 deaths, on the grounds that he or she preferred to have money spent on measures which could be seen over time to produce a tangible benefit, rather than invest it in an area where the benefits were uncertain and where one might never really know whether the expenditure had in fact been effective. In this case we would compute the 'minimum' scale premium as $[(12.5 / 27.5) - 1] \times 100 = -55\%$; the 'maximum' scale premium as $[(15 / 27.5) - 1] \times 100 = -45\%$; and the 'best estimate' scale premium also as -45%.

Prior expectations, based on the literature reviewed in the Phase 0 report, were that the former attitudes would outweigh the latter, so that overall there would be a marked premium on preventing fatalities in large-scale accidents. And indeed there were a number of participants who responded in this way. But it seemed that there were others whose *initial* reactions were of this kind, but who, upon reflection tended towards the opposite view.

Altogether, 54 people took part in the last eight group meetings and of these, 46 gave usable responses to the 'scale' question. And overall,

---

[9] In these calculations, 35–40 fatalities were treated as 37.5; 25–30 as 27.5; and so on. 'Best estimates' were derived from the mid-point of the range over which the participant was undecided or, if there was no indecision, from the point at which preferences switched from one option to the other.

the two opposing views outlined above largely tended to cancel one another out, so that in *aggregate* the premium associated with multiple-fatality accidents was substantially smaller than originally expected. The mean and median 'minimum', 'maximum' and 'best estimate' of the scale premium are reported in Table 13.2.

The format of the 'context' question was broadly similar to the one used in the 'scale' question, in that it offered a 'fixed' option – spending a sum of money to reduce the risk of single-fatality accidents on the Underground to an extent expected to prevent a total of 25 deaths over the next 25 years – and asked participants to weigh this against the alternative of spending the money to reduce the risk of such accidents on the *roads*, where the expected effectiveness of this alternative was varied.

As in the 'scale' question, respondents were asked to indicate those levels of road risk reduction at which they would definitely prefer the Underground option, those levels at which they would definitely prefer the road option, and at which levels they would be unable to state a clear preference. Again, these responses were used to derive 'minimum', 'maximum' and 'best estimates' of the context premium for preventing small-scale fatal Underground accidents relative to the value of preventing small-scale fatal road accidents.

For this question 52 out of 54 responses were usable and yielded the estimates summarized in Table 13.3.

Finally, the 'overview' question simply told participants in round numbers the amount that the DoT was prepared to spend to prevent a road fatality and asked them to say how many times smaller or larger

Table 13.2. Mean and median estimates of the 'scale' premium.

	Mean	Median
'Minimum' scale premium	−13%	−18%
'Maximum' scale premium	35%	9%
'Best estimate' scale premium	11%	−5%

Table 13.3. Mean and median estimates of the 'context' premium.

	Mean	Median
'Minimum' context premium	38%	0%
'Maximum' context premium	79%	20%
'Best estimate' context premium	58%	10%

they felt the figure used on the Underground should be. This is, of course, a very crude form of question; but interestingly, most people (47) gave an answer. Only two thought the Underground figure should be lower, 18 thought it should be the same as the one used for the roads, and the rest thought it should be higher, with the most frequent of the last group of responses suggesting it should be about twice as high. The mean response to this question would imply a premium of about 80%, while the median would give a figure of 100%, which is broadly consistent with the overall premium implied by the combination of the mean answers to the first two questions, namely 69%.

Details of the computation by which the 'scale' and 'context' premiums should be combined to derive an overall premium are given in Jones-Lee and Loomes (1992). In particular, for a scale premium that is relatively small and a context premium that is relatively large, the implied overall premium is approximately equal to their sum. This result is based on the assumption that, over time, the number of fatalities in large-scale and small-scale Underground accidents are approximately equal (see Appendix B). However, because in the event 'scale' effects turned out to be quite small, our results are relatively insensitive to this assumption. Thus, even if large-scale accidents account for only 20% of all Underground fatalities, the overall premium implied by the combination of the mean responses to the first two questions would be about 61% rather than 69%.

Conclusion

From Tables 13.2 and 13.3 it is clear that for both the 'scale' and 'context' questions the mean responses substantially exceed the medians, reflecting the fact that the distributions of responses are highly right-skewed, as is commonly the case in quantitative questions related to physical risk (see, for example, Jones-Lee, 1989, chapter 4; Miller and Guria, 1991; and Persson, 1992, chapter 4). Furthermore, given that for both questions the median 'best estimate' of the relevant premium does not differ greatly from zero, it is plain that those favouring a positive premium are roughly equal in number to those favouring a discount, but that the *magnitude* of the premium required by the former substantially exceeds the size of the discount sought by the latter.

This immediately raises the question of whether, in an exercise of this sort, one should be guided principally by means or by medians. Given that, as argued in the introductory remarks, the essential purpose of a WTP based value of Underground safety is to reflect customers' *strength* of preference for safety *vis-à-vis* other potential objects of expenditure, it seems clear that the mean, rather than a statistic such as the median, is the appropriate central-tendency measure. Indeed, insofar as a WTP based value of safety is intended to reflect *aggregate* willingness to pay on the part of those affected by the safety improvement concerned, then the underlying methodology of the WTP approach *requires* that the mean should be employed. In fact, as one of the authors has argued elsewhere (see Jones-Lee, 1989, chapter 4), the only grounds on which one might sensibly contemplate the use of medians within the context of the WTP approach would be if there were serious doubts about the reliability of 'extreme' responses, and we have no particular reason to harbour such doubts in the present study.

Focusing, then, on the mean responses to the three quantitative questions posed to participants in the Phase 1 study, it is clear that there is reasonably close correspondence between the overall premium implied by the combination of 'best estimate' answers to the 'scale' and 'context' questions (69%) and the premium implied by the responses to the 'overview' question concerning relativity with the DoT value of preventing a road fatality (80%). This suggests that an overall premium in the region of 75% may well be warranted for the value of preventing an Underground fatality in relation to its road counterpart. Applied to the DoT's pure WTP component of some £635,000, this would imply a WTP figure for the Underground in the region of £1.1m in 1991 prices. Adding a further £50,000 for avoided medical and ambulance costs and costs of legal compensation would then carry this figure nearer to £1.2m. Indeed, while we would not necessarily advocate that it should do so, were LUL to choose to take account of avoided costs of system damage and lost revenue by adding a further component to its WTP-based value to reflect such factors, then the resultant overall figure could well be in the region of £1.7m.

All of this having been said, we must stress that these figures should be treated with some caution. While participants in the focus groups spanned a range of ages and social classes, they were not selected by the kind of procedure necessary to produce a truly random sample. Moreover, there are indications that some groups tended to respond in rather different ways from others, which may reflect the possibility that some members of those groups influenced others to an extent that might not persist if participants were allowed to give further independent thought to the issues and then answer the quantitative question a little later in one-to-one interviews. In the light of this it is our intention to employ a sort of 'two-stage' procedure in the Phase 2 main study.

There is one more point to be made concerning the use of the DoT value of preventing a road fatality as an 'anchor' in determining a corresponding figure for the Underground. It may be worth bearing in mind that when the WTP approach was first adopted by the DoT in 1988, the figure was deliberately set at the lower end of the range of values that were considered – in order to temper a radical change of methodology with an element of caution – and since then this figure has only been increased in line with inflation and economic growth. It is not inconceivable that the DoT or the Treasury may become amenable to the idea that the figure was originally set *too* low and should be raised for that reason, though such a revision in the near future seems somewhat unlikely. Even so, when considering the figure it wishes to use for its own project appraisal, LUL may prefer to anchor the premium discussed earlier to a higher figure than the arguably conservative £635,000. An anchor of £1m, for example, would produce an overall figure for the Underground of something around £1.8m excluding avoided system-damage costs and lost revenue, or £2.3m if these were included, given the assumptions and estimates made above, and subject to the caveats already noted.

Finally, we feel bound to highlight the fact that, contrary to our prior expectation, it is 'context' rather than 'scale' effects that have done the lion's share of the work in producing a premium for the value of Underground safety in relation to the DoT figure for the roads. While we have always been sceptical of the argument – advanced in, for example, Wilson (1975) and Ferreira and Slesin (1976) – that scale, as such, provides a justification for treating the loss of *n* lives in a catastrophic accident as being significantly worse than the loss of *n* lives in separate small-scale accidents, we were prepared to entertain the possibility that people's aversion to the *ambiguity* associated with the probability of occurrence of large-scale accidents, together with the *uncertainty* concerning the extent of the consequent loss of life, might provide grounds for a significant 'scale' premium (particularly as Kunreuther *et al.* 1992, report clear evidence of ambiguity and uncertainty effects in the context of financial risk). In the event, however, as already noted, such aversion appears to have been largely offset by countervailing doubts about getting demonstrable 'value for money' from expenditure aimed at mitigating the risks of large-scale Underground accidents. This suggests that whatever justification there might be for setting the value of statistical life for catastrophe risks at a premium in relation to the value of preventing small-scale accident fatalities, anything other than a very modest premium may prove difficult to defend on the basis of the preferences and attitudes to risk of members of the public, *per se*.

Appendix A

While the Phase 1 study focused principally on Underground fatalities, some thought was also given to the value of preventing non-fatal Underground injuries. In recent work for the DoT the authors derived estimates of the WTP based value of preventing various severities of non-fatal road injury *relative* to the DoT's WTP-based value for preventing road fatalities. These estimates were obtained from responses to a nationally representative sample survey (see Jones-Lee *et al.*, 1993).

While it is argued in the main text that various factors can be expected to result in *absolute* values of safety that differ markedly as between the Underground and the roads, we have no strong grounds for supposing that the *ratio* of the value of preventing a particular severity of non-fatal injury relative to the corresponding value for a fatality will differ greatly between the two modes. If this is so, then the ratios estimated in the DoT road accident study can be used, at least as a first approximation, as a basis for deriving values for the prevention of non-fatal Underground injuries relative to the Underground figure for fatalities.

According to LUL statistics for 1992, non-fatal Underground injuries breakdown into 'No first aid rendered' injuries (14.5%); 'Minor' injuries (82.2%) and 'Major' injuries (3.3%). In terms of DoT's classification, all of the 'No first aid rendered' injuries would be treated as 'slight', as would many of the 'Minor' injuries. Furthermore, with the exception of injuries incurred in large-scale accidents such as King's Cross, 'Major' Underground injuries are apparently rarely worse than those classified as serious but involving no permanent disability in our non-fatal road injury study. Taken as a whole, therefore, it would appear that non-fatal Underground injuries are, in the main, substantially less severe than their road counterparts so that the weighted average ratio of the value of preventing these injuries – relative to the value of preventing an Underground fatality – will almost certainly be somewhat lower than the corresponding weighted average figure for the roads.

Appendix B

If one takes LUL's estimated $F-N$ curve (which gives the predicted annual frequency, F, of accidents involving N or more fatalities) and treats large-scale accidents as those involving between 10 and 100 fatalities, then an approximation to the ratio of fatalities from large-scale and small-scale accidents follows from a straightforward exercise in integral calculus. (For details, see Jones-Lee and Loomes, 1992.) However, if one considers historical accident data for the Underground the picture is somewhat different. Thus, data for the period 1948–1990 indicate that there were only three accidents involving ten or more fatalities on the Underground during this period, namely at Stratford in 1953 (12 fatalities), Moorgate in 1975 (43 fatalities) and King's Cross in 1987 (31 fatalities). These constitute only about 20% of the estimated total number of Underground fatalities for the period concerned if trespassers and suicides are excluded. The difference between the historical accident record and the implications of LUL's estimated $F-N$ curve in part almost certainly reflects the fact that an $F-N$ curve represents an attempt to predict and take account of all possible sources of system failure and hazard, including many that have, mercifully, not actually occurred and therefore do not show up in historical accident data.

References

Cummings, R.G., Brookshire, D.S. and Schulze, W.D. (1986) *Valuing Environmental Goods: An Assessment of the Contingent Valuation Method*. Rowman and Allanheld, Totowa, New Jersey.

Dalvi, M.Q. (1988) *The Value of Life and Safety: A Search for a Consensus Estimate*. Department of Transport, London.

Department of Transport (1988) *Valuation of Road Accident Fatalities*. Department of Transport, London.

Department of Transport (1991) *Highways Economics Note No.1*. Department of Transport, London.

Ferreira, J. and Slesin, L. (1976) *Observations on the Social Impact of Large Accidents*. Technical Report No. 122, Massachusetts Institute of Technology, Operations Research Centre, Cambridge, Massachusetts.

Health and Safety Executive (1992) *The Tolerability of Risk from Nuclear Power Stations*. HMSO, London.

HM Treasury (1991) *Economic Appraisal in Central Government. A Technical Guide for Government Departments*. ('The Green Book'.) HMSO, London.

Jones-Lee, M.W. (1989) *The Economics of Safety and Physical Risk*. Basil Blackwell, Oxford.

Jones-Lee, M.W. and Loomes, G. (1992) *The Monetary Value of Underground Safety Relative to Road Safety: An Exploratory Assessment (The 'Phase 0 Report')*. Report to London Underground Limited.

Jones-Lee, M.W. and Loomes, G. (1993) *The Monetary Value of Underground Safety: Results of a Pilot Study (The 'Phase 1 Report')*. Report to London Underground Limited.

Jones-Lee, M.W., Loomes, G., O'Reilly, D. and Philips, P. (1993) *The Value of Preventing Non-Fatal Road Injuries: Findings of a Willingness-to-Pay National Sample Survey*. Contractor Report 330. Transport Research Laboratory, Crowthorne.

Kunreuther, H., Hogarth, R. and Meszaros, J. (1992) *Insurer Ambiguity and Market Failure*. Wharton Risk and Decision Processes Centre Working Paper 91-12-02, University of Pennsylvania.

London Underground Limited (1991) *London Underground Company Plan*. London Underground Limited, London.

Miller, T.R. and Guria, J. (1991) *The Value of Statistical Life in New Zealand*. Land Transport Division, New Zealand Ministry of Transport, Wellington, New Zealand.

Persson, U. (1992) *Three Economic Approaches to Valuing Benefits of Traffic Safety Measures*. Swedish Institute for Health Economics, Lund.

Wilson, R. (1975) The costs of safety. *New Scientist* 68, 274–275.

14

Establishing Priorities for Valuation Research in Government

David M. Newbery

University of Cambridge

The value of practical research lies in the improvement in decisions that might be made, and can be quantified by the expected cost saved by finding less expensive solutions to problems, or by the gain in well-being resulting from better decisions. This suggests three criteria for identifying priorities – the size of the potential annual benefit, which will depend on the scope of the activity; the degree of irreversibility of the decision; and the extent to which there are likely to be serious misperceptions about the cost and benefits of action. The first criterion is obvious, the second and third less so. Consider a decision where the potential cost saving from improved decision making is £10m per year, but where the decision, once made, is irreversible. The present value of a better decision at the test discount rate of 8% is £125m, whereas if the decision were readily reversible, the cost of remaining ignorant would only be £10m per year. The argument that one should carefully consider cases of potentially serious misperception is that constituencies for policies are likely to reach biased conclusions unless these misperceptions are identified and corrected.

What makes for irreversibility? International agreements and EC Directives come high on the list, for to be credible they must involve a degree of commitment that makes them hard to renegotiate uni-laterally. Decisions involving large sunk investments with few alter-native uses provide another obvious category, as do those that involve closing down activities that cannot be readily resumed. Locational investment decisions may foreclose alternative choices, and may lock in a whole subsequent chain of investments.

What priorities does this suggest? Sulphur emissions are subject to international agreements under the UN ECE *Convention on Long Range*

Transboundary Air Pollution signed in 1979, and the EC *Large Combustion Plant Directive* (LCPD), signed in 1988. Under the LCPD, the UK agreed to reduce SO$_2$ emissions from existing large plants to 80% of its 1980 level by 1993, to 60% by 1998 and to 40% of its 1980 level by 2003. The new UN ECE *Convention* under negotiation early in 1994 was guided by the principle that emissions of SO$_2$ should not lead to depositions that exceed critical loads except for a minor fraction of land, and may be even more stringent – the initial UK target was a reduction to 11% of the 1980 base by 2003, but the most recent agreement seems to have been relaxed to 21% by 2005.

More immediately, power stations in the UK have to meet the conditions of the *Environmental Protection Act 1990*, itself a response to the EC Directive, as laid down in guide-lines issued to inspectors and local authorities for Integrated Pollution Control. Plant will only be authorized if they have installed pollution abatement equipment deemed to be 'best available technology not entailing excessive cost' (BATNEEC) by the year 2001. BATNEEC for existing coal and oil-fired plant is likely to mean installing expensive Flue Gas Desulphurization (FGD) at £150–175 per kW, which would reduce emissions to 10% of their former value. The major generators consider it not to be cost-effective to install FGD on 30-year-old stations, so they are likely to replace this capacity by further gas generation or by installing FGD on oil-fired plant to enable it to burn imported Orimulsion, in both cases essentially closing down most of the rest of the coal industry.

These international agreements have indirectly contributed to the 'dash for gas', in which the British coal industry has seen its market for coal for electricity generation drop from 65m tonnes to 30m tonnes. Some 12–16 deep-mined pits are being closed and their reserves thereby sterilized and effectively lost. The gas industry has invested in considerable off-shore exploration and development, and some 12 GW of gas-fired CCGT generation has been ordered (relative to a peak demand in 1996 of some 52 GW), at a cost of nearly £5 billion (a sum that should perhaps be more than doubled if the cost of the gas investment is included).

Are the rather substantial costs of reducing emissions to these targets justified? We do not know. The uncertainty surrounding estimates of the damage done by acid rain are so large that we cannot be at all confident that the required reductions are cost effective. What is certain is that the costs of reaching any environmental goal are not being minimized, since the damage done depends on location of emission, while the targets are uniform, but without better estimates of the damage the cost of the inefficiency cannot be quantified. There would therefore seem to be high priority in improving damage estimates and delaying any tightening of international agreements, though this would have been even more the case five years ago.

A similar argument could probably be advanced for tightening emissions for vehicles, where the costs visited upon motorists are probably excessive, at least in many countries. The costs in the UK might be £1.5–£2 billion per year, or up to twice the scientific research budget. Again, we lack the information to judge whether they are excessive, and whether policies are well directed. Again, decisions on standards will involve large sunk investments in research into low-emissions engines and in tooling up assembly plants to produce the vehicles, which themselves have lives of 10 years or so, though future investment costs could be avoided by reversing current policies.

In both emissions cases governments seem content to legislate costly changes as the costs fall on producers who are well able to pass them through to consumers with little direct resistance, as the consumers are unaware of the magnitude of the costs. In contrast, the costs of congestion are fairly well documented, and are large. This could be considerably cost-effectively reduced by road pricing, but this would be politically costly and highly visible to the electorate; and is, in consequence, less likely to be undertaken.

The next area of large sunk investments of doubtful merit concerns purity standards for water and rivers, mandated by EC rules, despite violating standard criteria of subsidiarity. The effects of nitrate levels in drinking water are very doubtful on any realistic risk assessment calculation, and similar arguments could probably be applied elsewhere. Whether research would improve the quality of the policy debate is itself problematic, but surely worth pursuing.

If we turn to areas of misperception, the most obvious is the considerable asymmetry in the cost required to compensate people for the loss of some amenity, compared with the amount they might state they are willing to pay to obtain a new amenity. Thus people may feel they need to be compensated four or five times as much when threatened with the removal of some scenic resource than they might have been willing to pay for its availability. The recent arguments over the preservation of Twyford Down illustrate this rather well. It has been seriously proposed that up to £80 million be spent on tunnelling rather than following the proposed road route in order to preserve an admittedly rather special natural resource. It is interesting to speculate what £80 million spent on enhancing the landscape elsewhere might produce, given that the whole forestry budget is £91m per year, with farm woodland schemes costing £6m. It is difficult to imagine such enthusiasm for providing comparable finance to create new resources, even when there are strong arguments for providing such sums to defend existing landscapes. The cost of re-routing and tunnelling for the channel tunnel rail link to avoid harm to parts of Kent might be as high as £1.5 billion, even more dramatically out of scale with potential benefits that a similar sum might generate if spent wisely elsewhere.

The asymmetry on public perception is often amplified by an asymmetry in public funding: it is hard to argue for spending public funds on creating new amenities which may be undervalued, while public protests at some investment have the superficial attraction of deferring public expenditure, often at the expense of increased private costs borne as continued congestion. I conclude that there is too little research on the potential benefits from improving the environment near areas of high population where the number of potential bene-ficiaries is large, compared with research into the value of protecting the existing environment; but again it may be hard to create a constituency to press for a reallocation of funds towards creation rather than preservation. One possible approach might be to create a land improvement fund financed by a levy on all land granted planning permission for new building, on the argument that the pursuit of private gain is likely to lead to underinvestment in amenity. Research into institutional design to redress these asymmetries in perception and financial allocation would seem to be well worthwhile.

If we return to the first criteria of the amount of money at issue and the potential for improvement, then the adverse effects of the Common Agricultural Policy must come high up on the list of welfare-reducing expenditures whose waste could be considerably reduced by intelli-gent policies. If it is impossible to argue on the principle of subsidiarity that each EU member state should choose its own agricultural policies subject to free trade at world market prices, then we should argue for ways of better meeting the political objectives at lower social cost and greater environmental gain. Raising the tax on all agricultural chem-icals to the same relationship to world market prices as agricultural products would do both, while more imaginative solutions than set-aside would be worth researching, though again within the context of identifying the constraints on economically rational action and work-ing within those.

Finally, the potential benefits from a more rational approach to accidents and risk are also likely to be considerable, though the causal chains are hard to identify. Some 4000 deaths occur in road accidents, which, at £2m each amounts to £8 billion per year, compared with road taxes of about £15 billion and estimated total road costs including congestion but excluding pollution and accidents also around £15 billion. What fraction of this £8 billion should be charged to road users to induce efficient accident reducing responses? It might lie anywhere between zero and the full amount, though it is doubtful whether it would be more than one-quarter of the total cost. The question we need to answer is how many extra accidents of what severity are caused by an additional million vehicle-kilometres travelled by different categories of vehicles (ideally further subdivided by location, time, and other observable characteristics). This apparently simple question is extremely difficult to answer because it depends on psychological responses to increased traffic, and the preferred level of risk chosen by other road users. Answering the question would have a high pay-off both in terms of identifying the correct level of road user charges, and more directly in finding more cost-effective ways of reducing accidents. Again, because the accidents happen to private motorists, rather than public transport users, there is little effective pressure to improve decision making, and hence a tendency to under-research the issue. Certainly the Transport and Road Research Laboratory has consistently under-researched this larger issue, rather than more narrowly focused on accident-reducing measures.

To summarize, there is remarkably little applied economic work directed to valuations of this kind, and most scientific work is not well informed by the economic principle of allocating effort to generate the most valuable information (in terms of improving decision making). Most environmental economics research is concentrated on global warming, and most of this is conducted largely independently of other scientific work, though making use of published dose–response relationships. What seems to be missing is genuinely interdisciplinary work involving scientists, psychologists and economists who are able jointly to identify the causal pathways, the behavioural responses, and the impacts on costs and welfare.

Acknowledgement

Support from the British Economic and Social Research Council under the project R000 23 3766 *The Impact of Electricity Privatisation on the British Energy Markets* is gratefully acknowledged.

15

Value for Money in Environmental Valuation[1]

Norman Glass and John Corkindale

Department of the Environment

Introduction

The publication of 'Policy Appraisal and the Environment' (PAE) (Department of the Environment, 1991) was the signal for a resurgence of interest in environmental valuation research. Although PAE was by no means concerned only with this subject, it argued the case for monetary valuation as a means of measuring public preference, for example, for cleaner air or water, within the framework of cost–benefit analysis.

There was nothing particularly new about this as such: after all environmental valuation is also advocated in HM Treasury's 'Green Book' on investment appraisal (HM Treasury, 1991) and it has been used in project appraisal for some considerable time. The report of the Roskill Commission on the siting of the third London airport (Roskill, 1971) is an early and celebrated example of the use of environmental valuation in project appraisal in the UK.

There are however perhaps three respects in which PAE broke new ground. First, the guide explicitly extended the potential scope of environmental valuation beyond project appraisal to the appraisal of policies, programmes and plans and, by implication, to strategic environmental assessment. Second, it advocated systematic appraisal as the best way of analysing policy options effectively. Third, it described a wide variety of monetary valuation techniques and the uses to which they might be put.

---

[1] Any views expressed in this chapter are those of the authors, and should not necessarily be interpreted as being held by the Department of the Environment.

The ways in which the principles set out in PAE are being applied in government-sponsored research is the subject of the recent publication, 'Environmental Appraisal in Government Departments' (Department of the Environment, 1994), Chapter IV of which is devoted to monetary valuation. Three general criteria are advanced as likely to govern the decision on whether to undertake a monetary valuation exercise. These are:

1. whether a conceptually sensible way forward can be found;
2. whether the required data are available or can be made available;
3. how expensive a valuation study is likely to be in terms of skilled manpower, etc. in relation to the intrinsic importance of the issue to be addressed.

The question of how to decide when monetary valuation is likely to be worth doing immediately confronts us with the possibly unpalatable fact that determining research priorities is an exercise in the allocation of scarce resources between competing ends: that is, it is in itself an economic problem.

The conventional approach to the identification of research priorities is to try to pin-point research gaps. If the gaps in our knowledge were small or unimportant in relation to what we already know, identifying such gaps might make some sense. The extent of our knowledge about environmental values is growing as is revealed for example by the OECD's recent publication on project and policy appraisal (OECD, 1994). The reality is however that, in the field of environmental valuation, what we know is probably rather insignificant compared with what we don't know. In these circumstances research priorities need to be set according to an assessment of where the returns are likely to be greatest rather than trying to identify research gaps as such.

Determining the Research Agenda

Since the publication of the Rothschild Report (1971) on government research, the customer/contractor relationship has been central to the establishment of research priorities in government. The practical effect has been progressively to ensure that the research agenda is determined by the needs of policy, though the identification of those research needs has often been the result of input from potential contractors. Sometimes these are specialists – economists, scientists, etc. – within government and sometimes they are their counterparts in academia, consultancy firms, etc.

There are ultimately two ingredients to successful research in the field of environmental valuation: marketing and analysis. Both are equally important. Without proper marketing, it does not matter how good the product, it is unlikely to be made use of. Equally, no matter how good the marketing, if the product is inferior it will not sell and will not deserve to.

How can we market environmental valuation research? How can we sell the idea? 'Policy Appraisal and the Environment' would probably not have happened, or at least happened when it did, had it not been for the interest of the then Prime Minister in establishing a framework for assessing environmental costs and benefits (Corkindale, 1993). Once that interest had been made known it was the task of the civil servants to provide the answers. A commitment to produce PAE found its way into the Environment White Paper (HM Government, 1990) and, as we have seen, it was published a year later.

Since that time the annual reports on the Environment White Paper (HM Government, 1994a), and the UK Sustainable Development Strategy (HM Government, 1994b), have included commitments to produce more guidance on appraisal in specific policy areas and to publish more case study material. The publication of 'Environmental Appraisal in Government Departments' was stimulated by this process. Rachet mechanisms of this kind are clearly helpful in promoting the general idea of doing environmental valuation, but the proof of the pudding is ultimately in the eating and it is with the content of environmental valuation research that we must mainly be concerned.

It might be useful to distinguish three dimensions to the problem of establishing priorities for valuation research. First, there is a consumption dimension: what is required will depend on the demand side – how useful it is likely to be both intrinsically and in terms of its 'sellability' to decision makers with political constituencies – and on the supply side – what it would cost in personnel and effort to produce usable results. Second, there is an investment dimension: immediate results may be few and far between, but there may be value in building up techniques and expertise for future use. Third, there may also be a distribution dimension: should we attempt to cover all areas of potentially useful application of environmental valuation? Or should we confine our attention to those areas where the pay-off is likely to be greatest or most immediate?

Marketing Valuation Research

The OECD appraisal manual distinguishes two categories of users of valuation studies: clients and general public:

> Information elicited on people's values for environmental improvement is often of greatest interest to a wide variety of groups in society. In

choosing a valuation technique, thought should be given to how the information obtained will be received by the public and interested parties other than the immediate client.

The OECD manual categorizes the differing perspectives on environmental valuation (Table 15.1).

It is part of the task of environmental valuation practitioners to try to increase the proportion of people in Cell A. Ultimately this will be achieved when environmental valuation comes to be seen as making an important contribution to the efficient allocation of resources. The key to this is to examine the uses, actual and potential, to which the various environmental valuation techniques can be put.

Environmental Valuation Techniques

The applicability of the different monetary valuation techniques is discussed in Appendix C of 'Policy Appraisal and the Environment'. The techniques listed are well known:

1. Conventional market approaches:
   - the dose response approach;
   - the replacement cost technique.
2. Household production function approach:
   - avertive expenditure;
   - the travel cost method.
3. Hedonic price methods:
   - hedonic house (land) prices;
   - wage risk premia.
4. Experimental markets:
   - contingent valuation (CVM);
   - contingent ranking (CRM) or stated preference.

The OECD manual shows that, in industrial countries, the major areas of application of these techniques have been air and water

Table 15.1. Economic values of environmental goods and services.

Economic values of environmental goods and services are:	Can be measured accurately and reliably	Cannot be measured accurately and reliably
Useful for policy making	Cell A	Cell B
Not useful for policy making	Cell C	Cell D

Source: OECD (1994).

quality, water supply (including ground-water protection), health risks, and recreation (including fishing, hunting, parks, wildlife preservation).

Also, different valuation techniques may measure different things:

> ... in this sense they should be considered complementary, not competing tools. For example, the contingent valuation method is the only available technique for measuring non-use (or passive use) values. Suppose that estimates of use value of a national park and wildlife reserve were obtained using a travel cost model and estimates of non-use value were obtained from a contingent valuation survey. These value estimates are not substitutes for one another; both are useful for policy makers. Similarly, revealed preference methods measure the perceived benefits to individuals; they do not capture the value of effects of which people are unaware; for example, if individuals do not know that a cancer-causing substance is in their drinking water, they obviously will not take action to avoid this risk. There will thus be no 'behavioural trail' that an analyst can follow to determine how much they would be willing to pay to avoid such a risk. However, using the damage function approach, an analyst could estimate the reduced cancer deaths that would result if the carcinogenic substance was removed from the water supply.

A full review of past experience with environmental valuation techniques is beyond the scope of this chapter. A recent survey (Hanley and Knight, 1992) reviews the reasons behind the expansion in the economic evaluation of environmental quality, and summarizes recent work in the UK with regard to three of the valuation techniques in most frequent use: contingent valuation; travel costs; and hedonic pricing. The authors conclude that contingent valuation seems likely to continue to dominate in terms of numbers of applications owing to: (i) its simplicity; (ii) the wide number of instances in which it can be applied; and (iii) that both the alternatives are restrictive in terms of potential applications. In addition, hedonic pricing studies require large data inputs.

The applicability of environmental valuation techniques is one thing; but the main difficulty in determining how far environmental valuation research represents good value for money lies in the fact that there is rather little information available on how far it has influenced decision making. In the absence of information of this kind, it is not possible to know the extent to which resources have been used more efficiently as a result of valuation research.

The Roskill Commission on the Third London Airport

One approach to the problem of evaluating valuation research is to examine past experience. In this respect, the experience of the Roskill

Commission is an interesting case. The Roskill Commission was set up largely as a result of controversy surrounding an earlier government decision to choose Stansted as the third London airport.

The report of the Roskill Commission is still fuelling a debate on whether cost–benefit analysis and valuation of environmental externalities can or should be done, more than 20 years after it was published. Among the criticisms of Roskill there are perhaps three that stand out:

1. The report was ridiculed on the grounds that, according to the criteria developed by Roskill for determining the siting of the third London airport, the obvious place for it was Hyde Park.
2. The report was criticized for being conceptually wrong in its choice of valuation techniques, in particular for valuing the environmental damage associated with the loss of a Norman church.
3. The report was held to be misguided in its findings because they were not accepted by the Government.

There was some force in all these criticisms. Despite the fact that the Roskill Commission report represented a significant advance in the application of cost–benefit analysis and raised the level of public debate about the third London airport to a higher plane, there is no doubt that the criticisms were a set-back to the cause of cost–benefit analysis. Yet we can now see, with the benefit of hindsight, that Roskill helped to diffuse the controversy about the siting of the third London airport by drawing attention to just how expensive, in economic and environmental terms, all the possible sites were likely to be.

The Community Forest Supplement

While environmental valuation clearly has its place in option appraisal, another important application is in the design of economic instruments for environmental policy. The Community Forest Supplement is designed to reflect the difference between the private and social costs and benefits of forests close to major UK population centres. The major social benefit in this case is recreation and the contingent valuation method was applied to determine just how valuable the forest resource might be in this respect (Forestry Commission, 1993). Without research of this kind there was no obvious way of determining the rate at which the Community Forest Supplement should be struck.

Exxon Valdez

A third use of environmental valuation which has already been of some importance in North America, though not so far in the UK, is in litigation. Perhaps the most celebrated case to date is the *Exxon Valdez* disaster which, among other things, resulted in the US National Oceanic and Atmospheric Administration (NOAA) commissioning a panel of specialists to report on the use of the contingent valuation method in the estimation of environmental damages (Arrow *et al.*, 1993).

The deliberations of the NOAA Panel are discussed earlier in this volume by both Michael Hanemann and Ken Willis. For the present purpose, the interesting point is that environmental valuation has already proved its usefulness in helping the courts in North America to determine the level of compensatory damages for environmental pollution incidents.

The Uses of Environmental Valuation

These three examples – Roskill, the Community Woodland Supplement, and *Exxon Valdez* – illustrate three important uses of environmental valuation, namely in option appraisal, in the design of economic instruments, and in determining compensatory payments for environmental damage respectively.

The last of these has not so far found application in the UK, but, as pressures on the environment from population and economic activity continue to increase, it seems reasonable to expect that, in due course, environmental valuation will come into its own in the resolution of environmental disputes in the UK and elsewhere.

In *Cost Benefit Analysis: An Informal Introduction* Mishan (1971) suggests an increasingly important role for compensatory payments in cost–benefit analysis. Even where cost–benefit analysis, by reference to the Pareto and Hicks–Kaldor criteria, can provide information about what is economically desirable in an overall sense, it cannot tell us what is politically possible or ethically desirable unless it goes a step further and addresses the question of what arrangements can be put in place to ensure that gainers will actually compensate losers.

The potential importance of this approach extends beyond the need to address NIMBYism and transboundary pollution. We also need to address sustainable development concerns; what exactly do we mean by intergenerational compensation? This issue has particular importance, for example in relation to decisions about nuclear power facilities. What does it actually mean to compensate future generations for the nuclear decommissioning costs that we impose upon them?

Value for Money

The applicability of the different environmental valuation techniques and the uses to which they should be put need to be distinguished from the question of where the value for money lies. All economic analysis is ultimately concerned with reducing or eliminating uncertainty. The importance of the analysis is a reflection of the importance attached to reducing the uncertainty. The reason is that uncertainty can give rise to political controversy and/or to poor decision making. The importance of environmental valuation in relation to the latter is discussed by Newbery who indicates some areas of policy where poor decision making could be rather costly. In general, the cost of carrying out a valuation study must be weighed against the likely value of the information on environmental values in helping to make better decisions.

Putting numbers on the value of valuation studies is perhaps an even more difficult task than doing the valuation studies themselves. But, if there is little information about the value of environmental valuation research in terms of its contribution to final output, what about measures of intermediate output? Measured in these terms, value for money might be defined in terms of the extent to which use is made of particular environmental valuation estimates. Against this criterion decisions on the collection of data on environmental valuation are in principle no different from those governing decisions about the collection of other environmental statistics. Such decisions need to be based on data requirements to meet clear policy needs and on the cost of the data collection involved (Department of the Environment, 1993).

Although most people would probably regard such a requirement as unexceptionable in itself, the practical implications are not necessarily obvious. In particular, it is by no means clear at what stage special data collection exercises designed to test particular hypotheses of interest to policy should give way to the creation and maintenance and upkeep of a data bank such as the Census of Population which can be used for a wide variety of purposes. In this connection it is relevant to note that the questions asked in the Census of Population are regularly reviewed to ensure that they are as policy relevant as possible.

Against this background it can be seen that the collection of environmental valuation statistics is at a relatively early stage of development. The need for environmental valuation data has been widely argued, for example in the OECD manual and in 'Policy Appraisal and the Environment'. Also a substantial number of valuation case studies have been carried out. The number of these is now such that databases are having to be developed for reference purposes.

In the UK such a database is held at the Centre for Social and Economic Research on the Global Environment (CSERGE) at University College, London. To a considerable extent these developments have been made possible in the UK by funding from the Economic and Social Research Council (ESRC). In particular, the ESRC has funded CSERGE and the Countryside Change Initiative based at the University of Newcastle upon Tyne, thereby helping to encourage the development of centres of excellence in environmental valuation.

The Way Ahead

The next steps in the development of environmental valuation are to some extent a matter of crystal ball gazing. Two important areas are the development of transferability of valuation estimates and values for environmental accounting. (The chapters by Willis and Garrod (chapter 12) and by Jones-Lee and Loomes (chapter 13) in this volume are of direct relevance to the former subject.)

The transferability of environmental valuation estimates, known in the literature as 'benefit transfer', is discussed at some length in the OECD manual. The two principal potential advantages of using a benefit transfer procedure over a new valuation study are likely to be speed and cost. Difficulties are likely to arise where there is a dearth of relevant high quality studies to draw on; where estimates are needed for new kinds of policies and projects; or where there are important differences between the context of past studies and the context of the analysis.

The OECD manual refers to the proposal of Boyle and Bergstrom (1992) for the establishment of a 'non-market valuation library', otherwise described as an 'environmental valuation reference inventory'. This would be a sophisticated database capable of expanding benefit transfers from known to planned studies. The long-run cost savings from such a library or database might well prove to be quite large.

The United Nations (UNSO, 1990) has proposed that its Member States should establish integrated economic and environmental accounts. Bryant and Cook (1992) have attempted, in a limited way, to apply the UN's guidelines in the UK context by exploring some of the basic ideas and concepts involved; by reviewing the environmental data available and likely to be required; by explaining the problems of evaluating, in monetary terms, the condition of the environment; and by illustrating the type of accounts which could be prepared for the UK.

Bryant and Cook identify three categories of problem for monetary valuation: depletion of natural resources; 'defensive expenditure' to prevent environmental deterioration or to rectify deterioration which has already occurred; and 'residual' environmental degradation such as the pollution to soil, air or waste which is not 'made good'.

Progress in developing monetarized environmental accounts has so far been limited. Internationally the principal efforts in the field of environmental accounting have been to develop satellite accounts. The essence of satellite accounting is that physical indicators of the environment are integrated into a wider accounting framework, but without monetarization of environmental and resource changes. A system of monetized accounts, based on the United Nations System of National Accounts (SNA), is supplemented by sets of physical accounts which show opening and closing stocks of natural resources and changes in environmental quality. The two countries that have gone furthest in this direction are France, with its 'natural patrimony accounts', and Norway with its 'resource accounts'. Full monetarization of environmental and resource changes would appear to be some way off.

Beyond these two areas, it is perhaps time to take stock of where we are on environmental valuation and the purposes for which it is used. The legitimacy of using valuations derived from economic methodologies is a controversial area. We need to take the larger non-economist community with us by demonstrating that such valuations are not only consistent with the sort of market valuations with which they are familiar in other circumstances, but can make a helpful contribution to the resolution of real policy choices. This can only be done if they are properly understood and acknowledged to be of high quality. Endlessly refining the unacceptable or collecting further examples of the irrelevant is unlikely to provide value for money. Identifying the market for high quality products and concentrating on producing these is likely to be much more effective.

Acknowledgement

Support from the British Economic and Social Research Council under the project R000 23 3766 *The Impact of Electricity Privatisation on the British Energy Markets* is gratefully acknowledged.

References

Arrow, K., Solow, R., Portney, R., Leamer, E., Radner, R. and Schuman, H. (1993) Report of the NOAA Panel on Contingent Valuation. *Federal Register* 58(10), 4601–4614.

Boyle, K.J. and Bergstrom, J.C. (1992) Benefit transfer studies: myths, pragmatism, and idealism. *Water Resources Research* 28, 657–663.

Bryant, C. and Cook, P. (1992) *Environmental Issues and the National Accounts.* Economic Trends No. 469, November 1992. Central Statistical Office, HMSO, London.

Corkindale, J. (1993) Recent developments in environmental appraisal. *Journal of Environmental Planning and Management* 36, 15–22.

Department of the Environment (1991) *Policy Appraisal and the Environment: A Guide for Government Departments.* HMSO, London.

Department of the Environment (1993) *Explanatory Memorandum on European Legislation: Amended Proposal for a Council Decision Adopting a Four Year Programme 1993–96 to Develop Regular Official Statistics on the Environment.* European Commission 10553/92 Cm. (92) 483 Final.

Department of the Environment (1994) *Environmental Appraisal in Government Departments.* HMSO, London.

Forestry Commission (1993) *The Costs and Benefits of Planting Three Community Forests: Forest of Mercia, Thames Chase and Great North Forest.* Forestry Commission, Edinburgh.

Hanley, N. and Knight, J. (1992) Valuing the environment: recent UK experience and an application to green belt land. *Journal of Environmental Planning and Management* 35, 145–160.

HM Government (1990) *This Common Inheritance: Britain's Environmental Strategy.* Cm. 1200. HMSO, London.

HM Government (1994a) *This Common Inheritance: The Third Year Report.* Cm. 2549. HMSO, London.

HM Government (1994b) *Sustainable Development: The UK Strategy.* Cm. 2425. HMSO, London.

HM Treasury (1991) *Economic Appraisal in Central Government: A Technical Guide for Government Departments.* HMSO, London.

Mishan, E.J. (1971) *Cost Benefit Analysis: An Informal Introduction.* Unwin Hyman, London.

OECD (1994) *Project and Policy Appraisal: Integrating Economics and Environment.* OECD, Paris.

Roskill (1971) *Commission on the Third London Airport.* Report. HMSO, London.

Rothschild Report (1971) *The Framework for Government Research and Development.* Cmnd. 4814. HMSO, London.

United National Statistical Office (1990) *SNA Handbook on Integrated Environmental and Economic Accounting.* UNSO, New York.

Index

Because they are so frequently referred to throughout this text, 'contingent valuation' and 'willingness-to-pay' are not separately indexed.